THE NOVELS OF RAJA RAO

THE NOVELS OF RAJA RAO

The Theme of Quest

ESHA DEY

PRESTIGE

Published by
Prestige Books
3/28, East Patel Nagar, New Delhi 110 008
in association with
Indian Society for Commonwealth Studies
New Delhi

ISBN: 81-85218-34-X

Jacket design by
3-A Corporation,
New Delhi 110 002

Phototypesetting by
data culture
New Delhi 110 065
Ph. 6431070

Printed at
Mehra Offset Press
New Delhi 110 002

Contents

Foreword

The project on Raja Rao was undertaken during the Seventies when the major works of all the Indian writers in English born in the first quarter of this century had already been written, appreciated and tabled as incontrovertible evidence of "Indianness." From its modest beginning in the preceding century, the subcontinent's creative effort in English has been for quite some time deeply involved in the question of national identity seeking expression in an alien medium. The historical background of European colonization naturally forced such concentration of nationalism, which, however useful in the politics of the period, gave rise to a maze of problems in every branch of intellectual and creative activity, producing a singular crisis in the Hindu psyche exacerbated by an almost universal notion of a permanent divide between East and West.

But human conquest of space has actually reduced the importance of the geographical divide, while at the same time new vistas of knowledge have opened up to emphasize the basic oneness of human civilization through a continuous process of evolution. In other words, immutable division in space may give in to fluid stages along the axis of time which admits change as the reality. The fact of this change is very much perceptible in every sphere of Indian life today and strives to find expression in all activities from politics and social reforms to literature and spatial arts. In this situation an Indian writer like Raja Rao who tries to establish a unique Indian identity based on a presumed polarity in an alien language develops an acute crisis of identity exaggerating the divide which ultimately assumes dominance over and above the native heritage ignoring the truth that such heritage continues in actuality through changing forms and signals of culture. This conclusion ran entirely counter to the critical opinion prevalent in India and abroad at that time. However, just before the submission of my thesis in December 1981, Salman Rushdie's *Midnight's*

Children was published. Its mature and confident acceptance of the West and its wide recognition as an achievement of undoubted excellence beyond the narrow colonial reserve of the "Commonwealth" have vindicated my thesis. In quick succession followed Vikram Seth's *The Golden Gate* (1986), Amitav Ghosh's *The Circle of Reason* (1986), *The Shadow Lines* (1988), and Upamanyu Chatterjee's *English, August: An Indian Story (1988)*; all widely appreciated works and without any "nationalist" pretension.Bharati Mukherjee whose short stories have attracted wide attention even declares that she is an "American" writer. This recent "Western" wave is not exactly accidental or a sudden happening; the ground for such development was indeed being prepared all along--which is my precise task to elaborate and establish in the works of Raja Rao, considered to be the most "Indian" of all Indian novelists in English. I have recast some of the material used in the original thesis so as to explain the present buoyancy and asssurance displayed by the Indian writers in English as a logical consequence born out of the agony and desperate groping which the older generation underwent.

Acknowledgements

The project on Raja Rao was largely facilitated by the grant of a long-term teacher-fellowship from the University Grants Commission which allowed me to rest from the duties of teaching and devote whole time to the work. I sincerely thank the Commission for the generous award.

I have received valuable assistance from various quarters which I take this opportunity to acknowledge with gratitude. Professor David Lodge of Birmingham University, a leading formalist critic of English fiction, very kindly read the central chapter of this work and offered his views and advice. The methodology of this project owes substantially to Professor Lodge's support and assessment of my use of recent critical and linguistic theories of the structural--formal kind.

In my explorations into the various aspects of Raja Rao's works it was the late Reverend Robert Antoine, S.J. (Department of Comparative Literature, Davpur University), who so very kindly offered himself as a spring-board for my ideas to venture into a wide expanse, with the firm support of his formidable scholarship in ancient literary forms, his authority in scholastic philosophy and his natural advantage as a native speaker of French. My debt to Father Antoine is simply incalculable. In this connection, I should also thank M. Georges Fradier, the translator of Rao's novels into French, who provided further impetus to my analysis of the inroads of Western culture in Rao's Indian identity by entrusting me specifically with the task of gauging the extent of French influence on Rao's novels.

I thank Shri Mulk Raj Anand, one of the foremost Indian writers in English, Professor Hiren Mukherjee, leading Marxist intellectual, and Shri Sudhi Pradhan, Cultural Advisor to the Government of West Bengal, for supplying me useful information about Raja Rao's past association with the socialist and progressive movement in culture and politics--an interesting phase in the life of an Indian author who is now usually appreciated as a traditionalist intellectual.

I sincerely thank M. Jean Herbert, the well-known Indologist, who very kindly provided details about Madame Camille Rao, Raja Rao's divorced first wife, who was M. Herbert's associate in the French translation of Sri Aurobindo's works.

Thanks are due to Calman-Levi, Paris, for supplying relevant material published in France on Raja Rao and for their kind gift of a copy of Rao's works in French translation; to the Alliance Francaise, Calcutta, for making available important texts in French literature, to St. Xavier's College, Bombay, for presenting me with a copy of Lois Hartley's review of Rao's novel *The Serpent and the Rope* published in America on 4 May 1963.

With pride and respect, I record my gratitude to Dr R.K. Sen, Professor and former Head, Department of English, Calcutta University, who supervised the whole project and arranged my consultations with experts like Father Antoine and the late Prof B.K. Sengupta, Head of the Department of Sanskrit, Rabindra Bharati, I consider myself fortunate to have received Dr Sen's invaluable guidance without which this work would hardly have been possible.

Esha Dey

Introduction

An Indian writer in English is a product of an encounter between the multilingual heterogeneous inhabitants of a subcontinent with the relatively homogeneous people of a nation-state. The encounter admittedly carried the stigma of colonial subjugation and exploitation, against which there surfaced the gradual resistance of a people inspired by their recently acquired idea of nationalism. Since the oppressors came from Europe and the oppressed belonged to Asia, there has appeared, as a matter of course, a full blown mythology of East-West confrontation. The British came to this subcontinent as merchants. Everything they introduced in the colony, from railways to English education, was geared to the commercial interests of the British people who were then at the penultimate stage of the capitalist economy. The success of a handful of merchants in such a vast country as ours perhaps depended on the acquiescence of the common people of this subcontinent who were not only fragmented by castes and creeds but also frustrated with outdated and decadent feudal heads, often worse tyrants than the new merchant rulers. This choice of the people is revealed best in the reaction to the educational system which was actually introduced half-heartedly by the foreigners as a response to the demands of a small group of vocal natives in Bengal. The British however did not destroy the institutions which carried on the ancient tradition of formal instruction prevalent among the Hindu upper-caste males, nor did they interfere with the medieval academic or theologic training of the Muslims. They simply offered an alternative in the model of the primary, secondary and higher education which they supplanted from their homeland. The new system, sometimes adopted even in the princely states outside British India, was not exactly forced down the throat of a subject people who actually preferred the new to the old for a number of reasons: firstly, the Western education was far broader based than any in the history of the subcontinent;

secondly, it offered new avenues of livelihood which soon created a professionally competent and economically self-sufficient middle class; thirdly, it opened up to us various new fields of knowledge with the potential of changing the quality of life; lastly, it presented a spectacular example of a very rich literature with various forms of both poetry and prose written in a language which happens to be the mother-tongue of a community.

We are particularly concerned here with the literary aspect of the situation. In theory, any writer born in this subcontinent may inherit two literary cultures, one ancient, e.g. Sanskrit, Pali, Prakrit, ancient Tamil etc., and the other modern, e.g. vernaculars like Assamese, Bengali, Gujarati, Hindi, Kannada, Malayalam, Marathi, Oriya, Punjabi, modern Tamil, Telugu, Urdu etc. This duality obviously suggests a European analogy with Greek, Latin or Hebrew as the ancient heritage and English, French, Spanish, German, Italian, etc. as the modern modes of expression. However a very significant historical fact marks a far-reaching difference. During the early stages of human civilization, the intelligentsia quite often consisted of an elect group of males who had the knowledge of a Second Language and disseminated it to other selected males to be used in specific areas of life like intellectual activities, religious and court ceremonies etc. In a few countries this exclusiveness, from the second half of the fourteenth century, started to lose its hold with the growth of a vibrant mother-tongue which ultimately led to its supremacy during the Renaissance. The ideal of the whole man valorized the mother-tongue as the appropriate vehicle for all experiences, emotional, spiritual and intellectual, and became a central factor in the growth of national consciousness. In the progress of human civilization the Renaissance marks the watershed ushering in the modern age. The following centuries saw in these countries an exuberance of human creativity in all fields of life, arts and letters, opening up new vistas of knowledge. This was accompanied, indeed propelled by, drastic changes in the concept of man, the rights of the individual in social, political and economic terms which gradually resulted in great upheavals in the form of civil war or revolution creating a new momentum in the socio-economic evolution. It is in the process of this transformation from the medieval to modern, that the colonial encounters between the people who participated in the Renaissance and those who had not, took place. Exiles from languages quite often belong to countries of the latter group.

Thus the transition from the supremacy of a Second Language used by an exclusive elite to the sovereignty of the First Language (as the mother-tongue is now called) shared by all irrespective of class or gender actually signifies a very basic change in the mode of human existence. This transition in the subcontinent of India has been fraught with what appears to be almost insurmountable problems. The Vedic language preserved in the memorization of the hymns of the *samhitas* by the brahmans was polished/perfected and standardized by grammarians notably Panini for all the ages to come in the form of Sanskrit to be used only by a male elite. Sanskrit has always been a Second Language, never spoken by the vast majority in the daily business of life, which is why even the upper-caste heroines in the classical Sanskrit dramas speak Prakrit, Sanskrit is used only by the upper-caste males. Since the Hindu Period, a great gulf has gradually separated the minuscule elite from the mass who spoke the vernaculars of various regions. From the tenth century onwards, in some cases even earlier, these vernaculars began to acquire literary articulation. As Sanskrit was the symbol of tyranny, the medieval rebels were often poets whose vehicle was the mother-tongue. Wherever the movement travelled it raised the vernacular literature to great poetic heights. At the same time existing essentially on the periphery of the society these poet-saints could not really change the basic hierarchical structure. Their influence only created yet another sect gradually assimilated in the amorphous structure known as Hinduism. The limitations of the *bhakti* movement--as it is now called--mark the underdeveloped stage of prose in modern Indian languages at the time of the arrival of the British. It is therefore a rather exaggerated nationalist myth that the cultivation of the native tongue was discouraged by the foreign rulers who forced English on a subject race. As a matter of fact the foreigners were far less hostile to the vernaculars than the brahmans in general had been in the past. Bengali for example was contemptuously dismissed by the brahmans as the language of women, children and low castes, and the listeners/ readers of the Bengali versions of holy texts were threatened with an indefinite sojourn in hell. So the example of English actually produced a great stir in the modern Indian literary scene especially in those communities where the ground had been already prepared through a strong undercurrent of popular striving towards a secular synthesis now aided by the newly set-up printing presses. As a result modern Indian literatures have gained new vigour and exuberance often leading to great and memorable achievement assimilating ancient and medieval heritage in modern forms. In other words the creative urge of the Indian people so far finds expression mainly in modern Indian languages.

Why do then some Indians, however small in number, write in English? A writer of Indian origin writes in English because historical circumstances force him to regard it as his First Language. He is not a successor to the Sanskrit writers composing for an elite of his own proto-feudal society, he belongs to that increasing fraternity of modern writers who are produced by a history of displacement. This displacement is first of all in geography or space. People in this country have often migrated from one language community to another, because in the succession of empires no community has been able to attain self-sufficiency in the economic and political spheres. Absence of clearly defined linguistic nation-states helped the migratory mobility. This fluidity was particularly manipulated by the British to evolve a unitary form of government for their own administrative convenience and maximization of financial gain. Since the newly emergent middle class comprising of English-educated people depended largely on jobs in the government or British-controlled mercantile houses, transfer from one language area to another became the practice supported by a framework of voluntary displacement. Professionals like doctors, lawyers, teachers often moved away from their places of origin to settle in areas which offered better prospects of livelihood. Indian writers in English perhaps with a few exceptions belong to this not inconsiderable class of internal exiles. Since independence the demand for linguistic states has been accepted although at the same time the unitary system of government has continued. Qualified people are almost invariably expected to serve anywhere in India. With the introduction of the three-language formula, a child of displaced parents may find the mother-tongue reduced to the position of a fourth language. The very concept of India today inheres the condition of exile insofar as it underrates the role of the mother-tongue in the evolution of man. Displacement in space causes not merely linguistic but also cultural alienation because one's roots lie in the actual participation of the life of a community which alone carries the tradition because it modifies ceaselessly the symbols and signals of culture. It is perhaps ironical that free India forces its elite to be alienated from the native speech and seek assurance of the First Language in English. Moreover, with such an Indian, it is quite often true that his or her own culture is passing through a period of transition from the medieval to the modern, whereas his or her intellectual discipline and literary sensibilities are shaped by that part of the modern West which has long passed this stage of transition. Hence such a person suffers from an acute problem of displacement in time as well.

With the fact of alienation in space and time one focuses on a groping for identity which is magnified in Indians who grew to maturity during the nationalist struggle for independence. Nationalism as an ideology was borrowed from the West and so the core of Indian nationalism has been largely determined by a reaction to the two major Western attitudes. The colonial ruler's contempt for the Indian, particularly Hindu, lack of egalitarianism forced the Indians into a defensive or even evasive stance towards the contemporary reality; at the same time the scholarly works of the Indologists--themselves products of European romanticism--created a profound nationalist pride in the ancient heritage. However the Indians, to this day, have never understood that these two apparently contradictory attitudes of the West towards India, its contempt for the present and veneration for the past, are complementary, the one being the obverse of the other. The actual oppression in the present is sought to be perpetuated by the creation of a mythical past when the oppressed can be presented safely as superior. The Indian past is therefore quite often tailored to suit the Western present. Most Indologists during the colonial period concentrated on the normative texts which were assumed to be the actual practice and tended to give rise to an idealized notion of spiritual preoccupation as the essence of Indian culture. The ancient civilization that arose in the cities, republics and empires of this subcontinent was a product of the concerted endeavours of kings and warriors, artists and craftsmen, traders and merchants, writers and philosophers and it was materialistic enough to repulse the aggressive Greeks and contribute significantly to the downfall of the Roman empire by inflicting on the mighty Romans an adverse balance of trade. The Western vested interests being primarily military and commercial, the myth of a brahmanic India with its halo of spirituality has satisfied both the oppressor and the oppressed and perpetuated an atmosphere of autocolonization in which the evolution from the archaic past to the modern present gets constantly retarded.

In this context Raja Rao offers a test-case as a major Indian writer who tries to face the complex problems of displacement in space and time with remarkable linguistic talent, artistic sensitivity and literary sophistication. Eldest son of an ancient brahman family, Rao was born in 1909 in the princely state of Mysore which is part of the peninsula, considered far more orthodox Hindu than the Gangetic valley in the North. At the time of Rao's birth, his mother-tongue Kannada was passing through an acute crisis which threatened its survival as the British had manipulated the feudal dissension of the Kannadigas to break up their land into odd parts and subject it to the onslaught of other languages to suit their own political ends. Besides, long before Rao's birth the escapades of his grand uncle had forced the family to seek shelter in the Muslim state of Hyderabad. Raja Rao, born to Kannada, the language of Karnataka of which Mysore now forms part, grew up in Hyderabad where two languages are used, viz. Telugu and Urdu. Right from his birth--so to say--Raja Rao has been an exile--linguistic, religious and cultural. He was the only Hindu pupil in the Muslim public school of Hyderabad where according to his testimony in the preface to *The Policeman and the Rose* (1978), the teachers who impressed him most were British. For his higher education he was sent to the Muslim University of Aligarh in British India. Here he met Eric Dickinson, poet, painter and professor, about whom Rao says: "He impressed me very much. I have been made by him. My literary sensibilities were formed by him." It was Dickinson who brought out the artist in Rao, teaching him to "love France" and "to appreciate Michaelangelo and Santayana." After his graduation with English and History, two typically modern or Western subjects, he left India to study at Montpellier, France, in 1929. Soon after his arrival, he married Camille Mouly, a highly-educated French woman who taught at a lycée in Menton. Apart from supplying the model for Madeleine, heroine of Rao's major work *The Serpent and the Rope* (1960), and the most profound and sensitive portrayal of a white woman by an Indian writer, she played a crucial role in her husband's development as an artist, insisting that he should explore the potential of his native language. He published a few pieces, articles and a long poem in Kannada

(*Jaya Karnataka*, Dharwar, Mysore 1931-33), which, significantly, did not evoke enthusiastic reception, although his first novel in English, *Kanthapura* (1931), written almost immediately after or during the Kannada phase became a landmark in Indian writing in English for its poetic realism and elaborate experiment in style. Obviously his "appropriate language of expression" can be only English since "to marry Sanskrit and Gide in Kannada and go further would have demanded an immense stretch of time." Some of the Kannada stories, translated, were later published along with others written in English in *The Cow of the Barricades and Other Stories* (1947)) with a dedication to Camille. Decades later he denounces these stories explicitly and appears only half-hearted about *Kanthapura*. The source of this rejection of the past lies as much in art as in life. A brahman's marriage with a foreigner happens to be in reality an act of rebellion against the Hindu orthodoxy which regards marriage not as a particular condition of two individuals, but as a duty to ancestors and society at large. The more exclusive the ancestry, the more restricted is the field of marital choice. As for Rao's personal situation in this regard, he himself is the best commentator: "We are Hoysalas of Karnataka, we marry only among ourselves," and "I was the eldest son's eldest son. In the south he has got a very special place, so I was chosen to continue the line. I was the specially favoured one."

How can a Hoysala of Karnataka married to a French woman fulfil his brahmanic commitment writing fiction in English? The trauma of falling apart caused acute restlessness in Rao which led him to abandon the research project entitled "The influence of India on Irish Literature" started under the guidance of Cazamian. His subsequent journeys to various ashramas in India presided over by gurus like Pandit Taranath, Ramana Maharishi, Sri Aurobindo and Narayan Maharaj bear eloquent testimony to the depth of his agony and desperation, his insistent search for the right path. At the same time the political turbulence of contemporary India was too overwhelming to be completely ignored. So in 1941 we find him with Gandhiji at Sevagram, and during the Quit India movement in 1942 with socialists as close associates. During all these years of restlessness, he edited with Iqbal Singh, *Changing India* (1939), a selection of writings by modern Indian intellectuals from Raja Rammohan Roy to Jawaharlal Nehru, then the journal *Tomorrow* (with Ahmed Ali). In 1947 at Trivandrum, he met Atmananda Guru and accepted him as his spiritual preceptor.

The immediate impact of what appears to be a grand brahmanic finale, was of a tragic nature--the formal dissolution of his marriage. This was followed by a long silence over more than a full decade during which Raja Rao devoted himself to an extensive study of philosophy. His major work and perhaps the most sophisticated exploration into the ambiguities of an intercultural encounter, *The Serpent and the Rope*, published in 1960, received wide acclaim and the Sahitya Akademi Award. He was invited to teach Indian Philosophy at an American University and in 1965 married Katherine Jones, an American stage actress. The same year he published *The Cat and Shakespeare: A Tale of Modern India*, a short novel of unique artistic achievement which attracted sharp controversial reaction from critics and readers. His next novel *Comrade Kirillov* (1976) delving into the ambiguous soul of an orthodox brahman Communist, evoked lukewarm reception. Critics have been further baffled by *The Policeman and the Rose* (1978) which incorporates some of the stories of *The Cow of the Barricades* and a few new ones. Rao's second marriage which gave him his only child also broke up leading to a third union with another American woman. His magnum opus *The Chessmaster and His Moves* (1988), purported to be the first part of a trilogy and awarded the prestigious Neustadt Prize by the Oklahoma University, repeats the theme of multicultural confrontation, whereas *On the Ganga Ghat* (1989), a collection of stories (meant to be read as a whole), presents a glimpse of that Indian reality which is beyond the conflicts of time with a quiet and objective stance.

The present study attempts to trace the growth of Raja Rao as a novelist from the beginning to full maturity, with an emphasis on his art. The task had its difficulties for Raja Rao himself appears to be his greatest enemy. "I had this conflict in me. Should a man be a writer first, then a man," ponders Rao, "or a man first and a writer afterwards?" Since according to him man is "a metaphysical entity" and he declares his writing to be "a consequence of a metaphysical life" his stand seems to indicate a surrogation of the writer by the philosopher. As India has epitomized spirituality to the sympathetic Western intellectual, it is this mental equation that tends to control the aesthetic evaluation of Raja Rao. Ironically enough it is the basic principle of utilizing abstract thought in the mimetic presentation of human beings that ties Rao irrevocably to the modern West. As Albert Camus perceives, "What distinguishes modern sensibility from classical sensibility is that the latter thrives on moral problems and the former on metaphysical." In the tradition of Sanskrit poetics the work of an individual is a composition, a *Kavya*, and a subject for evaluation and analysis according to the canons laid down by aesthetics which has very seldom regarded the use of metaphysics as a factor of primary importance. For centuries Indian literary criticism has been preoccupied with the poetics of expression--*laksana, guna, alamkara* and *vyanjana*--in the production of the aesthetic pleasure *(rasa)* which is the goal of every literary endeavour. The authorities on Indian aesthetics clearly state that according to our own ancient tradition the essential nature of the writer's vision is intuitive, spontaneous, unpremeditated which renders a literary utterance "the distinctive mark of aesthetic pre-eminence."

Against such a background Rao's repeated and much publicized "Indian" gestures, posing to reject the West and assert the superiority of "India" in metaphysical terms, may perhaps appear as a residue of colonization, since he himself at the same time admits the reality of his anchor in the alien ethos. In his article, "The books which have influenced me," the Indian works/writers are: *The Ramayana, The Mahabharata, Brihatstotraratnakara* (an anthology of Sanskrit religious verse), Buddhist texts in English translation, medieval Kannada mystical poetry, Mahatma Gandhi's autobiography and Ananda Kentish Coomaraswamy, the celebrated art historian and scholar who wrote in English. Among the Western authors/works he mentions are the Bible, Plato, Shakespeare, Dostoevsky, Malraux, Kafka, Valéry, Rilke, André Gide, Ignazio Silone, Gorky. From this brief summary it is obvious that Rao's Indian roots as specified by himself could hardly provide a model for his fiction. The novelists who might have supplied the literary model are mostly Europeans, none of them Anglo-American. It is this "Europeanness" of Rao that perhaps accounts for his uniqueness which quite often seems "Indian" to shortsighted readers and critics. Further if Rao needed a structural model from the West, it is because his artistic ambience, the pattern of his actual experience, even his point of view, cannot find adequate expression in his inherited and traditional idiom. Borrowings in literature or art are successful and justified only when embedded in life. Besides, to claim--as many have done--that despite his undeniable debt to the

Western literary tradition Rao as an artist remains essentially Indian is to deny the organic unity of art and erect a barrier between form and content. However sympathetic, such critics are unjust because they devalue Rao as an artist and his life-long struggle to grapple with an alien tongue which ties him almost inextricably to an alien ethos. His quest for identity is essentially a quest for form. More than any one else Rao realized the immensity of his problem and sought a solution. His colossal and heroic efforts are largely determined by one single factor--the impact of France, which has made him the most sophisticated Indian artist of his generation. In the preface to *The Policeman and the Rose* Rao himself presents his situation thus: "A South Indian brahmin, nineteen, spoon-fed on English, with just enough Sanskrit to know I knew so little, with an indiscreet education in Kannada, the French literary scene overpowered me."

We may remember that France in those days was the very heart of all modern European movements in art and literature. So Rao's heroes may refer to persons like Simone Weil or Poincaré, or books like *Le Silence de la mer* or use notations of Western music that are by no means familiar with other Indian writers in English. Rao arrived at a France which was not yet the France of Sartre and Camus, but a France of Maurice Barrès and Charles Peguy, where the residue of *la belle époque*--so wonderfully suggested in Oncle Charles' youth in *The Serpent and the Rope*--was still felt. The example of Barrés who started his career with an unabashed concentration of ego ("culte de moi") and found an anchor in nationalism, perhaps initiated a similar transformation in the disturbed soul of the South Indian brahman. Living in France, Rao's nationalism was converted into an adoration of a few selected principles of Indian ethos and developed into a metaphysic of India. This process was assisted by a particular wave in the turbulent crosscurrents of contemporary France, namely Catholic humanism. Rao himself says afterwards, "What I like in France is the Roman Catholic. It springs up in every intellectual and literary discussion. It is the background of France." It is Charles Peguy who is regarded as the very incarnation of the ideas and ideals of the French Catholic humanism and no wonder Rao calls Peguy "the human embodiment of the living force of Europe" and refers to him again and again in his works. The instance of Peguy's fervent Catholic faith and Gallicism helped Rao to merge Hindu nationalism and Advaita

Vedanta.

This mixture found a definite shape and contour in the nationalist historiosophy of Dostoevsky. Just as Slavophilia and the orthodoxy of the Greek Church combined in the Russian master's apprehension of reality, so did Indianness and Hindu orthodoxy--deemed to be expressed in one particular school of Vedanta--blended in Rao's mental equations. In the article, "Meaning of India," Rao justifies the Hindu hierarchy of castes and the deprivation suffered by the oppressed as a sacrifice to the Absolute Consciousness or Brahman of Advaita Vedanta; further, from the reports of foreign travellers he seeks to prove that during all these ages such operation of orthodoxy actually made people happy and peaceful. To him, Indian history is to be interpreted through a particular metaphysical system. Such a profoundly Western core of "Indianness" naturally moulds his art as a novelist. No doubt Rao's brahman heroes, all leading a very non-violent, sedate and calm existence, inhabit a world which seems so far away from the dim and murky atmosphere of the Russian author's violent underworld. But the fundamental principle behind the characters is not so different. One of Dostoevsky's various achievements was his tremendous power to transform ideas into living human beings, be it the Christian humility of Prince Myshkin or Alyosha or the dialectical atheism of Kirillov or the messianic slavophilism of Shatov. In Rao's novels too abstractions are embodied in flesh and blood--Indian nationalism in Moorthy, humanism in Madeleine, Indophilia in Ramaswamy, Catholicism in Georges and so on. It is these ideas in confrontation with the external world through the life and experience of the individual that constitute the basis of all Rao's novels.

Naturally enough, Rao's emphasis lies in the soul, not in man as a social being. Rainer Maria Rilke's assertion in the Seventh Elegy, "Nowhere beloved can world exist but within," describes exactly Rao's viewpoint. Hence the reality he depicts is multilayered so that the fictional characters engaged in mundane or even questionable activities are continuously lifted up on to a different plane altogether. The genesis of this transcendence owes substantially to Dostoevsky whose metaphysical preoccupation transformed a banal story of crime and punishment to a spiritual enquiry. No wonder his *Brothers Karamazov* had such a profound impact on Rao that he felt "as if it had all happened around" and to him in particular. Apart from numerous references to Dostoevsky's characters in *The Serpent and the Rope*, the very title of his novel *Comrade Kirillov* marks his debt to Dostoevsky. Even the famous double, the typical thematic pattern through which the divided Slav soul's dialectical torment found expression, seems to have guided the conception and presentation of Rao's characters, for example Pai and Nair in *The Cat and Shakespeare*. Moreover in following Dostoevsky Rao is in the tradition of the French novelists who from Malraux onwards may be regarded as direct disciples of the Russian master. When Rao declares, "The Indian novel can only be metaphysical in nature," he actually echoes Malraux's concept of novel as "an instrument of metaphysical consciousness." Hence the title of a French interview: "Raja Rao cherche un gourou et rencontre André Malraux" (Raja Rao searches for a guru and meets André Malraux).

It is imperative however to remember that being essentially an artist astride two modes of existence often presumed to be antithetical, no influence, no impact on Rao is unconditional or simple. He claims to revere the *Ramayana* of Valmiki, but actually uses the *Uttararamacharitam*--which is noted for its deviation from Valmiki--in his hero's critical situations. He extols medieval Kannada poetry, yet upholds that rigid brahmanic orthodoxy against which the Kannada saint poets dedicated their lives. He admires Peguy who was an anticleric humanist and at the same time stands by the institution of the Catholic Church justifying the ruthless extermination of whatever was deemed as heresy. When his hero Ramaswamy renews his "Indianness" through the love of Savithri, a line from Dante, the great Catholic poet, is found apposite ("From the most holy waters I came forth again remade . . ."), yet the same Dante's line spoken by Beatrice, who is essential to Dante's Catholic faith, seems to Ramaswamy so objectionable, "the inversion of truth." Even Dostoevsky's nationalist historiosophy had an intensely ethical aspect which has no relevance for Rao since his Advaita is supraethical. His characters therefore are propelled by a private code of conduct, close to the one preached by André Gide which sanctions a life free from all commitments except to onseself. Discovery of the true self is the goal of all Rao's heroes, if not of Rao himself. So Rao praises Gide for "a precise sense of the play of ethic" although at the same time presents him as a typically Western figure to be pitted against his "India" in *The Serpent and the Rope*.

The same principle of ambivalence operates in his celebrated creed as a writer. With deep roots in the Western literary, intellectual and artistic ambience, Rao declares: "An Indian writer in English must absolutely discover and identify himself as an Indian first." For him therefore "literature as *sadhana*--not a profession but a vocation" is superior to the Western writer's life "as an intellectual adventure." Writing for Rao is an "extremely severe discipline" which "is painful and exhaustive." The labour however does not lead to successful creation which remains as mysterious as ever. When the artist is in the throes of creation, at the crucial moment "suddenly a word comes from somewhere as if by magic, not something you thought of." One is reminded of the surreal writer as "a modest recording instrument" and the surreal creation as "psychic automatism in its pure state" when the writer is "suddenly seized by something stronger than himself." Rao admits, "Triple are the constituents of a book--the word, the author, the reader." In the centre is the word, rather the sound which is the Absolute *(sabda Brahman)*. The purpose of the writer is to reach that stage when "the eternality of the sound *(sabda)* will manifest itself." This happens when the writer turns himself into an ardent worshipper (an *Upasaka)* and realizes the Absolute or Brahman as his true self ("enjoys himself as himself"). So creation is impersonal--the Sanskrit equivalent of Rao's favourite word "impersonal" is not however very clear. As a writer of novels often considered "difficult" he brushes aside the responsibility of communication. The critic should "have the experience of the impersonal and the Absolute" since it is his duty, according to Rao, to conform to the exalted standard of the writer. Our ancient tradition, instead of requiring such metaphysical attributes for the connoisseur, emphasizes taste and aesthetic susceptibility. So the only critic who has met Rao's standard is Middleton Murry. Words like "the reading public" or "communication" seem meaningless to Rao since at the level of the realization of the word as Absolute the distinction between the reader and the writer ceases to exist. He states: "It is my firm conviction (basing myself on my Indian background) that you cannot communicate unless you have *no* desire to communicate." To convey meaning is virtually an anti-Indian act. He concludes: "Let us therefore not heed expressions like the reading public, communication etc. We in India need but to recognize our inheritance. Let us never forget Bhartrihari."

One wonders if Bhartrihari, the ancient monist philosopher of grammar, really suggested such complete denial of communication while enunciating the Word-Principle or *Sphota* as "indivisible and partless consciousness in essence" which "partakes of the nature of both word and import." It is as the medium of communication of knowledge that the experts affirm "the limitless power of the Eternal Verbum" because it "explains all our usages." Hence the *sphota* theory of Bhartrihari influenced a school of literary criticism known as *dhvanivada* which laid paramount importance on the connoisseur *(Sahrdaya)* who "through the function of *Vyanjana* (suggestion)" lying as a "latent impression" in his mind, cognizes aesthetic pleasure *(Rasa)* in a *Kavya* (literary composition) consisting of "*śabda* (word) and *artha* (meaning)." Occupied in the quest for word as an abstract, Rao inhabits the well known ivory tower of the lonely modern artists, for some of whom like Mallarmé, writing may approach the absolute state of Platonic ideas. Surprisingly enough Rao's "impersonal" utterances admittedly form a chronicle of his "*personal* philosophical quest." He confesses, "certain aspects of my life are emphasized in each book. So they are a fairly accurate statement of my life." But the crux of creation lies in the process of transformation of this whole corpus of subjective experience into a self-sufficient art form. Rao has so far remained silent over this fundamental issue. Nor has he established autobiography as an Indian traditional form of writing. The ancient Indian encyclopaedic works called *Puranas* (usually kept outside the scope of poetics), which Rao poses as his model, depended essentially on the lack of personal involvement of the writer/compiler, his complete absence of autobiography in passing on what he learned from a predecessor. However the role of autobiography as the source and spring of Rao's literary endeavour highlights the crisis inhering the encounter between two modes of existence, archaic-medieval and modern, for in a time when traditional values no longer correspond to the actual experience of life, the individual turns inward to seek a shadow of reality there. The life and work of Raja Rao is the testimony of a crisis in culture.

Kanthapura

1. *Myth and Reality*

With his background in the formal discipline of Western education, and a predominantly Western literary orientation, Raja Rao has been intensely aware of individual experience conditioned by historicity, as well as of the need for roots in the native tradition. Hence his whole endeavour has been to integrate into his consciousness of the past tradition, his present experience in time. Consequently, for his narrative form he chooses a mingling of myth and realism.[1] Behind the whole archaic existence of Indian life may be found an operation of the principle of myth as structural essence, denoting the metaphysical attitude of a traditional (and primitive) society towards time as a cyclical occurrence as distinct from the Western Judaeo-Christian concept of time as a straight line. The action narrated in legend or myth always happens in what Mircea Eliade has called "the Holy Time of the Beginning."[2] Holy Time belongs to Cosmos and thus the repetition of archetypes in the form of recurrent myths and legends represents the cosmic rhythm. The legendary structure is "sacred" and infinitely repeatable. In repeating the myth in actual life in the form of recital of the deeds of mythical heroes, the archaic man lives in Sacred Time.[3] Hence the ordinary story-telling tradition offers Rao a feasible narrative structure to present an "Indian" identity,[4] though the action is depicted not in the Holy Time, but in the historical present which is always sharply distinguished from the former. His first novel *Kanthapura* narrates the confrontation between the static, archaic existence of a Hindu village and the historical reality of the present in the form of the Gandhian socio-political agitation. In social and political manifestation, the historical preoccupation is undeniable. But the Indian ethos has always consistently attempted to perceive a historic fact, the existential reality of an individual life, in the mould of a set legend or myth so that the historical person may be annihilated in the archetype which is eternal. There lies the rationale of Rao's attempt to balance the two antithetical forms, the mimetic and the mythic.

The action of *Kanthapura* starts as a narration of how life in a remote Kannada village, protected in its static existence by the timeless figure of Kenchamma the presiding deity, revolves in peace and piety within the traditional, rigid, Hindu hierarchy of caste. Moorthy, who takes a prominent part in the religious activities which seem to constitute the very life of the village, is a "Gandhi-man," that is, a follower of Mahatma Gandhi, who organizes "Gandhi-business" in the form of teaching the untouchables the three r's and popularizing spinning as a means to economic independence. The opposition to the new ideology comes from the foreign authority represented by the policeman Badè Khan and also from the Hindu orthodoxy embodied in Bhatta, the rich moneylender and premier brahman of the village, from the fear that "the confusion of castes" will lead to the "pollution of progeny" and bring Brahmanism to an end. Moorthy, however, does not waver in his idealism and carries on his work with missionary zeal among the coolies of the neighbouring Skeffington Coffee estate, establishes the Congress committee of Kanthapura and courts imprisonment for seditious activities. On his release, he leads the people of Kanthapura to join the mainstream of the Indian national movement which, at this stage, takes the form of Civil Disobedience. The rest of the action follows closely the directives of the Indian National Congress, as the people rally for the enforcement of prohibition, refuse to pay taxes and attempt to establish a parallel government. In penal retaliation, the village is subjected to violence and humiliation. Ultimately, the very identity of the village is destroyed as the land belonging to most of the inhabitants is sold in auction to complete strangers. The uprooted inhabitants find shelter in the neighbouring villages where the middle-aged and barren widows go on living almost the same kind of life as at the beginning of the action, believing in the Mahatma as the saviour. Moorthy, along with many young people of Kanthapura, however joins the socialist camp, having lost faith in the efficacy of the Gandhian ideology.

The narrative structure that tackles this theme is mythic and realistic at the same time as Rao himself meant it to be "legendary history." A typical Indian archetype is that of an incarnation of

God as the saviour of people in distress, who establishes righteousness *(dharma)* and destroys the evil. Historical persons have often been deified to approximate to this archetype. The most important instance of such assimilation is perhaps the identification of Krishna the Yadava, the cowherd boy of Gokul, with the counsellor of the Pandavas, the charioteer of Arjuna and the expounder of the *Bhagavad Gita* and ultimately the incarnation of Narayana-Vishnu.[5] In *Kanthapura* Moorthy, the mover of action, is a devotee of the Mahatma conceived as an incarnation, a veritable *avatar* of the divine, born in this earth to end the suffering of Indian people under British rule. His life and deeds, as portrayed by the village bard, approximate to those of Lord Krishna, the archetype of the divine rescuer:

> You remember how Krishna, when he was but a babe of four had begun to fight against demons and had killed the serpent Kaliya. So too our Mohandas began to fight against the enemies of the country . . . and his voice was so pure, his forehead so brilliant with wisdom, that men followed him, more and more men followed him as they did Krishna the flute-player.

As the young Gandhi "goes from village to village to slay the serpent of foreign rule," the allusion to Krishna's victory over the serpent Kaliya cannot escape the villagers. Thus the historical person of the Mahatma is approximated to a well-known archetype and is accepted by the common men as reality but for the legendary parallel. To the people of Kanthapura, as in the vision of Moorthy, the Mahatma is "mighty and God-beaming." His words repeated by his devotee affect the villagers with the force of a divine edict. His socio-political ideology is reduced simplistically to a set of commandments, "spin and practice *ahimsa* and speak the truth." When Moorthy asks people to spin, the economic pragmatism turns into religious sanction "To wear cloth spun and woven with your own hand is sacred," says the Mahatma, and "Spinning is as purifying as praying." So Moorthy's brahman listener, Nanjamma, fully aware that it is deemed unseemly for her caste to spin, immediately agrees to spin and accepts the free gift of a spinning wheel. The real historical objectives of economic self-sufficiency and employment are thus totally subordinated to the transcendental halo surrounding a legendary incarnation. The profane or temporal reality of history is sought to be deprecated by emphasizing the mythological pattern of behaviour. So Patel Rangè Gowda agrees to help the Congress organization only because as a man belonging to the traditional Hindu society he cannot withstand the pull of the archaic mode of conduct which insists on absolute devotion to the incarnation. He transforms Moorthy's exposition of the Gandhian ideology to an assumption of obedience:

> All I know is that what you told me about the Mahatma is very fine, and the Mahatma is a holy man and if the Mahatma says what you say, let the Mahatma's word be the word of God.

With the Mahatma's political programme translated into the paraphernalia of worship as practised in the Hindu religion, the whole political action of *Kanthapura*, generated by an *avatar*, an incarnation, has to centre in a temple, the temple of Kanthapurishwari. The election of the Congress Committee is preceded by a god's procession and devotional song. The aim of the Congress has to be explained with an offering of camphor and coconut to the gods. It is right in front of the gods in the temple that the very vow of spinning, practising non-violence *(ahimsa)* and of speaking the truth, is to be sworn. The picket at the toddy-grove begins with auspicious decorations, the customary musical accompaniment and the offer of coconut-camphor to the gods. At the climax of the novel the final encounter between the people and the repressive force of the foreign authority starts with an elaborate ritual connected with the Satyanarayana Puja. The political programme of Gandhi, located in historical time, translated into paradigmatic ritual action, tends to conform to a mythical structure.

The question is whether the fictional events that constitute the plot correspond to the category of mythical actions which is a natural corollary of mythologizing a historical person. In legends and myths as in our *puranas*, all the actions and events serve to proclaim the glory of the deity (or the incarnation) who is above human beings in power, and the narrative reality always bears out the success of the *principle* which may underlie an archetype. In the realistic narrative of *Kanthapura* on the other hand there is almost total contradiction of the philosophy implicit in the new incarnation in the course of the actual translation of his precepts into the life of events. The ideology of Gandhi, in Moorthy's version, is a simplistic formula for the benefit of his illiterate devotees. But even the three cardinal principles are not obeyed. Rangè Gowda for example almost always deviates from the non-violent ideal. During the actual salt agitation, almost all incidents tend to descend into force. When Moorthy tries to explain the Gandhian ideal of loving one's enemy, even his docile women listeners are baffled. As the Grandmother comments on Moorthy's exhortation of universal love, "Rangamma did not understand this, neither, to tell you the truth, did any of us." When the police beat up Sidda who has thrown dung at a policeman for ogling at his sister, the villagers retaliate with a shower of old slippers, broom-sticks, rags and dung along with stones. Far more than passive resistance is put up when they face the attachment of their properties. During the frenzy of persecution unleashed by the government, the pent-up urge for violence and revenge is released through actions like setting fire to Bhatta's house. Bhatta has left the village long before the actual agitation and thus has no perceptible role to play in the police atrocities. Yet the Satyagrahis seem to have suddenly realized that he has been a skinflint moneylender and exploiter of the poor, neatly forgetting the Chetty brothers who exploit them even more. As they set fire to Bhatta's forsaken home, Gandhian morality is summarily set aside. Beside the ashes of Bhatta's burnt home and hearth, the repetition of the Gandhian injunction of universal love sinks to a hollow mockery of senseless mechanical incantation: "we are out to convert them, the Mahatma says we should convert them, and we shall convert them; our hearts shall convert them. Our will and our love will convert them."[6]

This sharp juxtaposition of the historic reality of vindictive violence and the ideal of non-violence and love indicates the deep gulf that separates the mythical category of action where such blatant contradiction is unthinkable and the concrete existential reality which is always a web of human complexities. Thus the two narrative structures, mythical and realistic, are constantly in conflict with each other, one trying to negate the other. In the climax of the novel, in the "hand to hand fight" there is such violence, hatred, and animosity that "men grip men and men crush men and men bite men and men tear men."

Moorthy, a devotee of the apostle of Truth, apparently takes a very firm stand on truth when during his trial he refuses to have a defence lawyer: "I shall speak that which Truth prompteth and Truth needeth no defence." Yet the conscience of the truth-loving Gandhians seems totally undisturbed when in the Gandhian resistance to the government, the people of Kanthapura take out a procession for an essentially political purpose under religious guise. The tactical value of the move is obvious, since the villagers would not have been allowed to approach the barricade without this religious camouflage. Their goal of putting up a resistance is no doubt justified, but the morality of their means is definitely questionable, in view of Gandhi's specific insistence on the ethics of method. This co-existence of tactical prevarication along with a high moralistic ideal of Truth brings us back to the reality of history, taking a cue from Gandhiji's own confession: "People describe me as a saint trying to be a politician, but the truth is the other way round."[7]

Hence we find Moorthy, true to the basic Gandhian ideology, avoiding any direct confrontation with unbelief or criticism. When he tries to preach, "the Mahatma says you must love even your enemies," Patel Rangé Gowda, the representative of Kanthapura's common men, straightaway rejects the Gandhian ethic of love and non-violence which, according to this man of the world, is meant only for superior human beings, besides being completely useless in day-to-day life. His criticism is never met by Moorthy who seeks and accepts his help knowing fully well his lack of faith in the Gandhian principles. Nor does he display the moral courage to adhere to the ideal of Truth which according to Rao himself should not accommodate any compromise.[8] There is, indeed, a total acceptance, in accord with the convention of the realistic novel, of the authority of the external world at all levels—social, political and economic. The Congress organization is constituted of leaders most of whom are drawn from an economically self-sufficient class. Thus Moorthy, the little Gandhi of Kanthapura, is not only a brahman and thus a member of the privileged class, but also the owner of 27 acres of wet land, 54 acres of dry land, a cardamom garden, a 25 tree mango-grove and a small coffee plantation. Rangamma, the brahman widow, who patronizes "Gandhi-business," has no financial problem. Not to speak of Rangè Gowda, the rock behind the Kanthapura Congress, who "has amassed solid gold in his coffers." In fact the legendary halo of the *avatar* around the Mahatma rises from the very solid and mammoth organization that was the

Indian National Congress, which could set up a wholly modern and efficient system replete with trained volunteers, medical units, a reliable and effective network of communication and even economic planning for the uprooted. This elaborate historical and contemporary structure leads inevitably to the ultimate negation of the myth. In the final criticism of Gandhi and his pact with Irwin which necessitates the withdrawal of the agitation that wipes out Kanthapura, Moorthy's bitterness echoes the frustration actually felt by a whole generation of Indians.[9] As Moorthy writes to Ratna: "Have faith in your enemy, he (i.e. Gandhi) says, have faith in him and convert him. But the world of men is hard to move, and once in motion it is wrong to stop till the goal is reached."

In this recognition of failure of a political programme at a specific point of history—which we find recorded in many Indian novels—the legendary pattern of the unvarying success of the divine saviour is completely shattered. Indeed, the fact that only the middle-aged, barren widows are left to believe firmly in the legend of the Mahatma's omnipotence is emphasized by their escape into a fantasy of hope which alone seems to enable the inhabitants of a traditional society to deprecate the historical present, so immediate and real with pain and suffering.

It is possible that this conflict in the interaction of the two narrative forms is intentional, but Rao's own avowed objective makes it rather unlikely since he proposes to show how *"the past mingles with the present"* in an unbroken continuity. What actually happens is not a harmonious transition but a violent break from a static and archaic existence amounting to an irrevocable uprooting: "nothing can ever be the same again" as even the old grandmother confesses. The life of Kanthapura, a hermetically sealed existence revolving eternally on its own axis, is destroyed forever at the end, and is drawn into the vortex of time with all the pain and suffering that such traumatic transition involves. The clear divison between the two kinds of existence, past or archaic and the present which is historical, is symbolized by the two temples, one with legendary timelessness dedicated to Kenchamma, the presiding deity of the whole Kenchamma hill (which includes not only Kanthapura but also the neighbouring Coffee Estate); the other the temple of Kanthapurishwari, a recent construction right at the centre of the village. To the people of Kanthapura, Kenchamma stands for their eternal agrarian existence. In all the activities that are *repeatable* and thus connected with the traditional, one may say mythical, life of Kanthapura, Kenchamma remains the presiding deity, invoked more often than the whole pantheon of gods and goddesses of the Hindu mythology.

But the historical action of the novel ushered in by the Gandhian ideology is *not* connected in any way with Kenchamma. It is significant that Kenchamma's traditional sanction plays no part in the introduction and dissemination of Gandhian thought, nor is it the scene of crucial happenings. It is the temple of Kanthapurishwari, which is entirely a construction of the present, that constitutes the centre of all activities relevant to the Gandhian theme. As the narrator says, this makeshift temple becomes "the centre of our life." In fact, it is with this new temple that "all the trouble" begins for it provides an excellent venue for the recital of Harikatha in which Gandhi is introduced as the new *avatar*. It is here that the members of the newly-formed Congress party take their oaths. When the Civil Disobedience movement starts, it is here that Moorthy calls for unity, and right here the villagers gather to consider the future course of action. It is from here that the signal for the last and ultimate action goes off. The hallowed timeless existence of Kenchamma is clearly conceived and presented as far above the blood and mire of the contemporary history which centres in the new temple. The past does not "mingle" into the present, cosmic time can never be the plane of existential history.

This gulf between sacred time and historical present is constantly evoked in the narrative tone of the whole novel which is a mixture of credulity and scepticism. The simple credulity of the archaic and primitive mind conditioned to accept myth as reality is always counterbalanced by reasoning and a critical sense of history: The red colour of the Kenchamma hill is explained by the myth that Kenchamma waged a furious battle with an evil demon for days and "the blood soaked and soaked the earth." Here the matter would normally have ended to the satisfaction of everybody since myth assumes absolute faith on the part of the listeners or readers. But the grandmother-narrator immediately seeks defence in geographical proof:

> If not, tell me sister, why should it be red only from the Tippur stream upwards, for a foot down on the other side of

> the stream you have mud black and brown, but never red. Tell me, how could this happen, if it were not for Kenchamma and her battle?

It is the scepticism of a critical and rational reader that Rao obviously hopes to negotiate with this defence. Such self-conscious over-pleading weakens the credibility of the narrator. The description of Moorthy's miraculous feat in sending back the flooded river water to its old course could have rested on the authority of a legend, but it is concluded thus: "And who will say the water did not sink back that very evening?" When it is expected that Moorthy in jail will be freed by the Goddess Kenchamma who "will appear before the judges," Vasudeva, a modern young sceptic, comments: "No, Sister, they will give him a good six months." Unlike his prototype, the puranic devotee Prahlad, who is saved by the Lord at every crisis, Moorthy however does get a prison sentence.[9] Even the glory of the *avatar* is gradually seen substantially tarnished by reality. Take for example the fervent fantasy the people conjure up on the eve of Gandhi's Salt March. The mythical pattern leads them to expect the Mahatma to be blessed by the gods as Harishchandra was in the legend and the Britishers to leave India by divine intervention. This exalted hope is punctured immediately by a thrust from reality as Dorè, the university-returned man of the village, comments: "This is all Ramayana and Mahabharata: such things never happen in our times."

And he is proved right, such things do not happen in the course of events that lead to the destruction of the village. In the archaic mind the pilgrim path of the Mahatma evokes an expectation of miraculous rescue which never materializes:

> People lie many a night in fearful fervour for some pointing finger of the Heavens—so did we lie all through that wakeful night, but no shadow ever flew across the stars, and no dreamer ever woke with a pointing dream.

This sense of frustration persists in spite of all protestation of faith in the Mahatma, climaxing in the last symbolic gesture of Patel Rangè Gowda who spits and throws a handful of dust at the "sunken wretch" that was Kanthapura, their archaic existence; his suffering so intense, "to tell you the truth, mother, my heart it beat like a drum."

This last note of agony is an admission not only of the historical reality but also of the ultimate predominance of the existential framework of the novel over the mythical. Here is thus a "creative acknowledgement of the data of social life at a recognizable moment of history"[10] which resolves the fundamental issue of the traditional and realistic form.

2. *A Stream of Action*

The principle of organization that seems operative in *Kanthapura* is in accordance with the traditional form of the novel. The exposition introduces the place, the main characters and indicates the historical background. Complications start with the activities of Moorthy. This leads to interaction between different characters and the tension builds up gradually in encounters between characters in opposition enhanced by significant alliances. Thus Moorthy is opposed by Bhatta, helped by Rangamma and Patel Rangè Gowda. This is a period of preparation for the community to imbibe new ideas as also for the main character to discipline himself for his Gandhian mission. He gets over his weakness for Ratna, tries to attain the ideal of universal love through the expiatory fast and meditation and overcomes the most powerful enemy that is within, viz. the hereditary brahmanic inhibition in regard to the untouchable. His social ostracism is compensated by his martyrdom of a short imprisonment necessary to make him the "little Mahatma" of the village. Now the action steeply climbs to the climax as the villagers led by Moorthy practically rebel against the government and, in the retaliatory violence, are thrown out from their ancestral lands. The tension of the climax is brought down to the placidity of normal life recording the aftermath of the disaster in terms of the reactions of the main characters. Thus in the very scheme itself, in its graded rise and fall, the pyramidal structure is that of traditional plotting.

The novel begins in the middle of the main character's life, not from the birth, and the past is evoked through allusions to lead to the crisis. The frequent shuttling back and forth in time, which has been noted by critics, does actually contribute to the exposition. Take, for example, the frequent shifts of chronology in the presentation of Moorthy. He is introduced as "Corner-house

Moorthy, who had gone through life like a noble cow, quiet, generous, serene, deferent and brahmanic, a very prince." Nothing is said about his past and the narrative progresses to set the base of future happenings. It is only when Bhatta the first brahman determines to put his foot down on this "Gandhi-business" that the narrator goes back to the past to project Moorthy's vision of the Mahatma so that the bonafides of Moorthy's idealism are convincingly established. The detail of his high status as an heir to considerable property would naturally justify to the readers his mother's death from the shock of his excommunication. When Moorthy's proposed entrance into Skeffington Coffee Estate causes an act of violence and leads to his expiatory fast, the narrator goes back to the past to recount Moorthy's experience to suggest his present spiritual preoccupation as a manifestation of a permanent trait of his character. Thus every shift of chronology is guided by a thoughtful consideration for the aesthetic effect so as to complete the portrayal of Moorthy with those necessary details of his past which will explain him in the present. Further, these details are presented not in a mass or in strict sequence, but in isolated emphasis on each occasion to create the most vivid effect in a particular situation. The same conscious manipulation of chronology is revealed in connection with the presentation of Rangamma and Bhatta.

In fact the narrative form is consciously mimetic or representative of the reality in its evocation of setting and environ in the digressive descriptions of the outbreak of the monsoon, the Kartika festival of lights, the planting ceremony etc.[11] The elaborate digression on varieties of snake poison is offered obviously for the benefit of non-Indian readers. It is however not only the physical reality, but also the ethos which is being presented in the celebrated recital of the glory of Kenchamma which sets the tune at the proper key for an archaic existence.

Within the dominant realistic structure, Rao adapts some well-known instrumentalities of modern fiction but hesitates to exploit them fully. Take, for example, Rao's handling of a dramatized first person narrator which has an established lineage in Western fiction. Rao has apparently adapted it as a suitable substitute for the *skaz* or oral tradition of storytelling by a common man which he clearly has in mind for he mentions Grandmother as the typical narrator. The advantages of a first-person narrator who is a participant in the action obviously lie in a heightened realism and closer intimacy with the reader. But in the literary tradition of the Indian *puranas* where action takes place on a different plane altogether, the narration is impersonal and distant from the action as well as from the readers.[12] To achieve perhaps a compromise between the two opposed modes, Rao tries to impute a semblance of impersonality on the first-person narrator by adopting a constant plural point of view which has perhaps led some critics to find in the village the novel's true protagonist. Since in first-person narration the point of view tends to gravitate to the dramatized narrator, this plurality raises a serious problem of narrative focus in the novel. In *Kanthapura* there is a distinct impression in the first two stages of the novel, judging from the attention of the narrator as well as the source of action, that Moorthy is the focus of narration. Yet at the climax of the novel, as the village is wiped out, he disappears. In other words, his character is not allowed its expected growth and evolution through encounters with crises. Yet the end again is mainly concerned with his reaction to the disaster that has befallen them. At the beginning, it is he who is the chief devotee of the Mahatma, at the end he is the most vocal detractor. The transition from one pole to the opposite should have been the focal point of the crises of repeated violence which occupy almost one-third of the novel. In fact, not only Moorthy, but all the characters—Rangamma, Patel Rangè Gowda, Bhatta, Waterfall Venkamma—with whom the action starts and develops are suddenly withdrawn at the climax. In their place we find a mass of strangers, little-known persons described in fragmentary detail. We get glimpses of Vedamma, Timamma, Puttamma, Satamma, Nanjamma, Laksamma etc., but the characters with whom the readers have identified themselves, who have constituted so long the main focus of Kanthapura's fictional existence, are nowhere. No doubt there may be some very "real" explanations, for example the fact that all the leaders were actually often arrested on the eve of an agitation: that Bhatta, the most important brahman and the richest man of Kanthapura, may have left the village for Benaras, being too sensitive to the critical disapproval of the Gandhians. But these "real" explanations are not enough to rationalize the narrative imbalance.[13] The *mythos* or the structure here demands the known characters to be fully realized in action. But Rao's literal transcript of reality goes against the grains of the tradition established by the specific form he has adapted.

This gradual blurring of focus is accompanied by a distinct change in the narrative technique which is discernible especially in the marked difference in presenting the scenes of violent physical action with the portrayal of static behaviour patterns or repeatable occurrences. In the first two stages we get mostly the narration of the second type and it sets the fictional tone. Every novel creates its own fictional world, the rules of which are set down at the very beginning: "each work promises in its early pages a further provision of distinctive qualities exhibited in those pages."[14] The distinctive quality that has characterized Rao's technique in the early pages of *Kanthapura* is a wealth of concrete details intimately related to the milieu in the presentation of characters, their behaviour and activities. The fictional world is so solidly entrenched in the concrete that the reader is plunged into the living world of a Kannada village at a specific point of time. Take, for example, the description of the encounter between Patel Rangè Gowda and the newly arrived policeman Badè Khan. The fact that Badè Khan, being a Muslim, is none too welcome in a Hindu village is revealed not in an abstract statement but embodied in a concrete situation. The Patel is "a veritable tiger" and the most powerful man in the village, being also a government employee, and his cold reception is detailed in gestures and actions—he goes on in his leisurely ritual preparing a betel leaf with all proprieties observed while the worthy representative of the government is kept standing right in front; unhurriedly he performs his daily routine ordering Chenna to go to the Big Field to "see whether those sons of concubines are planting well," and instructing Mada to come back early with the cattle which are described then by name, while he amuses himself fondling his little grand-child. The request of Badè Khan to find him a house not only meets a flat refusal from the Patel but the worthy person himself is reduced to nothing when he is dismissed with a warning not to take bribes.

In this description, all is particular and singular, from specific gestures and concrete actions down to Badè Khan's kicking the one-eyed pariah dog in impotent fury. Yet the gestures and sounds carry further implications. In the contempt of the Patel, we read the script of a people, a whole community, reacting against British rule. When the Patel sarcastically suggests that Badè Khan is most welcome to rent any house he can get and turn it into a palace, he is completely secure in the knowledge that no one in a Hindu village will extend this kind of hospitality to a Muslim constable. This concrete presentation, further, is geared to show that the heart of the Patel is in the right place, so that his support of Moorthy in the "Gandhi-business" is received in the proper perspective. The same technique, embodying a general idea or ethos in concrete details, individual and telling, is evident in various happenings, usually habitual or common visits to each other, village-women's meeting at river steps, their gossip and squabbles, nuptials and marriages, replete with personal idiosyncrasies, as well as expressive details of the mundane, perceptible reality. In none of these descriptions Moorthy is completely bypassed; most often, he is the centre. Yet at the climax of violent actions there are neither concrete details nor is there a focal point. Take, for example, the following description of physical persecution:

> There are cries and shrieks and moans and groans, and men fly to the left and to the right, and they howl and they yell and they fall and they rise and we rise, too, to fly, but the soldiers have seen us, and one of them rushes towards us, and we are felled and twisted, we are felled and kicked, we are felled and the bayonets waved over our faces—and a long time passes before we wake and we find Satamma fainted beside us, and Madanna and I, who were soaking in a ditch, crawl past him. And then there is a shot, and a fleeing man nearby is shot in the chest and he falls over us, and the moon splashed on his moustached face, his peasant-blanket soaked in blood.

It goes on and on in this unfocused manner of narration for pages. No doubt the situation has all the terror of a real human tragedy, but the question is, does it find realization in distinct and clear terms? With the importance that violence has in the novel the defect in the narrative technique amounts perhaps to a failure. In presenting the behaviour pattern of the villagers, Rao has scrupulously exposed their weaknesses, their inhibitions, their age-long prejudices, their penchant for material well-being; but the delineation of political action takes no account of the different shades of the reality. Take, for example, the instant success of the Satyagrahis in dissuading the coolies of Skeffington Coffee Estate, from drinking. The picketers are beaten up by the police before the toddy-booth at the Estate and "the coolies rushed again towards us, and called upon us, 'Sister, sister, brother, brother,' and we said, 'Do not drink, do not drink, in the name of the Mahatma,' and they said, 'By Kenchamma's name we shall not.''

One almost expects these wretched addicts to live abstemiously ever after. This summary ''telling'' is in complete contrast to the concrete ''showing'' that has dominated in the early stages of the novel. Indeed the nuptial of Waterfall Venkamma's daughter has far more concrete realization than this picket at the toddy-booth although it is the latter that relates more closely to the Gandhian thesis than the former. The campaign for prohibition remains sketchy and totally unrealized because of a deliberate evasion of all the complex problems involved in such an issue, for example the problem of alternative employment for the makers of liquor who incidentally form a particular caste in the Hindu hierarchy and are thus completely protected and justified in their particular means of livelihood by the Hindu tradition. Nor is one allowed any glimpse of the most substantial opposition to prohibition which may arise from the addicts of alcohol, who, like most human beings, with the highest regard for the Mahatma, may be found weak in flesh. In a realistic delineation of external action, the competence of veracity can derive only from actual experience of life, and one wonders if Rao's situation as an exile has not already alienated him from the inter-related problems of the contemporary Indian reality. During the actual agitation of the thirties he was thousands of miles away, not even a spectator to those happenings, a verisimilitude of which he seeks to present. He himself admits that *Kanthapura* was written in a thirteenth-century French castle in the Alps. Hence Rao's ''telling'' belongs to a mythical plane and the historical theme gets lost in generalized abstraction, a contradiction in itself and a deviation from the literary convention that he has adopted earlier in the novel—that of detailing, concretization and firm focus.

The uninterrupted flow of monologue which Rao has adapted from the modern Western tradition of the flux of consciousness is particularly suited for psychological analysis, to reveal realistically different levels of consciousness in the continuous monologue which imitates the flow of speech.[15] But the action of *Kanthapura* happens very much in the external reality and these events cannot possibly be as continuous, as uninterrupted as the technique of the interior monologue would suggest. Applied to events in the external world, this technique robs the description of clear and sharp definition. This becomes so marked in the climax when a series of violent, physical actions are described in a flow of long continuous paragraphs that one never gets the hang of what is really happening. The edges are all blurred, one action imperceptibly flowing and mingling into another. The whole reality is turned not only fluid but also indistinct and vague. The following passage is a typical example of the surrender to an unfocused flux of happening presented apparently with all the immediacy of actual experience:

> And suddenly a boy rushes to the flag and a host of bayonets are thrust at him, and another boy rushes up behind him, and at him the officer aims his pistol, and then others cry and rush at the flag, and the parrots and the bats and the crows come screeching out of the bel tree; and the coolies are now running down the Bebbur Mound, and there is a hand-to-hand fight, and some frightened, fall into the canal, and others go rushing this side and that, but the city boys, they squat down, they plop on the harvests and they squat down. But someone has hit the officer and he falls, and then curses and bayonets fly, and the coolies of Bebbur Mound have arrived, and they are holding the gas-light boxes in front of them, and some carry gas cylinders on their heads, and they carry sickles and lathis in their hands.

This passage is totally vague because it raises so many questions like (a) Why does the boy rush to the flag which has been planted by soldiers to make the rebels salute it? (b) Do the bayonets keep on in a Freeze of thrust at him? (c) Does the officer just aim the pistol and stand still while all sorts of cries, human and of nature, go on? (d) What is the relation between "some frightened" and "(they) fall into the canal?" (e) Why do they rush "this side and that?" (f) Who exactly are carrying sickles and lathis? The fragmentary details heaped on without interruption and balance render the whole delineation of disaster a failure in narrative technique.

3. *A Stylized* Skaz

It is widely recognized by critics that the language of Rao's first novel *Kanthapura* is a remarkable experiment. His Foreword, which is now famous and oft-quoted, reveals very clearly what kind of task he has set for himself. English, according to Rao, is "the language of our intellectual make-up" but it is not "the language of our emotional make-up." His main object is therefore to find stylistic equivalent in an alien language, of emotion and feeling, in other words, of the modes of actual and direct apprehension of life. With this specific object, his experiment in style is bound to be fundamentally realistic in nature, since it tries to find a form for felt experience at a given context. At every level of linguistic structure that is available in fiction, namely, lexical, syntactic and metaphoric, Rao proceeds to dissociate the English language—as far as possible for an individual—from those palpable aspects which habitually identify it with a mode of experience supposed to be Western and antithetical to the Indian and to project an alternative stylistic organization based on specific devices. Although Rao is definitely not the first Indian writer to have felt the need for a distinct Indian identity, there can be absolutely no doubt as to the fact that no Indian writer so far has extended the experiment to the whole language structure and, what seems to me far more important, has tried to find a meaningful relationship between the narrative form and the stylistic experiment. Form in *Kanthapura* tries to perceive a mythic design in an actual happening. An archaic, timeless existence on the point of transition into a specific historical situation has to find an adequate correlative in language. With this objective in mind, Rao has to combine two experiments; one, to present an intense and particular experience delimited in time and space; the other, to denote a general, timeless and eternal perspective and, if possible, to mingle the two in a golden mean.

The first part of the experiment has already received some critical attention and is obviously based on realism. The first thing which strikes even a casual reader of *Kanthapura* is the profusion of what is known in stylistics as "local colour," in the form of extensive borrowings from his native language, Kannada, in various forms. There are, as we have been told by competent critics, a great number of idioms and phrases literally translated into English as well as speech function and phatic communion, like characteristic habits of speech, modes of address, greetings, prayers, and imprecations which are peculiar to the Kannada-speaking community.[16]

The most important aspect of this experiment is what appears to be Rao's total reliance on the *spoken* medium of Kannada. This point needs emphasis because what Rao is trying to accomplish is not so much an abstract and theoretical model for Indian English to be emulated by all and sundry in various literary efforts, but a very individual and particular style to inter-relate a definite narratology. In other words, Rao's attempt to infuse Kannada into English is an inevitable concomitant of his adaptation of a realistic narrative form which happens to structure the actual experience of a Kannada-speaking community at a specific point of time. This experiment in local colour or linguistic realism is abandoned by Rao himself when his narrative ceases to be realistic. In *The Cat and Shakespeare* the milieu is Trivandrum, the capital of Kerala, and many characters are supposed to be Malayalis. But there is hardly any distinguishable Malayali linguistic feature against the overwhelming Kannada elements in *Kanthapura* because the narration of *The Cat and Shakespeare* is *not* traditionally realistic. In the first phase of Rao's development, the basic principle that guides his experiment is derived entirely from the Western tradition of linguistic realism which started with Romanticism and is now, more or less, taken for granted in the general run of fiction. It may sound strange, but we have to place Rao's Kannada experiment side by side with numerous experiments in dialects in the presentation of the lives of common people in the traditional nineteenth-century fiction, e.g. the Scottish brogue in Scott or the Cockney in Dickens.

The ancient literary tradition of India, as embodied in the classical Sanskrit, was dominated by classical theories of aesthetics and as such hardly ever recognized local colour or linguistic realism as a valid stylistic experiment, since the realistic portrayal of the life of the common man at a particular point of time did not provide the focus for any major literary effort. It would seem ironic no doubt, but inevitable nonetheless, that in order to achieve a particular *Indian* expression, Rao has to depend on a specific Western tradition. Even the principle of incorporation of the features of one language into another which we find followed in *Kanthapura* has specific Western predecessors. We have only to remember the exploitation of *alien* items by French writers like Stendhal, to evoke the spirit of Italy in *La Chartreuse de Parme*, or Mérimée to create the Spanish atmosphere in *Carmen*, or Vigny to build up a particularly English climate in *Stello*.[17] To conclude, Rao's experiment in introducing items of one language into another has been undertaken specifically to achieve a contextualization and intensification of the realistic narrative structure, the basic principle of which derives from Western practice. Rao has mostly translated the Kannada items into English following the practice of Indian writers in English as evident in the very first novel by Lal Behari Dey. An earlier model however would be Rudyard Kipling, the very representative of British India, in novels like *Kim*. For example, the rudimentary pattern for the use of Kannada elements in *Kanthapura* is already there in Kipling's address ("Ohè Mahbub Ali"), imprecations ("God's curse on all unbelievers"), translations of Indian idiomatic usage ("I am thy sacrifice"), deliberate dissociation from usual English ("Be still, no harm comes to thee, my son"), typical modes of phatic communion particular to the Indian ("What is your caste? Where is your house?") etc.[18]

Rao's linguistic realism, however, does not expend itself on the evocation of local colour alone. He maintains it unobtrusively in the use of quite a number of idiomatic and colloquial expressions in English which readers and critics of *Kanthapura* are apt to miss. Take, for example, his frequent use of tag questions: "Nanjamma does not know what all this is about, brahmins do not spin, do they?" "No one ever goes like that to far Kashi, do they?" "Nor like Bhatta do we go on Kashi-pilgrimage with toddy-contract money, do we?" or the typical idiomatic use of English expressions like *not bad to look, so much the better, drops in* to see them, *some two years ago,* and for the evening meal . . . soup *will do, to top it all,* I see no fault in khadi and *all that, bloke, kid, thank heavens, better not bother*. Some of these are repeated, as the *not . . . for nothing* pattern, e.g. "God has *not* given me a tongue *for nothing,*" "It was *not for nothing* she had borne eleven children. . . ."

In order to emphasize the Indian reality, there is sometimes a conscious avoidance of common English terms in favour of less common ones to convey alienness, for example *crow-and sparrow story* for *cock-and bull story, crush it in its seed* for *nip in the bud.* Then there is a sprinkling of words connected with the physical reality of India and Hindu behaviour patterns, like *pollution, caste, coconut, camphor, lantana, bamboo, ablution, banana, puffed-rice* etc., in short the items which "Indianize" the language essentially for their semantic function in respect of Hindu/Indian culture. But the linguistic principle remains the same, in the effort to present reality as actually perceived by the senses.

This realistic emphasis is considerably intensified in the *infor-*

mal and *intimate* tone of the whole narrative. The relationship between the narrator and the listener/reader is conceived as personal and intimate as though shared by each other. Hence the prevalence of direct address to the reader who is not only asked to enter the fictional world of Kanthapura's life, but actually made to participate in the action. It is here that we may contrast the style of the ancient *puranas* with that of *Kanthapura,* to indicate the fundamental difference in stylistic presentation. The style of the *puranas* is simple, impersonal and formal unlike the intimate, personal and carefully evolved style of *Kanthapura.* We present here two passages, one from *Siva Purana,* the other from *Kanthapura,* to bring out not only the essential difference between the two styles, but also the fact that the very *form* is controlled by different aesthetic values. Both the passages deal with anger and indignation, yet the stylistic expression is totally different, because the plane of representation is realistic in one and mythic in the other. Daksa, hearing that his sons have become ascetics under the persuasion of Narada, feels righteous anger and addresses Narada thus:

> "O, foremost among the base, disguised in the garb of a saint, what is it that your have done to these good people—my sons? To those engaged in good actions, the accursed path of mendicant has been shown by you.
> Ruthless rogue that you are, even when they are not free from three debts you put obstacles in the path of their progress both here as well as hereafter.
> He who renounces the world desiring salvation, without repaying the three debts and departs from the house forsaking his parents surely courts downfall.
> You are unkind, shameless, distorter of the tender intellect of children, and a destroyer of fame. Why do you, a foolish fellow, move about among the attendants of Visnu in vain? Frequently you have committed offences against me, O basest of the base, hence roaming over in the world your feet will never be steady anywhere (1969 edn., Vol. I, Ch. 13, 34-38)

Here is a passage from *Kanthapura* on a similar theme of righteous indignation felt by the Waterfall Venkamma at the threat of excommunication which Moorthy's association with untouchables might bring to the village:

> Venkamma plants herself like a banana trunk in front of her (i.e. Moorthy's mother) and cries out: "Hè Narsamma! Do you know what your son is bringing to this village?" "What?" trembles Narsamma. "What?" "It's for nothing you put forth into the world eleven children, if you do not even know what your very beloved son is always doing. I will tell you what he is doing: he is mixing with the pariahs like a veritable Muhammadan and the Swami has sent word through Bhatta to say that the whole of Kanthapura will be excommunicated. Do you hear that? A fine thing, too, it is, you with your broad ash-marks and your queer son and his ways. If he does not stop mixing with pariahs, this very hand—do you hear?—this very hand will give him two slaps on his cheeks and one on the buttocks and send him screaming to his friends, the pariahs. Do you hear? And I have daughters to marry, and so has everybody else. If you have none, *so much the worse for you.* And we shall stand *none of this pariah affair*. If he wants to go and sleep with these pariah whores, he can *do so by all means*. But let him not call himself a brahmin, *do you hear*? And tell him, the next time I see him in the Brahmin Street, he will get a jolly fine marriage-welcome with my broomstick."

The theme of both the passages centres round a feeling of indignation at the "irreligious" ways of a person who is criticized. Narada is denounced because he has deviated from the sanctified Hindu tradition by tempting young men to become mendicants before their duties as householders are fulfilled. Moorthy is condemned for having brought disgrace to the brahman community by caste-pollution. Yet the two outbursts are essentially different, stylistically.

The portion from the *purana* is divided into small units which renders the rage controllable and stylized. Though the cause is intensely personal—relating to a father's loss of son —the emphasis is on the impersonal. Narada is upbraided for the harm he is supposed to have done to the community as a whole. The emphasis in the passage from *Kanthapura* is over-whelmingly on the personal. For Moorthy's "fault," his mother is the victim of all kinds of taunts and humiliation. Her very motherhood and religious observances are brought to question. In order to be personal Venkamma even exaggerates the threat of excommunication to cover the whole village although the Swami has specifically mentioned Moorthy alone as the culprit. It is by inflating her sense of grievance that the eventual "jolly fine marriage-welcome" is imagined with Venkamma's own precious hands and broomsticks. So concrete and personal a discomfiture is a sharp contrast to the fate that awaits Narada as the result of the curse which may be seen as impersonal and general and conceived altogether on a different plane from the mimetic fictional world of *Kanthapura.* Further, Venkamma's outpouring consists of an unbroken flow in far closer—imitation of speech, replete with colloquial idiomatic uses, than the stylized units of the *purana.* Even the solidity of Venkamma's pose is conveyed to the reader through an image drawn from a familiar field of experience ("like a banana trunk") which is far more vivid in sensuous appeal than Daksa's "grief-stricken" appearance, "lips throbbing with fury." It is obvious even in translation that there is a fundamental difference between the distant and authoritative style prevalent in the *puranas* and the personal and informal representational mode in *Kanthapura.*

There may thus arise a reasonable suspicion that Rao's language in so far as it is contextualized, realistic and personal, can present only a realistic narration of actual events happening in a fictional world. But Rao's aim, as I have repeatedly maintained, is to combine myth and realism, and so the second part of the experiment, namely, the careful incorporation of specific linguistic items to represent the mythical and the archaic ethos is by far the more difficult one. The fundamental principle which proves Rao's linguistic talent is his instinctive realization that it is in accordance with the specific tradition of a language that experiments are to be conducted. Therefore he does not rely on translation, or transfer of devices alone.

This purpose is sought to be achieved by an extension of the scope of realism which is, in my opinion, a far more important endeavour than the borrowing from Kannada. This experiment is carried out with the help of two devices, archaism and conventional figures of speech. Deliberate archaism in vocabulary is used to suit recitation of legend, also to suggest the archaic nature of Indian reality. It has thus two functions in *Kanthapura* in the use of items like the following: *prompteth, needeth, doth, ye, so be it, wench, concubine, recompense, kine, obsequy, veritable, laved, verily, babe, breathful, bejewelled.* Take for example this passage:

> "O Brahma! deign to send us one of your gods so that he may incarnate on earth and bring back light and plenty to your enslaved daughter."
>
> "O sage," pronounced Brahma, "is it greater for you to ask or for me to say 'Yea'? Siva himself will forthwith go and incarnate on the earth and free my beloved daughter from her enforced slavery."

The expressive elements which are noticeable here are the words *deign, forthwith, incarnate,* none of which usually occur in the colloquial mode of daily life nor does the obvious rhetoric in *light and plenty.* The intimacy and the personal touch which predominate the narration of the grandmother give way to a different style altogether, where specific items are deliberately used to effect a distance from the mundane existence. Besides, the Indian reality itself cannot be fully contained in the historical present of the West, as it is conceived essentially different in its insistence of tradition, on timelessness. Archaism can thus define a sensibility which inheres in an archaic world. Bound to the eternal repetition of nature's cyclical events, the mythical pattern of recurrence predominates the peasant sensibility. Rao uses the Holy Bible as a source for the characteristic syntactic pattern of *Kanthapura,* namely, the repetition of short, regular structures connected with *and.* Here are two parallel passages, the first from *Kanthapura,* the second from the Bible:

1 Everybody goes from this side to that *and* Rachanna swears he has seen the light *and* Rachanna says he has seen it too, *and* they all rise up *and* Rachanna says he will go *and* look near the gate, *and* Madanna says he will go too, *and* young Venku and Ranga both say, "I'm coming with you, uncle," *and* when they are all at the gate they hear a grunt and a growl, *and* a soft whispering answer, *and* Rachanna cries out.

2 And his concubine played the whore against him, *and* went

> away from him unto her father's house to Bethlehem Judah, *and* was there four whole months. *And* her husband arose, *and* went after her, to bring her again, having his servant with him and a couple of asses; *and* she brought him into her father's house, *and* when the father of the damsel saw him, he rejoiced to meet him. *And* his father-in-law, the damsel's father, retained him, *and* he abode with him three days: so they did eat and drink and lodged there." (*Judges,* 29: 2-4)

The resemblance between the two passages, especially in the use of the connective *and,* combined with the fact that modern English style prefers the complex pattern of the periodic sentence to the linking of clauses with *and* has led Indian critics to conclude that Rao's use of *and* is un-English and therefore must be Indian. They fail to perceive the conscious pattern that he is trying to evolve in which this connective has a place in the total design. One should not also miss the interplay that he aims at between the linguistic experiment and the mythical part of his narrative structure. His use of repetition, also claimed to be Indian, echoes the Biblical style. Here are some passages from *Kanthapura* and the Bible which should make the point of resemblance obvious:

> he slips back into the foldless sheath of the soul, and sends out rays of love to the north, rays of love to the west, rays of love to the south, and love to the earth below and to the sky above. *(Kanthapura)*
>
> It stood upon twelve oxen, three looking toward the north, and three looking toward the west, and three looking toward the south and three looking toward the east: and the sea was set above upon them and all hinder parts were inward. (1 *Kings,* 7: 25)
>
> They say Rangamma is all for the Mahatma, we are all for the Mahatma, Pariah Rachanna's wife, Rachi, and Seethamma and Timamma are all for the Mahatma. They say there are men in Bombay and men in Punjab, and men and women in Bombay and Bengal and Punjab, who are all for the Mahatma. *(Kanthapura)*
>
> And when the king was come from Damascus the king saw the altar: and the king approached to the altar, and offered

> thereon. And he burnt his burnt-offering and his meat-offering, and poured his drink-offering and sprinkled the blood of his peace-offering upon the altar. (2 *Kings* 16: 12-13).

It was only too natural for Rao to look for the linguistic correlative of an orthodox Hindu sensibility in the timeless classic of the English language. The style of the Bible can be more fruitfully adapted to express the concept of an archaic ethos which is presumed to have remained the same for centuries and embodies a lifestyle closer to the ritualistic society found in the presentation of the primitive and close communities of the Biblical time than the complex linguistic structures of modern English which arise from a mode of life fully defined by the historical, existential present. Besides, when Rao started writing, there was already a very impressive body of work utilizing exactly the same elements of Biblical style in some of the English translations by eminent English scholars of the life of the Buddha, the one edited by Max Mueller, and the other by T.W. Rhys-Davids. Even the repeated references to Rao's Moorthy as the *Learned* One may be found echoing these scholars who describe the Buddha as the *Blessed One*. To claim Rao's use of *and* and repetitions as examples of Kannada influence is nothing short of sheer absurdity, since these very same elements are found in those renowned scholars who cannot possibly be proved to have been influenced by Kannada in their English rendering of the Buddha's life.[19] Besides, if these two characteristics are really derived from Kannada, these would form a part of "local colour" and would not be normally present in any non-Kannada context. But these linguistic features are permanent characteristics of Rao's style. Rao always falls back upon this style composed of repetitive short simple sentences connected by *and* with consciously-employed archaic flavour in words and turns of phrases whenever he writes ostensibly on fabular or mythical themes, e.g. *The Fables for the Feeble*, the legend of Rama in *The Serpent and the Rope*, of Kanyakumari in *Comrade Kirillov*. In these later examples, all these linguistic features are present, though the realistic Kannada context is absent. Indeed, in so far as the whole Indian ethos is conceived as static and archaic, Rao's exploitation of archaism serves for a stylistic device, connected essentially with the concept of the Indian ethos as an archaic existence and his search for a specific Indian identity which is static.

Since colloquialism and archaism may be antithetical, as myth is opposed in principle to reality, Rao attempts to enlarge the whole realistic mode with the help of some of the rhetorical devices of poetry. Take, for example, a portion of the celebrated beginning of *Kanthapura:*

> Roads, narrow, dusty, rut-covered roads, wind through the forests of teak and of jack, of sandal and of sal and hanging over bellowing gorges and leaping over elephant-haunted valleys, they turn now to the left and now to the right and bring you through the Alamba and Champa and Mena and Kola passes, into the great granaries of trade. There, on the blue water, they say, our carted cardamoms and coffee get into the ships the Red-men bring, and, so they say, they go across the seven seas into the countries where our rulers live.

The stylistic elements of this passage are not related to local colour, i.e. Kannada elements; these consist of evocative and expressive features, exploiting devices which are usually more closely associated with poetry than with prose. The use of sensuous images, "bellowing gorges," "leaping over elephant-haunted valleys," a marked preference for the concrete ("Red-men," instead of "British," "blue waters" for "sea"), conscious and careful manipulation of sound through alliteration and assonance ("teak and jack," "sandal and of sal," "Alamba and Champa and Kola," "great granaries," "carted cardamoms and coffee"), reveal unmistakably Rao's interest in rhetorical manipulation. It is here, specifically in this concept of the novel as primarily a verbal construct, that Rao stands apart from the puranic tradition where language is diaphanous and the whole motive of creation entirely content-oriented. It is this emphasis on language which is here not only a carrier, a vehicle, but the form inextricable from the narrative structure, which explains why Rao's novel, claimed to be so very "Indian," has not yet found an adequate translation in any Indian language.

This "poeticization" in *Kanthapura*, as we find in this passage, helps to distance the reality which is otherwise so dominant in the use of local colour. In other words, the function of Rao's rhetorical use of language is to counteract linguistic realism, in establishing the distance from the actual which is an essential requirement of mythical representation. At the same time, the poeticization enables Rao to make syntactic deviations for stylistic purpose.[20] Take, for example, Rao's careful use of what is known in stylistics as Inversion. The most common word-order that prevails in English (and French) prose following the speech habit is the subject-verb-object/complement pattern. But the simple fact that Rao is sometimes found to deviate from what is called the "normal" standard, does not necessarily establish his deviation as in consonance with Kannada or Sanskrit habit. The same deviation in fact is a very important stylistic device in English as well as French fiction which started in the Romantic age and—particularly in French—has continued to the present day. From Chateaubriand, Hugo and through Balzac the tradition comes down to Proust and Gide.[21] Rao's use of inversion is actually conditioned by a long and established Western practice. In the actual adaptation, Rao falls back upon the convention of English poetry which can very well supply him the required model. Take, for example, the opening line of *Kanthapura*, the very same that Indian critics have found abnormal: "High on the ghat is it, high up the steep mountains . . ."—so close in its pattern of construction to the well-known line of English poetry: "Delicious is the lay that sings" with the same kind of syntactic deviation from the normal, i.e. placing at the beginning the complement that normally comes at the end *(High* and *Delicious)* and the *be* verb *(is, is)* followed by the subject *(it, lay)*, thus reversing the normal order. This kind of inversion of the customary word-order has been widely practised in English poetry, e.g. in (a) "Fled is that music"; (b) "Tender is the night," (c) "Dull would he be of soul." In other words, Rao's "abnormality" in syntax draws entirely on the English literary tradition. Compare, for example, the following lines of *Kanthapura:* (a) "never has she failed us in our grief"; (b) "never has anything better been seen"; (c) "never was there a man in Karwar that had risen so quickly in public esteem": with these lines from a famous English poem: "Never did sun more beautifully sleep . . . in his first splendour/ Valley, rock or hill/Ne'er saw I, never felt a calm so deep."

Of course, one may present the exigencies of rhyme as the guiding principle of poetic inversion. But in Shakespeare's blank verse, the use of inversion is essentially an evocative device. Compare these examples from *Kanthapura:* (a) "Never will I sell my soul to a pariah"; (b) "Truth must you tell"; (c) "Him they put in morning bus"—with the following from Shakespeare: (a) "For

Banquo's issue have I fil'd my mind"; (b) "No sweet aspersion shall the heavens let fall"; (c) "But this rough magic/I here abjure." No wonder that Rao has always regarded Shakespeare as a major influence on him as a writer. The utility of inversion as deviance however is not merely decorative, but ingrained in the whole poetic technicality of *Kanthapura*, for, by placing the words in unusual position, at the rhythmic peak of the sentence for example, inversion becomes a means of focusing attention.[22] In sentences a, b and c, our attention is drawn to focus on *never, truth,* and *him*. Besides, inversion adds to the richness of description by allowing for actual experience to be impressionistically presented through this device. The oft-quoted opening of *Kanthapura* is a good example of the impressionist value of the device: "High on the Ghats is it, high up the steep mountains that face the cool Arabian seas, up the Malabar coast is it, up Mangalore and Puttur." Here the inversion creates a sense of actually seeing the whole scene that would have been lost in the ordinary word-order.

In fact this emphasis on the actual process of sense-experience leads to a marked degree of impressionism in *Kanthapura*. Since the theme of the novel is the actual destruction of a village in a series of violent actions, the verbs which recur again and again usually convey a sense of physical action. No one *goes* in Kanthapura, but *tramps* or *jumps*, often *thumps*, mostly *rushes*, though sometimes *crawls* or *creeps*. The rain never just *falls*, but *swings* and *swishes*, the light *leaps*, the dust *rises*, the road *hangs, rises, dips, turns* and *skirts*. It is to this purpose that most pathetic fallacies of the discourse are employed. So the night *tiptoes, hangs clawed up*, the rain *paws* and so on. Take, for example, the description of the onset of the monsoon in the Skeffington Coffee Estate:

> The darkness grows thick as sugar in a cauldron, while the bamboos creak and sway and whine, and the crows begin to wheel round and flutter, and everywhere dogs bark and calves moo, and then the wind comes so swift, and dashing that it takes the autumn leaves with it, and they rise into the juggling air, while the trees bleat and blubber. then drops fall, big as the thumb, and as the thunder goes clashing like a temple cymbal through the heavens, the earth itself seems to heave up and cheep in the monsoon rains. It churns and

> splashes, beats against the tree-tops, reckless and wilful, and suddenly floating forwards it bucks back and spits forward and pours down to the earth, and then playfully lounging up, the coffee leaves rising with it, and whorling and winnowing, spurting and rattling, it jerks and snorts this side and that.

The purpose here is obviously to convey an immediate, actual experience with an emphasis on the sensuous. In order to create an impression of actuality, the images are mostly kinetic, formed with verbs or verbals conjuring up sensations, some auditory *(creak, whine, bleat, blubber, clashing, cheep, rattling, snorts)*, others visual *(sway, flutter, churns, floating, bucks, back, spits forward, lounging up, whorling, winnowing)* which also convey a sense of motion. The violence of a tropical storm is seen and heard in concrete and physical terms, supported by the figures of sound-onomatopoeia *(moo, whine, bleat, blubber, cheep, thumping, rattling)*, alliteration and assonance *(bleat and blubber, temple cymbal, bucks back, spurting and rattling, jerks and snorts, heave and cheep, whorling and winnowing)*. While the intricate interlocking of senses and sound does indeed remind one of Hopkins, what interests us more is the extreme concentration of rhetoric in a limited area, here, for instance, a tropical storm which however is in no way related to the theme. With the emphasis thus overwhelmingly on the evocation of atmosphere, the principle behind the imagery of *Kanthapura* is to rely on the concrete and actual: old Ramkrishnayya reading chapter after chapter with such a calm "bell-metal voice," "their mouths touching the ears with delight," "stood fleshy with joy," "long barricades that lie like an elephant's carcass." The whole novel predominantly embodies an attempt to imitate a sensuous apprehension of the external world in the form of insistent onomatopoeia (the rain *patters*, the water *churns*, *swirls*, bamboos and gates *creak*, birds *screech*, monkeys *chatter*, autumn leaves *crunch*, fire *crackles*, wings *flap*; or the *flip-flap* of the whip, *pat-pat-pat* of rain) as also in the frequent coining of compounds which mostly appeal to the actual experience (*blue-spreading, tight-lipped, nine-pillared, puffy-cheeked, wind-swung, gap-toothed, goat-eyed*).[23]

At the same time there is a continuous straining for sound-effects in alliteration and assonance with which almost each page is replete, e.g. *sumptuous smell of cardamoms, grinned and grit, shim-*

mer and shake, a fuss and a flutter, hair and home, bright and benign, slipping seeking feet, not to mention an almost habitual repetitive grouping of *g* and *r*, e.g. *gropes and gurgles, gurgle and grunt, a grunt and a growl, grumbles and groans, groaning and grunting, grunting and grovelling,* and so on.

Such elaborate and persistent manipulation of sound points towards an aesthetic intention of impressing the reader rather than of conveying a meaning. Indeed for Raja Rao alliteration at this stage is almost a fatal Cleopatra for whom the world of meaning may often be well-lost. The oft-quoted line "there's neither man nor mosquito in Kanthapura" is obviously not to be appreciated for its informative value, but as an essentially "literary" presentation of the end of a village. Such a rhetorical style is hardly in keeping with the assumed spontaneity and artlessness of the unlettered grandmother's narration that *Kanthapura* is ostensibly supposed to be.

Besides, Rao's rhetoric often leads to a verbalization in excess of the actual experience. In the passage on the tropical storm analyzed, we find darkness compared to sugar burning in a cauldron. One may wonder if the image is really as sensuous as it appears. For, just before the monsoon breaks, the darkness that spreads all around grows distinctly ominous in its slate grey colour, very much unlike the melting of sugar in a cauldron, which starts with a golden caramel and turns into a quick brown-black. Rao's image suggests inadequate intimacy with the real experience that he tries to convey. Even if its domestic dimension relates to the fact that the speaker is a female, the sombreness of the piling clouds can hardly be associated with the melting of sugar, usually connected with gastronomical delights. In the thunder clashing "like a temple cymbal," the notion of the "Indian"/Hindu scene painting robs the actuality of the thunder that breaks in a series of almost stereophonic reverberations, one sound leading to another, pervading the whole auditory area of sensation, which gradually grows feebler and feebler till it merges into silence; the cymbals on the other hand produce clearly defined sounds at the same key and from a definite point, monoaural so to say, and the lingering reverberation can hardly be compared to the intensity and graduation of thunder. The verbal expression thus tends to be dislodged from the actual experience which it presumes to imitate. One wonders if it is not already the exile's enthusiasm to emphasize "Indianness" that produces such over-wrought sensuous exercises.

In his paragraph construction Rao handles too many diverse, even contradictory, elements in juxtaposition—local colour, short syntactic structure, repetition, rhetoric and archaism. The main charge against Rao's experiment in *Kanthapura* is of monotony and artificiality and these arise, not so much because of his Kannada elements, as Indian critics have offered as defence, but because of his assemblage of mainly poetic and archaic elements into a paragraph structure which is not suitable for including these specific features. In a long uninterrupted flow, his construction imitates *speech* as it is used in stream-of-consciousness novels, and is essentially modern. To put it rather simplistically, Rao incorporates essentially formal and conventional stylistic features in a modern, realistic paragraph unit geared to the oral. His inability to maintain a balance which is in any case precarious in such a bold adventure, comes out specifically in the long paragraphs delineating physical violence:

> We all groaned and shrieked and sobbed, and we rushed this side to the canal-bund and that side to the coconut garden and this side to the sugarcane field and that side to the Belfield bund, and we fell and we rose, and we crouched and we rose, and we ducked beneath the rice harvests and we rose, and we fell over stones, and we rose again, over field-bunds and canal-bunds did we rush, and the children held to our saris and some held to our breasts and the night blind held to our hands.

Thus it goes on and on in a paragraph of 43 lines to be followed by many more paragraphs, each made of more than 40 lines in exactly the same style. The aim is to convey a physical motion of speed as well as of diffusion over a large space. It is sought to be presented through a repetition of the same rigid syntactic pattern (subject-predicate) joined by *and* in the whole paragraph with a single variation ("over field-bunds did we rush") of inversion. This variation, first of all, is insufficient in weight considering the volume that has preceded. Besides, it is wholly obscured by an impression of being an extension which the use of *and* here in this clause produces. There should have been a stop, a breathing space here to allow the new idea in "children held" to commence and register in the mind of the reader. The artificial continuation of one sentence through these phases with the help of *and* distracts attention from the fact that there are different actions described here. In other words, the contour of thought, of narration, is obscured in the syntactic repetition, till the impression of speed becomes a mechanical process. The inverted sentence sounds abnormal in speech, for inversion is always distant from the spoken form. The very length of the paragraph is at variance with the device adopted in regard to its various components. In a passage like this, the attempt at rhythm is so obvious and deliberate that the effect is marred by an excess of stylistic parallelism. The aesthetic strategy of prose rhythm lies in the manipulation of similarity in the context of difference. "The essence of rhythm is," says Whitehead, "the fusion of sameness and novelty; so that the whole never loses the essential unity of the pattern, while the parts exhibit the contrast arising from the novelty of their detail."[24] The incessant repetition of short syntactic structures joined by *and* irrespective of the diagram of meaning in lengthy paragraphs only re-affirms that a mere repetition kills rhythm. No doubt there is a feeble attempt at creating balance, by incorporating inversion, but the aesthetic function of the latter is severely limited because it emphasizes the formal and literary aspect whereas the whole attempt is supposed to be informal and colloquial.

It has of course been claimed by Rao's Indian (and Kannada) critics that he has captured the "natural rhythm" of "Indian" speech in the English of *Kanthapura*. This however raises a fundamental question as to the basic components of rhythm whether these are freely interchangeable from one language to another as different as English and any Indian tongue. As a matter of fact, the rhythm of a language depends on its phonetic structure which is ultimately rooted in the speech habits of the speakers of that language alone and as such the rhythmic properties are peculiar to a language:

> We should not forget that these sound-figures will vary in their effect from language to language, that each language has its own system of phonemes and hence of oppositions and parallels of vowels or affinities of consonants.[25]

The claim that the rhythm of Rao's English in *Kanthapura* is a faithful reproduction of any speech rhythm in India can hardly be accepted without a detailed analysis which has to prove that the trinity of English rhythm, namely time, stress and pitch, have exactly the same or similar values and relational pattern in an Indian language. In fact, it is quite clear that Rao himself intends only to infuse a sense of speed, a heightened *tempo* which he feels to be the nature of Indian life. Tempo is of course not a factor of rhythm, but definitely its regulator. We are told that "an increased tempo tends to level down the stresses, to hurry over the unstressed elements, and so, increasing the distance between pauses, diminish the marks by which rhythmic groups are signalled."[26] Let us apply this formula to a typical passage in *Kanthapura* delineating action:

> And then more and more men crawl up, and more and more wounded are brought up, on shoulders and arms and stretchers are they brought up with dangling legs, dangling hands and bleeding hands, and with bleeding mouths and bleeding foreheads and backs are they brought up, city boys and peasant boys are they.

Instead of levelling down the stresses, we find an increased emphasis on them because the rhythmic groups with parallel construction and inversion are so distinctly sought to be signalled in a regular order. The monotony thus produced can hardly be conducive to increasing tempo or even imitating speech. The artificiality of this experiment can only lead to an overwhelming preponderance in *Kanthapura* of a specific metrical pattern which may be presented thus, "and we rush/and we stumble/and we rise/and we duck"; "and we fell/and we rose/and we crouched/and we rose." Stevenson's position— "prose must be rhythmical but it must not be metrical"[27]—need not be accepted literally, for metrical patterns are discernible in the best of English prose. But in a literary tradition the metrical form, even when latent, is compatible only with *formal* writing as we find for example in Burke, Swinburne or Ruskin. The presence of such an insistent metrical pattern in Rao's informal prose, a prose which aims at the rhythm of speech, may be totally unacceptable from an aesthetic point of view. The attempt to evolve a language stylized and natural at the same time arises out of the urge to combine the two forms, archaic/poetic and realistic or modern, ingrained in the very concept of the structure of

Kanthapura as a stylized *Skaz*.

A *skaz* is "an orientation toward oral speech," a narrator's narration "which is socially distinct" and carries with it a particular viewpoint that the author needs for his purpose.[28] The grandmother narrator of *Kanthapura* thus performs the function of the story-teller of a *skaz* who belongs "to the common people (precisely the quality the author values in him) and he brings with him oral speech." Hence the colloquialism, extensive borrowing from the Kannada speech habits, as also the characteristic pattern of the paragraph imitative of the continuity in the flow of speech. But the main point, as Mikhail Bakhtin emphasizes in discussing the stylized *skaz*, lies in the "double voiced quality, the intersecting of two voices and two accents within it" which arises because the author produces here in the narrator's name "a certain specific literary style" which belongs to the sophisticated and conscious writer and not to the common story-teller working in an oral medium. In *Kanthapura*'s narration and language, those two voices are clearly distinguished, the orientation to a spontaneous oral speech is juxtaposed by a whole paraphernalia of essentially literary devices of careful manipulation. But the problem is, both the voices are presented with equal authenticity and weight and so confront each other instead of being placed in the graded order essential in a structure. The rhetorical devices predominate in *Kanthapura*'s assumed oral texture and tend to confuse the identity of design. The artificiality of the stylistic experiment here lies, not only in the excessive repetition of one particular syntactic pattern, but more in this unassimilated opposition between different modes which stretches the limit of literary freedom available in a tradition.

4. *The quest begins*

In his very first work of fiction, Rao's fidelity to experience, to a presentation of actuality, is found to be in disjunction with the required recognition of the ambivalence of the total design. For Rao, the Indian ethos in so far as it is archaic is essentially brahmanic and must therefore be orthodox; while the Indian nationalism with which Rao seems to identify through Moorthy is, to a great extent, against brahmanic vested interests. Nationalism in India came through Western education as a longing for independence against British rule. The consciousness of India as a *national* entity is perhaps alien to Hindu orthodoxy. This fundamental disjunction is accepted by Rao in *Kanthapura*, for orthodox Hindus led by Bhatta, the leading brahman, oppose Gandhian nationalism. But the mythical design, in which Rao desires to perceive Gandhi as an *avatar*, can be derived only from orthodoxy. It is significant that the famous lines of the *Bhagavad Gita* describing the eternal recurrence of the archetype which so obviously underlies Rao's presentation of Gandhi is uttered by the representative of Hindu orthodoxy who denounces the Mahatma: "Whensoever there is ignorance and corruption I come, for I, says Krishna, am the defender of *dharma*." The contradiction in the author surfaces once we remember that the prevalence of "ignorance and corruption" which is the primary requirement for incarnation is nowhere to be seen in the village which, at the beginning of the action, is presented as a veritable haven of peace and prosperity where every one—from the privileged brahman at the top to the deprived pariah at the lowest rung—lives happily within the age-old rigid hierarchy. Hence the appearance of the Father of the Nation poses actually a threat by "meddling with the *dharma sastras*" which will lead to the greatest disaster constantly feared by the brahmans, namely "corruption of castes." Moorthy's orthodox mother moans, "Oh, this Gandhi! Would he were destroyed!" Whenever there is a direct confrontation, the orthodox brahmans emerge superior to the Gandhian nationalists in objectivity and rational power. So instead of an *avatar* who appears to establish the right order, Gandhi is ultimately found to be a catalyst who disrupts a static existence. The failure of the mythical pattern to prefigure the apostle of nationalism is thus embedded in Rao's unconscious identification of brahmanic orthodoxy with the whole Indian ethos and impedes the full development of narrative technique, especially the growth of characters required to show not only Moorthy's disillusionment in detail and in concrete terms but also the brahmans's active role in the destruction of the Hindu/archaic existence of *Kanthapura*. Rao's failure in the delineation of the crisis is a consequence of this fundamental contradiction. Even a small episode like Moorthy's expiatory fast which follows the Gandhian moral exactitude appears isolated and abrupt because of the *metaphysical* element incorporated in it, which is outside the domain of the Gandhian thesis, but related to what seems *Hindu* to Rao.[29] The total design or *mythos* is effected in two ways in fiction: "One is the continuous recognition of credibility, fidelity to experience, and of what is not so much life-likeness as life-liveliness. The other is the recognition of the identity of the total design, into which we are initiated by the technical recognition of the plot."[30] In *Kanthapura*, Rao's fidelity to the experience of Indian nationalism is set against the mythical design associated with brahmanic orthodoxy. His style reflects this fundamental dissonance, and the attempt to strike a balance between the opposed modes fails to attain the harmony of a total design. Thus the quest of an Indian writer for a specific "Indian" identity to be embodied in the novel form in English arises out of and falls against a deep-set disjunction between the contemporary Indian reality and the inherited concept of tradition.

NOTES

1. The same experiment is discernible in the stories published in *The Cow of the Barricades and Other Stories*, 1947, seven of which reappear in *The Policeman and the Rose*, 1978. These can roughly be divided into three groups: a) Realistic, e.g. *Javani, Akkayya, A Client, The Little Gram Shop, In Khandesh;* b) Mythic, e.g. *Companions* and *The True Story of Kanakapala;* c) Realistic-Mythic, e.g. *Narsiga* and *The Cow of the Barricades.*
2. For details see Mircea Eliade, *The Myth of the Eternal Return or Cosmos and History*, 1949, trans. 1954, p. xii.
3. Mircea Eliade, *Myths, Dreams and Mysteries: The Encounter between Contemporary Faiths and Archaic Realities*, 1957, trans. 1960, p. 23.
4. Raja Rao, *Kanthapura* (1938), 2nd ed. (rpt. Madras 1974), p. vi.
5. For details, see A.D. Pusalkar, *Studies in the Epics and Puranas*, 1953, p. 36, where he deals with the problem of historicity of Krishna and concludes that Krishna was "originally a real man" and deified gradually later on. As Mircea Eliade says: "The historical personage is assimilated to his mythical model (hero etc.), while the event is identified with the category of mythical actions." *The Myth of the Eternal Return*, p.

43.

6. Also *Kanthapura*, pp. 166, 93, 208, 252.
7. Recorded in *The Gandhi Reader*, ed. Homer J. Jack, 1956, Introduction, p. vii.
8. "No moral code is too severe for the people It is too severe only to those who have lost their dharmic role in society." Raja Rao, *The Illustrated Weekly of India*, Feb. 14, 1965.
9. In the *purana*, on the other hand, the incarnation always saves the devotee-in-distress like Prahlad for example, who never abandons the principle embodied in the incarnation. *Visnu Purana*, trans. H.H. Wilson, 1840, rpt. 1972, p. 119.
10. J.P. Stern, *On Realism*, 1973, p. 94.
11. In puranas however the digressions are mainly didactic in function. Thus in *Siva Purana*, the story of Devadatta is linked with the central theme because Devadatta, despite his grievous sins, goes to heaven, having listened to a recital of *Siva Purana* albeit accidentally. *Siva Purana*, B Kunst and S.L. Sastri eds., 1969, Vol. I, V; 37, p. 9. For details on the role of setting in the traditional novel., see René Wellek and Austin Warren, *Theory of the Literature*, 1949, 1976, pp. 220-21.
12. The Puranic narrator is "supposed to communicate what was imparted to him by his preceptor, as he had heard it from *some other sage." Preface to Visnu Purana, p.x. He can never be personal, nor can be ever involved in the events described by him.* Rao admits that he was inspired by Ignazio Silone's *Fontamara*, 1934, trans. S. David and E. Mospacher, 1948, which is narrated by three characters, husband, wife and son, each in first person.
13. Northrop Frye, *Fables of Identity: Studies in Poetic Mythology*, 1963, p. 36. Also, cf. George Levin, "Realism Reconsidered," in *The Theory of the Novel*, ed. John Halperin, 1974, p. 240.
14. Wayne C. Booth, *The Rhetoric of Fiction*, 1961, p. 128.
15. The Puranas on the other hand restricted by the frame of verse are further punctuated by divisions into units which are called variously, *Khandas, Samhitas, Padas, Skandhas, Amsas*, not to speak of well-known divisions in the great epics, the *Ramayana* into *Kandas* and the *Mahabharata* into *Parvas*.
16. See for details G.B. Patil, "The Kannada Element in Raja Rao's Prose: A Linguistic Study of *Kanthapura*," Dharwar;

The Journal of Karnatak University, Humanities, 1969, Vol. X, pp. 143-67.

17. For an authentic and detailed analysis of "local colour" as an essential aspect of romanticism in French Fiction, see Stephen Ullman, *Style in the French Novel,* 1957, pp. 41-80.
18. Rudyard Kipling, *Kim*, 1901, 1970, pp. 24-26, 11, 195.
19. Take for example any random passage from T.W. Rhys David's translation of Buddhist Suttas from the Pali *The Sacred Books of the East*, ed. Max Mueller, 1888, Vol. I.c. Ch. II: 21.2.
20. For details on the aesthetics of linguistic deviance, see Jan Mukarovsky, "Standard language and Poetic language," ed. and trans. Paul L. Garvin in *Linguistics and Literary Style,* ed. Donald C. Freeman, 1970, pp. 41-56.
21. For Inversion as a well-known device in the traditional realistic fiction, see Ullman, *Style in French Novel*, pp. 173-74.
22. *Ibid.*, pp. 103-11.
23. C.W. Turner points out the poetic possibilities of coinages as "an intentional catching of the specific situation," in *Stylistics,* 1973, p. 111.
24. Quoted by Paul F. Baum in *The Other Harmony of Prose*: *An Essay in English Prose Rhythms,* 1952, pp. 10-11.
25. René Wellek and Austin Warren, *Theory of Literature,* pp. 159-60.
26. Baum, *The Other Harmony of Prose*, p. 50,
27. Quoted by Baum, p. 29.
28. For details on *Skaz*, a narrator's narration, see Mikhail Bakhtin, "Discourse Typology in Prose" *Readings in Russian Poetics,* eds. K. Matejka and K. Pomoroska, 1971, pp. 181-82.
29. Mahatma Gandhi told Muriel Lester that he "never heard a voice, saw a vision, or had some recognized experience of God." See Louis Fischer, *The Life of Mahatma Gandhi,* 1951, p. 266.
30. Northrop Frye, *Fables of Identity,* p. 29.

The Serpent and the Rope

Part I

1. *Fissures in being*

In *Kanthapura* a gulf yawns between the Indian heritage conceived as mythical and the demands of the historical present. If the Indian ethos, that is essentially beyond time, structured on the principle of the myth of the eternal return, appears as a metaphysic of eternity in his second work, *The Serpent and the Rope* (1960), twenty-two years later, the credit perhaps should go to Rao's exile in the West. While the West's colonial interest in India is practical and derisive, the intellectual interest remains romantic and reverent. It is with the latter that Raja Rao chooses to identify himself. This choice is not only natural but also convenient for the brahman aspirant towards an "Indian" identity. From the turbulence of the contemporary Indian reality—as depicted in *Kanthapura*—in which the very foundation of Hindu hierarchical orthodoxy is being challenged by a new concept of national solidarity, Raja Rao the brahman sails to an apparently safe refuge, carrying with him the brown man's spiritual burden to the materialist West.

Hence the theme of *The Serpent and the Rope* is overwhelmingly serious—an Indian's quest for truth in his encounter with the spatio-temporal reality, growing into an acute crisis of identity because the hero, an orthodox brahman who claims to belong to a timeless ethos, is found however immersed in the modern Western culture dominated by historicity. This theme is presented through a movement running between the actual situations in life embodied in human relations and a development of the hero's particular philosophy of history, with an obvious suggestion that a necessary correspondence exists between the former and the latter.

Ramaswamy, a consumptive South Indian brahman, a descendant of a medieval Vedantin, is a research scholar in France, married to a French intellectual, Madeleine, who teaches history. Their first child dies of lung-complication, the shadow of death affecting Rama no less than Madeleine, for he feels at home only with his stepmother and stepsister in India, deriving from them "the *delire* (i.e. rapture) of immortality" when the wife mourning the death of a son seems "very far." At this point, he meets a north Indian princess, Savithri Rathor, a young student at Cambridge, engaged unwillingly to Pratap Singh of the Political Service, and impresses her with his "affirmation of Indian values." This meeting acts as a catalyst in the disintegration of his marriage, when Ramaswamy, drawn to Savithri, feels Madeleine's inadequacy. Two other exiles join them, Georges, a devout White Russian convert to Catholicism, and Lezo, a Spanish refugee and a socialist with an interest in Buddhism. Their discussions rouse Madeleine's interest in Buddhism though according to Ramaswamy's thesis, Buddhism is too historical, whereas India belongs to eternity. Madeleine's wholehearted attempts, her feminine instinct and love result in a second pregnancy. At this point Savithri lands up, "to know India" from Ramaswamy, who immediately recognizes in his role of guru, the spiritual affinity with Savithri. Frustrated in his sexual relationship with Madeleine, he escapes into the undemanding Platonic assurance of Savithri in Cambridge. Since Savithri is convinced of his "Indian interpretation of history" seeking to define the Western ethos as moralistic (and personal) against the Indian as metaphysical (and impersonal), their ritual wedding at London symbolizes the victory of India over Madeleine and the West. Back in France, he finds Madeleine's calm and perpetual sadness intolerable, as well as a constant reminder of her instinctive knowledge of his rejection. So he escapes to India ostensibly to attend his stepsister Saroja's marriage. He advises Savithri to marry her fiancé Pratap, just as he makes Saroja marry a person totally unsuitable, ostensibly because in his view Indian tradition is "impersonal," above egotistic preferences. Madeleine's second child dies. The actual marriage of Savithri plunges Rama into a short affair with Lakshmi, married to a friend. On his return, he finds Madeleine a true Buddhist *sadhaka* set on a severely ascetic path in the quest for transcendence. Rama now develops his thesis, justifying the ruthless extermination of the pure and noble Cathars by the Roman

Catholic Church. He tries to destroy Madeleine's new faith by declaring that India separates them for ever; as Buddhism has been "driven out" by Vedanta, Madeleine with her Buddhism must necessarily remain an outsider to Rama's Vedantic world. Leaving her to a lonely withdrawal, he goes to England where a flare-up of consumption leads to thoracoplasty. When Savithri offers to leave her husband, Ramaswamy realizes at last that their separation is ordained by the very nature of love which must have distinct entities, and accepts the separation as permanent in this existence. Invoking the "Impersonal" as *dharma* he attempts to come back to Madeleine, but fails, since his love for her remains subordinate to the personal to "the eighteen aggregates." The marriage ends in divorce. The loneliness and misery of Rama stretches to a point of desperation heightened by the fact that his thesis, an "Indian" attempt to philosophize history, is regarded deficient in "historical discipline." We are informed that within a short time (three days as the entries in the diary show), the crisis is resolved in his submission to a guru as disciple and Ramaswamy is freed for ever from the anguish of time.

The theme, to begin with, purports to be the "history" of a brahman who is however "never contemporary" and thus starts on the principle of paradox. Ramaswamy, conscious of his privileged position as a brahman in the Hindu social hierarchy, constantly aspires to realize the full metaphysical connotation of true brahmanhood— "a Brahmin is he who knows *Brahman*"—with which his quest starts and also ends. This Brahman, in Hindu thought, is the Ultimate Reality, the Absolute Consciousness beyond time and the world of phenomena. So the brahman's lifestory starts with a sage as ancestor, who as legendary is lifted to eternity beyond historical time; and the story ends at the feet of the guru who alone can lead the brahman to the true brahmanhood which "commences when you recognize yourself in your eternity." Surprisingly Ramaswamy is writing a record of happenings in time, "the *chronicle* of a life," with the discipline of "the historical sciences." The brahman and Vedantin Ramaswamy, supposed to be a pilgrim of eternity, is ironically a historian, his identity thus split between the two opposing modes of time and eternity, of history and tradition, the former always representing to him the modern Western existence, the latter the Indian ethos:[1] "There never was time, there never was history, there never was anything but *Shivoham*,

Shivoham, I am Shiva, I am the Absolute." At the same time he knows: "By taste and tradition, I am only a historian."

The historical self of Rama is very much rooted in the Western mode of Judaeo-Christianity which cannot be synthesized with Indian timelessness. For the Vedantin Rama, time should be a perspective belonging to the cosmic illusion of *maya*, that is the phenomenal world; the Ultimate Reality is eternal, beyond time. On the other hand, the modern Western ethos, in so far as it is permeated with the spirit of Christianity accepts time as real and final. Christ died for our sins once only, once for all. It is not an event subject to repetition, which can be produced many times. For the modern man in the West, life in this world is a unique event in history without the assurance of periodic return which demolishes time in the archaic and primitive faith. Ramaswamy's tragedy lies precisely in the fact that he aspires towards timelessness, assumed as his "Hindu" identity, whereas he is actually engrossed in historical time which is deemed to be the reality only for the Christian.

Little Mother's precept, "Birth and death are the illusions of the non-Self" is evidently derived from the Vedantic concept of the Self or the Ultimate Reality as transcending the time cycle of birth and death—mere happenings on the empirical plane. As Rama himself declares, "I do not believe that death is"; his remote and distant ancestors "did not die." He is fully aware that death cannot be "real" in the sense of being the ultimate. To Catherine, Ramaswamy repeats Little Mother's dictum self-consciously, "Death and life are not opposite things but alternate events, like spring and winter, heat and monsoon." Yet the very first concrete picture of Ramaswamy that is presented to us is that of a four-year old orphan mourning over the death of his mother. This is not merely a motherless child's normal reaction of grief at the moment of loss, but a preparation for a continuing inability to integrate death into the scheme of things, because Ramaswamy the Vedantin never gets over the death of his mother which pursues him throughout his life with unquenchable anguish.[2] Even at the age of twenty-two, when the action of the novel takes place, he sits at a hotel in the Pyrenees and sobs, "I know I would never see my mother again." The anguish of this sentence derives its strength from the irrevocable significance of death in the plane of time, because, "the historicity of every human existence directly implies the anguish of facing death."[3] Ramaswamy himself feels, "There is no pain more acute than a pain unnameable, and all the shine of the world is only a prophecy, a shout that *death* is, that one loses another. . . ."

The Vedantic concept which he believes to be the essence of India, realized so concretely in Benaras, the Eternal City, remains an intellectual conviction totally unrelated to his own experience and feeling.[4] Indeed the historical finality of his mother's death opens up a permanent fissure in his being which is fundamental in his life, "I know my mother Gauri is not dead, and yet I am an orphan" Throughout the novel it is the lament of an orphan that persists: "Where, I ask you, where was I to build a house, a home?" and "I must have a home, I must get back home." This intense and gnawing feeling of rootlessness arises out of his fundamental inability to accept the death of his mother, that is, from his self that is bound to time. Hence in his exile he longs for India as a home which he specifically identifies with the mother, "I would go back to India, for that India was my breath, my only sweetness, gentle and wise; *she was my mother.*"

The bondage to time naturally determines the nature of self or identity which reveals itself "only against the background of temporal moments."[5] Ramaswamy therefore undertakes an autobiography to reconstruct the passage of time, *à la recherche du temps pérdu,* an essentially Western task. Hence the adventures through which the temporal progress of Ramaswamy is recorded, centre round an existential concept of human relationship—Man and the Other. Ramaswamy exists in so far as he is not himself, that is, in so far as the Other exists. Man is man, because there is non-man, the woman. His consciousness defines itself by knowing what it is not. For Ramaswamy, woman is "the other" as he himself elaborates this essentially existential theme, "Man sees himself in woman as essence, the fact of womanhood is the meaning of his life. *If there were nothing other, you could not know that you are.*"[6] This need for woman as the other has nothing to do with the worship of woman as the feminine principle, but is directed entirely to a coincidence of man's own self. Indeed Ramaswamy has just reflected Sartre's metaphysical principle, "I need the other in order to realize fully all the structure of my being." To realize his being in the existence, Ramaswamy must be free, which in existential jargon means the right to be a subject. He can be a subject and free, only if the other, the woman, is not so. Hence for Ramaswamy, "The object, I thought, is woman." For him therefore, Savithri is the "true woman" because she professes to see the world through him alone. She has no independent subjecthood, for she embodies in her total dependence, the absence of freedom of choice, "For a woman to choose is to betray her biology." All his "equations in history" may leave the Cambridge undergraduates cold, but completely overwhelm Savithri. In this imprint of self on Savithri as an object, Ramaswamy feels confirmed in his "centripetal being."

In relation to Madeleine however Ramaswamy is unable to locate himself as a free subject dominant over her. Whenever he impresses her, as with the dialectic with Georges, he feels assured because he establishes his dominance, "This time I had really *won* her." And "Madeleine was *won*. So I felt free." But this dominance is essentially an intellectual victory. As Madeleine is his wife, Ramaswamy must prove himself the husband and consequently father to her children. But he is consumptive, and, in the Hindu mind, resisting no doubt Western medical knowledge, consumption is a serious disqualification.[7] So even the faint suspicion of a desire for active sexual participation in Madeleine hurries him away to seek assurance in the Platonic consolation of Savithri to whom he is safely a guru. Indeed, Ramaswamy is happy only in that kind of relationship with a woman which is predominantly non-sexual. With his sister Saroja he feels so assured because "She with the woman in her (is) without the woman's demands." Entries in Ramaswamy's diary reveal his deep obsession with such "demands" and the frustration that he experiences whenever he feels inadequate. At the same time he is sensitive enough to be aware that he has failed Madeleine, for, as a man, "his defeat is the defeat of her womanhood." This sense of inadequacy of manhood prevents him from reacting to the death of their children. Unlike the heroes of Indian epics who have always strongly reacted to the death of sons and gone to all extremes to demonstrate their respect for grieving mothers,[8] Ramaswamy has nothing to offer his wife in her loss although he knows, "the sorrow of woman be indeed the barrenness of man." The more desperate Madeleine becomes in her attempt to transcend the death of her sons, the more emphasized is Ramaswamy's "barrenness," his inadequacy of manhood. It becomes his aim to prove Madeleine's Buddhist path of non-becoming as wrong, to "destroy her theogony."[9] But the determination in her renunciation reveals "the assuredness that this identity nobody could remove or corrupt" and such a display of spiritual freedom makes Ramaswamy "ashamed" of himself. This is intolerable. The rejection of Madeleine therefore is inevitable, not because of what Madeleine is, but for what Ramaswamy is not. "You are more of a Brahmin than I," admits the brahman husband to his non-brahman wife.

The basic principle which underlies Ramaswamy's relation with Woman as the Other is existential for it is based on, what Sartre would call "a certain art of forming contradictory concepts which unite in themselves both an idea and the negation of an idea." The two aspects which are not co-ordinated or surmounted in a synthesis are facticity and transcendence. It is only *mauvaise foi* or *bad faith* that seeks "to affirm their identity while preserving their difference." Ramaswamy's relationship with Madeleine and Savithri provides a classic example of *bad faith*. He continually claims that in "Hindu" tradition it is the "impersonal," the Self, that underlies the love between husband and wife. "So no man can love a woman for her personal self." Yet Ramaswamy confesses, "Did I love the Self in Madeleine? I know I did not." To the very end of the novel his love remains rooted in her personal self alone, and so inevitably "It must go as it came." Bad faith, however, differs from a common lie because the person concerned tells the lie to himself, he deceives himself in deceiving others, as Sartre comments, "in bad faith it is from myself that I am hiding the truth." So the fact that Ramaswamy fails Madeleine in his adultery with Lakshmi is consciously ignored by himself. In the bed of Lakshmi he wonders whether he is Rama, "Saroja's loved brother, Little Mother's stepson." He does not appear to remember himself as Madeleine's husband because it is precisely this identity which is lost in his faithless act. The conscious defence of his Platonic relation with Savithri marks another aspect of the same self-negation. Lying by Madeleine, Rama has to convince himself that he is "overtaken by no remorse, no inhibition, no eating back of my own sorrow on thinking of Savithri" for he has been aware of Madeleine's instinctive knowledge of his new love. When he is heading towards the ritual union with Savithri in London, Madeleine's letter is eloquent with "calm desperation": "I lose you—I know I will lose you. And yet where can I go but to you?" Ramaswamy, proclaimed repeatedly as an ideal husband, has however no assurance to offer. Her sad eyes haunt him, so does her silent question: "Rama, tell me—tell me, that you love me." Instead of a decisive answer Ramaswamy peters into an elaborate prevarication of non-commitment, "I am mine and you Madeleine are a chunk of truth—as the sun, the moon, the space of the stars." The evasion is "exact," indeed he "would have betrayed no one," it is only himself that he is deceiving, not Madeleine whose knowledge of her rejection is instinctive, not dependent on his justification of duplicity. Ramaswamy's behaviour as husband may easily appear as an illustration of Sartre's perceptive analysis of *bad faith*..

> As for his flaunted intention of telling the truth ("I'd never want to deceive! This is true, I swear it!"), all this, of course, is the object of an inner negation, but also it is not recognized by the liar as his intention.

This compulsive self-deception manifests above all in Ramaswamy's relation with Savithri, a love supposed to be on a transcendental level, from which it derives its whole justification. Yet whenever Savithri is surrounded by her admirers—her "paramours"—Ramaswamy's ostensibly "Impersonal" love gives way to jealousy. Her calm acceptance of Pratap as her future husband makes him absolutely furious and he does not hesitate to make the reader see how he hates this resigned attitude of the Hindu woman. In the ritual wedding itself, when Savithri's resignation to her future role as wife of Pratap is made quite clear, Ramaswamy, the worshipper of Orthodoxy and the Impersonal, is in visible pain. Above all, the actual ceremony of Savithri's marriage drives his spirituality to an act, very much phenomenal in nature, in the bed of Lakshmi. This affair is a deliberate act of will: "since there was to be no Savithri any way." With such deep roots into the existence of flesh and blood, of phenomenality, this love continuously refuses to stay bound to the facticity. In the development of the Ramaswamy-Savithri theme there is thus a continuous see-saw movement between facticity and transcendence. When Savithri acts in accordance with the notion of transcendence, that is, accepts Pratap, Ramaswamy slides to facticity—feels jealous and pained. When Savithri holds down to facticity—offers herself to Ramaswamy, leaving Pratap—Ramaswamy leaps up, distant on the perch of transcendence, and advises her to marry Pratap. For a moment he seems to stabilize in the height, asking Savithri to be a true wife to Pratap. But as soon as the advice is obeyed, he is drawn back into the abyss of facticity. He has always associated the concept of paradise with facticity or phenomenality. "There can never be a paradise" because paradise is "the inversion of truth" and is promised by heresy. Yet as soon as the news arrives that Savithri has at last become the true wife of Pratap, his whole being is turned upside down, "Paradise, I thought, does, does exist." The brahman who would annihilate time is constantly defeated by it. In the grip of the existential anguish of the Western man, "without house/orphaned, alone, impotent" (Tiutchev, "The Abyss"), the identity of Ramaswamy is for ever lacerated, the gulf between "the Brahmin and I" is never bridged.

But the same man, so typically Western and historical here, is also successor to an archaic ethos which is assumed to be a hermetically sealed existence of timelessness outside historicity. The tragedy of Ramaswamy springs from the fact that being a man of the archaic world of eternity, so to say, he is ejected out into the course of time, placed in the stream of existential history which carries him irrevocably away from his native ethos. When at the end of his encounters with the Other he laments, "There is nobody to go to now: no home, no temple, no city, no climate, no age," the terror of rootlessness strikes him with such finality not because of his broken marriage, or death of children, or unfulfilled love, or even a physical stay in an alien land, but because of his anguish in a basic and fundamental alienation from his native heritage. If Rama cannot come back to his India, this is not merely because of the present degradation of Indian people, the poverty ("those ladle hands and skeletal legs"), the vulgar pride of the "new India," but because time has impinged upon him, changing his eternal brahmanic self imperceptibly but definitely into a new entity which is for ever isolated from the archaic ethos. The tremendous nostalgia which breaks through again and again in the novel in a wholly unjustified and partial manner, glorifying his ancient lineage in an ancient civilization, is the surest proof of the implicit knowledge that Ramaswamy can never come home. Therefore "home" becomes an abstraction built on an exclusive principle derived from a particular system of thought, so that he can carry this "metaphysic" of India within him: "I was born an exile and could continue to be one. My India I carried wheresoever I went." The phenomenal reality of India, "wheresoever you see, hear, touch, smell" is lost to Ramaswamy, for time has crept into his identity. And yet the brahman strives so desperately to cling to his brahmanic tradition:

> I found myself saying the Gayathri mantra as we landed at Santa Cruz. I had said it day after day, almost for twenty years; I must have said it a million, million times: "OM, O face of Truth with a disk of gold, remove the mist (of ignorance) that I may see you face to face."

He seems to be so very brahmanic, secure in traditional habit, for the recitation of the *Gayatri* is the exclusive privilege of the brahman and indeed constitutes the very symbol of brahmanhood. There is however one small catch—the *mantra* he recites is not the *Gayatri*, which is: "We meditate on the adorable glory of the radiant sun. May he direct our intellect."[10]

A brahman who does not know the *Gayatri* is damned for ever. Alienated from the archaic Hindu existence, he expounds his philosophy ostensibly "Indian," not in the context of the Upanishads like his glorious Hindu predecessors, but in relation to Plato and Nietzsche, contrasting non-dual "impersonality" with a dualistic "personality cult," hero-worship, "poetry" etc. It is for a man who believes in Plato that Jesus and the Buddha are outsiders to the "impersonal," perfect civilization for they are "poets." But in the age of the *Mahabharata* that Rama claims to belong to there is neither Plato nor Nietzsche. To try to interpret Vedanta in relation to the West is by itself an admission of the irrevocable fact that the brahman can no more transcend time than leap over his own shadow.

Rama's alienation from the traditional brahmanic life suggests thus a fundamental disjunction. Sometimes he muses on the typical life of a brahman that the centuries-old tradition of the Hindus has pre-assigned him. He would be a premier brahman in the village, study the ancient texts in Sanskrit, read the *Ramayana* for the villagers's benefit, earn fees and feasts at various rituals, remain satisfied with a docile Rukmini or Kaumudi in kitchen and in bed. But he wakes up from the wistful thinking with a jolt, with the sharp realization that this pre-fabricated life of a brahman is not for him, because he has been stirred by a force which is stronger than the whole strength of an ancient tradition: "Something hypostatic calls me. Mother mine, I will go." This hypostatic call makes it urgent for him to go in quest for the Absolute not because the Hindu in him is secure in the assurance of eternal return, but because *this life here and now is unique and final.* It is time and history which impel Ramaswamy out of the hermetically sealed world of the Hindu ethos and draw him into the vortex of existence.

Since the impingement of time on Ramaswamy's identity is undeniable, the more absolute is the opposition between Time and Eternity, between the West and India, the deeper is the crisis in our "European Brahmin." When he takes a rigid stand— "The one cannot be many, but the many can be one"—and rejects Madeleine's "dualistic" Buddhism, he has to deny the existence of the world altogether: "There is no world," the only reality being the Absolute. Ironically this is precisely the position of the Buddha. As a devotee of Sankara, Ramaswamy along with the Buddha must necessarily and logically "exclude forever a reconciliation of eternity and time, of religion and world."[11] This reconciliation is no doubt effected in the *Bhagavad Gita* as also in the Mahayana Buddhism, which proclaims the identity of being and becoming, of *Nirvana* and *Samsara* and insists that notwithstanding the world is but a Becoming it has a meaning. But the great dialectician Ramaswamy, who is always victorious over everyone, fails to establish this synthesis in his attempt to return to Madeleine. When Madeleine asks the reason of his return, he can offer her no assurance of that love which has dissolved duality, but admits that his love belongs to this world alone, a composite of duality. "The meaning of life," says Rao himself, "reveals when the duality resolves into non-duality."[12] But this resolution does not take place in Ramaswamy's encounter with either Madeleine or Savithri. He has to accept the duality between himself and Savithri which is revealed in their separate existence bound by time as human condition, a "mortal paradox." Does Ramaswamy then end his pilgrimage to eternity in the reality of time, maya?

The surest proof of the reality of Time is the profound and pervading melancholy which permeates the whole novel in all the situations and all the characters.[13] The whole chronicle of Ramaswamy is "sad." At the very root of his being is sorrow: "I feel the word *Dukka* (sorrow) almost with the entrails dropping into my hand," because "*Dukka* is the very tragedy of creation."

Starting as a sobbing child, he ends rolling in bed, sobbing and crying. Throughout his life, "deeper down was sorrow." It is only after Savithri becomes a "true wife" to Pratap that Ramaswamy realizes the full existential nature of this sorrow, "man's sorrow is not to belong to this earth." As there can never be a feeling of rapport between him and the world, there is an urgent and desperate need to effect the dissociation. Sorrow is the background of all situations in this novel because they exist in the momentary, and the moment in its very transience is cut off from Eternity. Thus sorrow is, because of Time. The question is, does Ramaswamy succeed in transcendence catapulted to "the other shore" with the help of the guru?[14] We are, however, not sure if Ramaswamy's leap is a realization of Time as Eternity or an escape from time into self. He has himself declared that "the meaning of life is *lila*, play," yet he remains groping for a meaning: "There must be something that exalts and explains why we are here and what is it we seek."

The question remains unresolved in *The Serpent and the Rope*. Ramaswamy himself voices the agonized suspicion: "Would the angels shut the fissures in our being that the world know not when we take the leap?" It is in this unanswered question, this suspicion which formulates the tragedy of a brahman face to face with time, that the real significance of *The Serpent and the Rope* lies, for, in no other Indian work do we find the portrait of a brahman caught so irrevocably in the anguish of time.

2. *The dialogic monologue*

An analysis of the theme of *The Serpent and the Rope* shows clearly that the hero Ramaswamy tries to progress through his relationship with women, especially his wife and his beloved, towards his true "Indian" identity that seems to reside in the realization of a metaphysical concept. This mingling of love and quest is derived from a literary convention wholly Western in definition.[15] But Rao's object is specifically to reveal the distinctive ethos of India as traditional and classical, contrasted against the West as romantic and historical. The "Indian" assumption for him is: "Man is ever lonely" which is enunciated by Ramaswamy in the novel itself. However, the spiritual recognition of the non-duality of self or Atman of Vedanta philosophy is reserved exclusively for the male, "Eternity is a masculine concept," "woman will die at the opportune time." It follows that logically, neither Madeleine who is rejected as wife nor Savithri who is extolled as beloved can be a companion on the way to the Absolute, nor can anyone of them lead him to his Ultimate. The question is: since there can be no companion in man's pilgrimage, since "strait is the gate," too narrow to accommodate more than one, how can any woman fail or succeed in being a "true woman" for Ramaswamy on his spiritual journey? The very fact that the ultimate realization is to be found nowhere but at the feet of the guru perhaps indicates the futility of all Rama's encounters with women. If the Indian identity is pre-empted to a consonance with a paradigm—beginning with a legendary ancestor and ending with a guru—how does any encounter with woman come into the picture at all?

It is precisely to solve this problem of a Western narrative framework being used to reveal an "Indian" identity, that a parallel schematization of an intellectual thesis is sought to be incorporated into the narrative structure. For Ramaswamy, there can be only two logically tenable attitudes towards the world, one Vedantic, the other materialistic. The former identifies the Absolute Consciousness (Self/*Brahman*/*Atman*) as the Ultimate Reality and the empirical world as only an appearance, an imposition on the Reality. The opposite is the Western "materialistic" view which culminates in Marxism, and states that the empirical world is the only reality. Ramaswamy further believes that there can be no compromise between these two opposite views. All other philosophies, religions, ideologies are "poetic," placed in-between these two mutually exclusive views, and are regarded by him as instances of "inversion of Truth," the same as heresy, defined as "near-truth seen as truth." Applying this subjective formula to history Rama finds that the Absolute Consciousness is symbolically manifested in the human organization of orthodoxy, since, like the Absolute Consciousness, Orthodoxy also is Impersonal. All deviations from orthodoxy are personal rebellions and treated justly as heresies. Since the concept of Brahman is connected by him to the organizational orthodoxy, Ramaswamy's thesis in history justifies the ruthless extermination of heretics by the corrupt Roman Catholic Church.

The human situation involving Ramaswamy's encounter with woman as the other is to be understood as an illustration and a viable proof of this abstract thesis.[16] These two schemata are sought to be presented as parallels through a number of equations. The Absolute Consciousness, the Truth, the Reality, is also orthodoxy in human history. Since the Absolute is non-dual (*advaita*), a belief in dualistic philosophy amounts to heresy. Madeleine's Buddhism in its altruistic orientation seems to Ramaswamy an acceptance of the existence of the world as real and hence being dualistic runs counter to the non-dual belief of the husband. Equating the Buddhist Church with Buddhism and Vedanta with Hinduism. the text seems to suggest an analogy: as heresies have been crushed by the orthodox Catholic Church, even so Buddhism has been driven out by Vedanta and it is natural and justifiable therefore for a Hindu Vedantin husband like Ramaswamy to cast out a Buddhist (and hence heretic) wife from his life. Savithri, who has believed in all these "equations in history" formulated by Ramaswamy, is the "true woman" for him since she submits totally to Ramaswamy's metaphysic of the Impersonal, manifested in historical reality now as *dharma* which, Ramaswamy concludes, constitutes the acceptance of the human condition.

It is obvious that the main artistic problem of the novel lies in finding an adequate correlative in form to structure the interaction between a concrete situation in human life and an intellectual, abstract thesis. The narrative form of *The Serpent and the Rope* has therefore necessarily to be a mixed one, as a combination of realism in the form of a flowing, continuous, interior monologue which offers a mimetic presentation of personal experience happening in a historical, spatial context, and a discursive mode of intellectual speculation. The thesis that Ramaswamy writes functions as the bridge to join these two forms and is derived from an established Western convention which starting with Raskolnikov's paper "On Crime" in Dostoevsky's *Crime and Punishment* continues as Edouard's journal in Gide's *The Counterfeiters* or Roquentin's thesis in Sartre's *Nausea*. A common genesis, which supplies these two forms its main strength, lies in the autobiographical inspiration. In Rao's novel this mixture is indicated clearly as he declares again and again that the work is autobiographical and "essentially metaphysical."[17] It is the autobiographical aspect that justifies the incorporation of the metaphysical. The life-story of an individual is often considered to be worth writing about because of the experience that the author undergoes trying to integrate his ideas with the world. The very motive of writing, the source of creativity, lies in a preoccupation to link idea to life. As has been noted by Northrop Frye, the confessional or autobiography is not only realistic in its dependence on history, but is also marked by a consistent preoccupation with the theoretical and the abstract,[18] the abstract functioning as a means to present an intensely subjective apprehension of reality which is the key to Rao's handling of the form of the novel. To adopt a realistic-dialectic confessional form, Rao has to depend exclusively on Western literary tradition since Indian aesthetics never accepted autobiography as a recognized form of human creativity, nor would it allow intellectual speculation based on a particular system to be manipulated as a formal device to present a personal view of reality in a literary effort (*Kavya* in Sanskrit). It is ironic that Rao's quest for form to structure an "Indian" identity has to find a literary habitation in a thoroughly Western convention.

The mixed form of *The Serpent and the Rope* is an intensely subjective flux of reminiscence in which narration of experience mingles with speculation, cerebral in nature. The mimetic aspects of the form are clearly discernible in the technical devices adopted in the narration, for example, the use of a first-person narrator-protagonist and the device of incorporating a diary; the former directly introducing the reader into the fictional reality whose representational aspect is thus firmly established; the latter, a residue of the documentary, of memoir or chronicle, which is almost photographic in its relation to the reality. The technique of block-characterization that Rao follows, introducing his characters by a descriptive paragraph on the physical or moral identity of an individual, is also a part of convention. Take, for example, his introduction of Madeleine as a grieving mother. Her beauty, her innocence, are all presented in detail so that her ascetic endeavour to go beyond the frustration of life may have a convincing and tragic development. The same technique is employed to introduce Georges, Lezo and Catherine and prepare us for the further growth of these characters into the directions implied at the outset. Thus the cause-effect relationship underlying the essential hypothetical nature of fiction is always adhered to.[19]

Even more significant is Rao's intense involvement in the present temporal reality. The novel as an essentially modern form is rooted in historicity. All the characters of Rao's novel are deeply entrenched in the contemporary reality. Ramaswamy himself, a pilgrim of Eternity, incessantly gets into arguments over the present—Superman, Fascism and Communism, His attempts to distinguish Vedanta from Buddhism is perhaps directed by the contemporary confusion between the two in Theosophy.[20] Even his obsession with the philosophy of history is a historical phenomenon borrowed from the West since it has no precedence in Indian or Hindu thought. At the level of actual experience, we find him deeply rooted in time, wondering over the Korean War which has led the French countryside "stock-piling sugar and paraffin, potatoes, wine and motor-car tyres," receiving as the guardian the progress reports of his stepsister, signing property transfers. All the characters are markedly connected with history. We hear again and again of the White Russian Georges's participation in the Resistance, the Spaniard Lezo's persecution by the fascist regime, Madeleine's experience of German occupation. Oncle Charles and Tante Zoubie are, of course, relics of the famous *la belle époque*, "the France of Monsieur Poincaré, of Déroulède and of Maurice Barrès."

This preoccupation with the temporal is rendered solid and visible in the emphasis throughout the novel on the spatial context. Although Rama says, "For Madeleine geography was very real," it is no less real for the narrator in him. Take, for example, his description of Madeleine: "Her *Savoyard* ancestry must have mingled with a lot of *Piedmontese* so that this girl from *Charente* still had thyme and lavender almost at the roots of the hair." The concept of India is "vertical to space and time," but the spiritual affinity between Ramaswamy and Savithri, presumably based on it, has to be revealed in the moon-lit wandering very much in space "all along the road, over the Rhone bridge, and by Montmajour, through *Beaucaire, Arles, Vauvainargues*, to the ruminant foothills of *Mont Sainte-Victoire.*"

This presentation of a fictional world—detailed, solid and concrete in time and space—belongs essentially to the mimetic convention. Hence the action, that is recorded or represented, is totally dependent on the external reality in so far as it is based on an acknowledgement of the Hindu social life at a clearly recognizable point of time. Ramaswamy's relation with Savithri betrothed to Pratap and later married to him and bound by the contemporary Hindu social rigidity never outweighs the proclaimed omnipotence of the spiritual affinity.

No less important however is Rao's evocation of an authentic atmosphere in consonance with the mood of the major character—a well-established nineteenth century convention. All the "settings" in which Ramaswamy is placed appear as extensions of his character. Take for example the portrayal of Ramaswamy's visit to Benaras. In this Eternal City we never know "where reality starts and where illusion ends":

> In Benaras there be many dead, and all the dead of all the ages, he successive generations of manes after manes after manes, have accumulated in the sky. And you could almost see them layer on layer on the night of moon eclipse, fair and pale and tall and decrepit, fathers great grandfaters.

If Ramaswamy's striving towards transcendence finds expression here, his bondage to the phenomenal world is recognized at the same time. He is fully aware that in the same Benaras only fifty rupees make the sacred brahman happy. On "these very banks" of the Ganges, he feels the presence of his Upanishadic ancestors along with the crocodiles and fragments of half-burnt bodies floating down the holy river. If the limit of the senses is stretched in the sensuous experience appreciating the "magnificent copper work inlaid with lacquer and ivory," "multi-coloured bangles," "rich, fervid smell of *bhang*," the description of Benaras establishes the desired atmosphere as an extension of the two fundamental aspects of Ramaswamy's character. This attention to atmosphere unfolds the world through a subjective sensibility and holds the key to Rao's handling of the mixed form of the novel.

Since the end of the novel seems to state the stasis—the protagonist's realization of true self—the plot bears the hallmark of all confessional forms.[21] But this realistic preoccupation is considerably defamiliarized and distanced by a consistent preoccupation with the theoretical and intellectual. The lineage of Ramaswamy's display of wide scholarship over a cup of coffee or at a dinner table lies in the Western literary tradition of the encyclopaedic farrago represented by writers of antiquity continuing through Rabelais, to Voltaire, Sterne, Melville, Mann or Joyce.[22] In Rao's use, the form however is distinguished by its entirely argumentative and dialectic bias reminiscent of Dostoevsky. In the *Puranas* (which are distinguished in Sanskrit aesthetics from literature or *Kavya*), there are philosophical disquisitions, though not necessarily in all. But the Puranic form is overwhelmingly narrative as the glory of the deity is revealed in an endless succession of stories, legends and myths. In the meditative portions, the form is expository, either teaching the ignorant or recording the mystic experience of the devotee.[23] There is never a continuous debate between philosophy and reality, the form in which Ramaswamy's remembrance of the past is presented. The function of intellectual speculation in this work is to emphasize an intensely subjective interpretation of reality and in the process to defamiliarize the shabby and the unpleasant. A deliberate retardation by complicating the form lengthens the perception.[24] Take, for example, the presentation of Ramaswamy's relation with his father. Hindu orthodoxy has a definite code of conduct regulating the relation between son and father in which the father is considered equivalent to "heaven, to *dharma*, to supreme discipline and to satisfy father is to please all gods." How does this paradigm presented by Ramaswamy's avowed ideal of orthodoxy, coincide with his reality? All that Ramaswamy says is "I have little to tell you of my father's death except that I did not love him." It is, so to say, a typically Western, Gidean situation. How can Ramaswamy the brahman be completely engrossed in such a contingency? Hence the sentence continues, "but that after he died, I knew him and loved him." Even this declaration cannot counteract the rebellion of reality against the paradigm of the orthodox ideal. Since the "fact," the "experience," cannot prove his "Indianness," his orthodoxy, he digresses from the situation in fictional life and tries to negate the realistic core with the help of abstract speculation:

> I cannot repent, as I do not know what repentance is. For I must first believe there is death. And that is the central fact—I do not believe that death is. So, for whom shall I repent?

The Vedantic concept that death is illusory is offered here not for the edification of the ignorant readers, but to justify Ramaswamy's attitude towards his father. The characteristic mark of the discursive mode is thus to suggest a confrontation with the realistic and the narrative. In other words, Ramaswamy's monologue is essentially dialogic in nature, a perpetual encounter with an invisible but ever-present other self. So Ramaswamy continues:

> Of course, I love my father *now* . . . left to myself, I become alone and full of love. When one is alone one always loves. In fact because one loves, and one is alone, one does not die.

The use of a digressive abstraction lessens the emphasis on the real life situation which is thus distanced, and suggests that somehow, though inexplicably perhaps, Ramaswamy's love for his dead father being presumably connected with his "Indian"/Vedantic metaphysic is far more important than Ramaswamy's failure as a Hindu son in real life. The question is, who is the addressee of Ramaswamy's dialectic here? None but Ramaswamy himself. This is the typical relationship between the narrative and the discursive modes in the novel which is magnified in the larger structure, the human situation of triangular love enveloped in the gossamer-thin but voluminous gauze of speculative digression which totally distances the blatant reality that is unpleasant to Ramaswamy, namely his utter failure as man and husband which we have seen in the previous section. So his "Indian interpretation of history" is an essay in self-justification. The rejection of Madeleine is defensible if she is proved inadequate or wrong. Hence her Buddhism is under Ramaswamy's dialectic fire. His equations in history form a series of parallels based on the principle of binary opposition. Roman Catholic Church: Cathary; Orthodoxy: Heresy; Vedanta: Buddhism; Non-dual: Dual, etc. which may suggest equations like: Buddhism = Dualism = Heresy, and Vedanta = Non-dualism = Orthodoxy. So Madeleine as a Buddhist is cast out by her orthodox, Vedantin husband with poetic justice. This kind of extrapolated homology[25]—to use a bit of jargon—ignoring qualitative differences in the pairs, is offered as a tenable "Indian" approach, and assumes dominance over the narrative by transforming or distorting other elements in the novel's structure.

To effect this domination, the intellectual analytic, first of all,twists and perverts the stages of the normal development in the plot.[26] Ramaswamy believes, "The god of Woman must be the God of her man" echoing Raja Rao's own view, "A woman can only find her God through Man. But the 'modern woman' thinks she can reach the Ultimate directly. This is heresy." Even if we accept

Rao's "traditional" view of male supremacy over the female in the spiritual domain one may logically ask at least one question: who is this man to lead the woman to the Absolute? Since Madeleine in her Buddhism refuses apparently to be led by her Vedantin husband and is branded heretic, it seems logical to deduce that for Rao this man is the woman's husband. This is strengthened by the orthodox Hindu concept of husband as the supreme guru which is referred to in the novel, explaining Sukumari's faithful obedience to her husband's communism as a behaviour proper for a Hindu wife. So the husband's right to lead his wife to the Absolute should constitute a categorical imperative. Yet, Savithri's husband Pratap is considered a "mere stump." How does Ramaswamy's neat formula, "He (i.e. Pratap) is your husband and you are mine," conform to the husband's role as guru in Hindu marriage? Since being a woman, Savithri cannot possibly "choose," what gives Ramaswamy the right to lead her in spirituality, since his right is not sanctioned by Hindu dharma? The only sanction lies in Gidean morality—the duty to the ego. Hence: "the fact that I was a Brahmin by birth and a South Indian seemed to have given me a natural superiority:" Therefore, Madeleine's Buddhism is automatically assumed to be her failure as a Vedantin's wife. There is an elaborate description of Madeleine's journey along the ascetic path—ostensibly Buddhist—which culminates in a momentous dialogue extending for pages. Apparently this is the crisis which should reveal a turn in the action, the anagnorisis to lead irrevocably to the conclusion. Of course, Madeleine learns that her Buddhism separates her forever from her "Indian" husband who identifies India with Advaita Vedanta which in turn is equated with brahmanic orthodoxy. But the protagonist of the novel is not Madeleine but Ramaswamy, for whom there is no revelation, no anagnorisis in this carefully prepared crisis. Has Ramaswamy not known from the very beginning that Buddhism is "too historical" for his "India," a concept of Eternity, or that Madeleine as a Christian is a humanist? Why does he wait hundreds of pages to deliver this denunciation of altruistic Buddhism? It is to inflate the importance of Madeleine's Buddhism in the breakdown of the marriage, that this crisis is faked, for Rao himself intends to lay the fault with Madeleine's conversion to Buddhism: "Madeleine, through her own Catholicism (by going back to it through it and beyond it) would have reached Rama better."[27]

Strangely enough, Madeleine is not even permitted to retain her own traditional Christian food-habit. Since for a Christian "to abstain from meats which God hath created to be received with thankfulness" is to heed to "seducing spirits and doctrines of devils" (1 Timothy, 4: 1-3), Ramaswamy's persuading Madeleine to become a vegetarian strikes at the very roots of her own native heritage which resides not so much in metaphysics as in the concrete life of a human community.[28] Ramaswamy uproots her from her background and then refuses to let her grow new roots. It is however necessary to emphasize that Ramaswamy's thesis is an elaborate fabrication to hide the fundamental realistic core of difference between an orthodox Hindu and a Christian. Madeleine is actually condemned as much as a Buddhist as a Christian. When she asks, "What was Christ?" Ramaswamy answers, "A poet like the Buddha, and with the great Indian to be banished from the perfect state of Plato," which is for Ramaswamy also Vedantic. "The perfect civilization, then, is where the world is not, but where there is nothing but the 'I'."

According to this argument it follows that as a Christian she is no less an alien to the orthodox Hindu world of Rama than she is as a Buddhist. Indeed her story, ostensibly Buddhist, has quite a few marks of a classic Christian pattern—conversion, mortification of flesh, miracles, mystical substitution, her taking upon herself the suffering of Ramaswamy's disease.[29] She is even wounded by a thorn and her supernatural power emanates from a black Madonna. It is before the chapel of this Madonna that Ramaswamy utters the Hindu decision of his ultimate rejection of Madeleine. The whole paraphernalia of Ramaswamy's thesis condemning Madeleine's Buddhism appears a mask of equivocation which completely hides the reality, where Madeleine as a Christian faces the blind wall of an orthodox brahman husband, that stone wall against which her love can only batter its own self in despair and futility.

So despite all his loudly professed enthusiasm for the Roman Catholic Church, Rama can notice only the bad architecture of a cathedral while attending a Mass. We never find him in any Catholic observance throughout his stay in France. For his single act of prayer at a chapel he is in anguish and this "Christian becoming" has to be atoned by an intellectual victory over the Catholic Georges ("my sins were washed away"). As a matter of fact it is at the very beginning of the action when Madeleine is neither a

Buddhist nor a rebel "heretic," but a Catholic and unquestionably a devoted wife (as her letter unmistakably proves), that Ramaswamy rejects her on his return to France after his first visit to India. He himself declares, "You have failed me," because he has met Savithri. Savithri acts as a catalyst in the disintegration of the Hindu-Christian marriage that stands completely negated in the ritual wedding of Ramaswamy-Savithri accepted by the protagonist himself as the final determinant in this human story. So as a narrator he states, "the rest of the story is easily told," because what follows is Madeleine's Buddhism, the inevitable result. The stipulated holiness of Rama's union with Savithri nullifies the sanctity of his marriage with Madeleine, for he is led to consider the unborn child Madeleine is carrying as a "bastard," the relation between man and wife merely "fornication." Rejected as wife and mother, Madeleine's irrovocable destiny lies in renunciation.

As the thesis blaming Madeleine dominates, the readers are apt to miss the real crisis of this human drama—the last meeting between our hero and Savithri when the brahman finally realizes that despite all his Platonic aspiration for a spiritual love, there can be no transcendence in human relationship. This is the "mortal paradox" of the human condition. But we have seen that the thesis decrees that the union of Savithri with Pratap is the fulfilment of Rama as well. So the last meeting is sought to be presented as a resolution. Although he himself has proclaimed the very awareness of the *other* in the humanism of his Christian-Buddhist wife as "anti-Indian," "dualistic" and so on, Ramaswamy professes to rejoice "in the rejoicement of the *other*." This inconsistency makes his subsequent agony not only inexplicable from the point of view of the thesis, but even incomprehensible as the need to end at the feet of the guru grows desperate. On the other hand if we perceive the real crisis to lie in this last meeting, then his misery, his vain attempt to return to Madeleine, will appear as a causal development, and the leap to transcendence at the end, an understandable attempt at a stasis. But the thesis confusing the stages renders the end totally gratuitous.

The imposition of the meeting with the guru which formally constitutes the end of the temporal journey of Ramaswamy is represented beyond temporality, and appears more of an epilogue than resolution. We are informed that somewhere, some time, somehow Ramaswamy the brahman devoted to Truth arrives at the enlightenment, guided by the guru. One wonders if there is really a true resolution in the novel, for the inter-relation between the two forms, one realistic and temporal, the other abstract and paradigmatic, results in a total impasse, despite all the attempts at a dominance of the latter and at a unified vision by the expedient of a protagonist-narrator. The employment of such a narrator to advocate a personal thesis results in an irritatingly fixed centre of vision which tends to become an obstruction in the aesthetic experience with the additional burden of an inflated hero who is supposed to be an ideal son, an ideal husband, an ideal brother, an ideal patient, even an ideal neighbour and tenant.[30] There is a distinct impression of a confusing interaction of two voices, in the two forms which consistently refuse to arrive at a resolution.

3. *A Structure of Discord*

The formal expression of this impasse may be seen in the employment of the protagonist-narrator who is, like a number of his modern sophisticated companions, "unreliable" as a narrator. Ramaswamy as narrator is "fallible" not because he "lies," but because he is genuinely self-deceived and pretends to qualities which the author denies him. Take, for example, the seemingly innocuous statement: "Madeleine had never participated at first in my superstitions, though I had in hers." Critics, who have accepted Ramaswamy as a reliable narrator, have, for this statement, been led to blame Madeleine and praise Ramaswamy. Yet in the happenings recorded by Ramaswamy we rarely find him participating in any "prejudice" of Madeleine's. There are on the other hand detailed, elaborate and recurrent references to Madeleine's participation in Hindu prejudices. This tendency of the narrator to depart from the implied author's norms holds a significance tinged with irony because the narrator comes very close to representing the author. When Ramaswamy declares Travancore to be his real home at the end of the quest, we find a complete substitution of life for art because Travancore has had no role to play in the fictional reality of Ramaswamy which is an artefact and as such must be seen separate from the life of Raja Rao who found his guru in Travancore. Such a fundamental overlapping of perspectives is the cause of the main technical problem that involves Rao's adaptation of interior monologue. This technical device is obviously suited to his purpose since it traditionally provides "a concentrated fusion" of the two forms, autobiography and intellectual analysis, according to Northrop Frye.[31] No doubt Rao takes full advantage of this instrument of psychological realism in a direct introduction of the reader into the interior life of the character, without any interventions in the way of explanation or commentary on the part of the author. The success of this highly valuable technique lies, however, in the author's power of objectivity, a clear distance from the subject of analysis which alone enables him to present a complex human psyche. Rao keeps the whole inner life of Ramaswamy strictly limited to one area, that of reminiscence, but at the same time constantly interrupts the flow with conclusions drawn from the other parts and levels of the psyche. These readymade conclusions are incorporated mainly in mythical substitutions for analysis of psychological phenomena. Take, for example, Ramaswamy's mental state awaiting Savithri's arrival at Kensington. He feels totally bound to the past and thinks: "You cannot escape time." Here he is an existentialist, bound to the Western preoccupation with history. The next moment, however, he is seen transformed into an Indian Vedantin, demolishing time: "There never was time." How does this basic and very important transformation from one ethos to another take place? In between the existential premise and the Vedantic conclusion, there appears a series of imaginary pictures of Ramaswamy cast in legendary roles: the exiled prince Satyakama entering the Kingdom of the Seven Sisters, a Cathar entering Grotto D'Orlac, a Manichean, a Parsifal carrying the Holy Grail—brief allusions presented in an unmistakable scale of ascendancy as they end in a purely formal expression of a piece of Western musical notation. Psychological analysis is thus sought to be substituted by a series of allusions. If we take each allusion apart and look for its meaning in relation to Rao's metaphysic, the result is confusion. Thus Cathar and Mani are heretical and hence cannot lead to Truth which is for Ramaswamy, Orthodoxy, nor can Ramaswamy be a Satyakama who is led to fulfilment by a woman. The conclusion, "I am the Absolute," is actually foregone, without logical development, or a convincing preparatory process. This absence of analysis shows a lack of essential objectivity. Hence Ramaswamy's height of spiritual realization of the Impersonal is immediately succeeded by his intense egotistic feeling—he hates Savithri's resignation to her marriage with Pratap. Again, the interior monologue conceals, instead of revealing, the mental process that dislodges Ramaswamy from the sublimity of the Impersonal and plunges him into the abyss of egocentric passion. In the delineation of the Rama-Savithri relationship, the interior monologue fails to analyze the complexity of Ramaswamy's mental state—how, through what alchemy, an ostensible aversion to Savithri's Westernized ways can harmoniously or convincingly coexist with the realization of a deep affinity strong enough to destroy his marriage. Their first meeting, which, technically, should be as important as Hans Castorp's glimpse of Clavdia Chauchat, goes without a concrete correlative in analysis or narration, anything comparable to Thomas Mann's description of Hans Castorp's subsequent dream in the snow. "What happened" between them leading to the ritual wedding is presented thus:

> Nothing more had happened, in fact, than if you look deep and long at silence you perceive an orb of centripetal sound which explains why Parvathi is daughter of Himalaya, and Sita born to the furrow of the field.

An analysis of the psyche is avoided by mere references to myths, neither developed in the course of the novel nor fruitful in the immediate context. Whether this results in a romantic lifting of the level of reality or a spurious deepening of significance, depends of course on the reader's viewpoint. But the conscious and deliberate identification of Ramaswamy and Savithri by themselves with their supposedly mythical prototypes is only an extreme example of Rao's confusion in perspective and subsequent failure in concrete objectivization. They constantly seem to be acting out roles, as though pre-assigned as Radha-Krishna, Tristan-Iseult, Savitri Satyavan, Shiva-Parvati, before a non-existent but ever-present audience. Such complete substitution of reality by myth reveals that the use of myth here is compulsive, not an aesthetic choice. In other words, here is an artist, who has failed to find an adequate fictional correlative of his intention. In the ritual of *padapuja* or feet-worship, which is the "wedding" between Ramaswamy and Savithri, the mythic pattern is carried to a point where the manipulation of symbolic formulae seems to have wholly substituted itself for the felt experience. The instinctive and emotional dialectic of a complex human relationship is displaced by a very conscious operation of intellect which through the technique of interior monologue turns the interpenetration of myth and experience potentially gratuitous and leads to total artistic failure in this situation.

The operation of such a confused perspective can be best perceived in Rao's particular employment of myth as a pre-figurative technique to define the love-and-quest theme. It is of utmost importance for the thesis to glorify the Ramaswamy-Savithri love. Hence a large number of myths and legends drawn from both Western and Indian tradition have been used repeatedly to indicate a parallel mythical structure which could illuminate the present situation. But these myths are often opposed to one another and some, more frequently used ones, to the professed "philosophy" of the novel. An extramarital relationship involving Hindus in fictional reality can hardly be explained by the two legends of Radha-Krishna and Savitri-Satyavan at the same time, without confusing the levels of interpretation and violating some of the cardinal principles of the Hindu concept of marriage. At the symbolic or spiritual level the Radha-Krishna myth evokes the eternal longing of the individual soul *(Jiva)* for union with the Absolute *(Paramatma)* and the eternal separation between the two. This legend thus offers an imaginative expression of a dualistic philosophy, which, according to Ramaswamy, is "anti-Indian" since for him the Truth is non-dual. As a basic pattern which may underlie a specific human situation, the myth was hardly ever used in classical or even medieval literature, perhaps because the Hindu view of marriage, which has no concept of original sin, never idealizes a transgression of the marriage vow for a spiritual goal. The legend of Savitri-Satyavan, on the other hand, is one of the archetypal patterns found early in the *Mahabharata* and is repeated again and again in traditional Hindu literature through the ages. Savitri's victory over death turns the legend to a plot structure essentially geared to a "happy" ending. As a formulation of invigoration and fulfilment, its pattern is opposed to the structural mould of Radha-Krishna as also against the novel's tragic end in Rama's agony of loneliness. Besides, the metaphysic of man's supremacy over woman in spirit as enunciated by Ramaswamy and Rao is hardly in consonance with the essence of the Savitri legend which emphasizes the dominance and power of woman.[32] Savitri's victory over the god of death is the reward of both her devotion and irrefutable dialectic power stemming from her fierce independence. For Rama, woman as the "object" has neither freedom nor power to lead man to overcome death as Ramaswamy confesses: "I'm a Brahmin, and for me touch and knowledge go with the holiness of surrender, of woman not taking me there, but I revealing to her that."

How can his Savithri be prefigured by the ancient Savitri who led her husband through death and beyond it? The impression of ambivalence which is inseparable from such incessant disjunction between the thesis and the mythical formulation is further strengthened by the persistent evocation of another legend, that of Tristan-Iseult. No doubt the real life situation involving the two pairs comes closest to the Tristan-Iseult set-up, indeed so much so that this one-to-one correspondence with a medieval European pattern cannot be ignored. In the Western literary tradition the Tristan-Iseult legend has always been the symbol of romantic passion.[33] Raja Rao himself, extolling the Indian view of love as "traditional," finds it totally opposed to the Western concept of love as "romantic." Since his intention, as is clear not only from his own admission but also from the novel's triangular plotting, is to show the "Indianness" of the Savithri-Ramaswamy love as superior to the "Western" pattern of the man-woman relationship, his employment of the same Tristan-Iseult legend to reveal a presumably "Indian" and therefore anti-romantic love cannot escape ambiguity. Conscious of the disjunction between the thesis and the mythical prefiguration, Rao tries to subordinate the Western myth to the thesis and to contain it within the straitjacket of his metaphysic when in the last climactic meeting with Savithri, Tristan, the romantic and passionate hero, is turned into the "Impersonal," the Truth-that-is-non-dual. Therefore, the following conversation between Savithri and Ramaswamy takes place:

> "Iseult was death itself when death dies?"
> "Tristan is born. And there never, never is an Iseult."
> "What happens to Iseult, then?"
> "She is Tristan."

The understanding of the above equation depends wholly on Rao's metaphysics—Iseult as the world ("the woman is the world"), and as such *maya* or imposition on the Truth, as the Serpent is on the Rope. When *maya* or Iseult dies, Tristan or Truth is revealed. The illusion and the knowledge here is realized to be one. The context of metaphysics thus attempts to transform the myth. But Ramaswamy has always held the Truth to be the "Impersonal" Principle and has already specifically stated that it is King Mark, husband of Tristan's beloved Iseult, who being a king like Shri Ramachandra, represents the Impersonal. This lack of consistency even at the intellectual level is however less disturbing than Rao's attempt to root out the Tristan-Iseult myth from the Western ethos in which it is embedded. A myth is integral to the ethos of a community which it formulates in an archetypal pattern, going so deep into the thought and modes of behaviour of a people that it is considered by Northrop Frye as a "pre-literary category."[34] The concept of the Absolute Consciousness as the Non-dual Truth is essentially Indian and as such can hardly be adequately revealed through any Western mythical correlative in so far as the modern Western ethos, influenced by Christianity, is centred in the very concept of a personal God. It is therefore inevitable that in the whole account of the Ramaswamy-Savithri love, the "Indian" intellectual formulation may be seen confused with a typical Western literary convention, that of courtly love in the non-sexual nature of the man-woman relation (never found among the ancient Hindus), the evocation of a constantly hierarchical relation between the two, the concretization of the non-physical relation in a distinct ritual, the sealing of love in the presentation of the ring and a single kiss, and above all, the vow of life-long devotion transcending actual separation.[35] The basic notion behind the Ramaswamy-Savithri relation, based on a dichotomy between marriage and love, is essentially Western and necessitates a literary formulation that is found contradictory to the Indian tradition.[36]

If the Western love-theme presents such an acute problem in Rao's attempt to relate it to his thesis, no less acute is the mythical formulation of his theme of quest. The autobiographical form which Rao has adopted in this novel depends for its narrative articulation on the Christian story of redemption and atonement which St Augustine in his *Confessions* recognized as the pattern of his life. For Rao the problem is to find an Indian equivalent of Christ's archetypal role in the Western tradition, and he cannot find it in the specifically "Hindu" figures of Shri Ramachandra or Lord Krishna, but in the immortal legend of the Buddha's renunciation, quest and fulfilment. So from the beginning to the end it is the legend of the Buddha that occurs again and again.

This recurrent use cannot but reflect its inextricable connection with Ramaswamy's situation. Indeed, his goal is admittedly the same as the Buddha's, to seek that "from which there is no returning." As Ramaswamy articulates, "There must be a way out, Lord, a way out of this circle of life." The Buddha's path of renunciation haunts him through all his encounters with Woman. He leaves the bed of Lakshmi remembering the Buddha's renunciation. He advises Savithri to wed Pratap, because of the Buddha's renunciation, which makes him realize that the path to the Absolute is lonely. Indeed it is in the figure of the Buddha-to-be that Ramaswamy finds the archetypal pattern underlying man's existence in the cosmos; "We are all Bodhisattvas." Yet, the Buddhism of Gautama is supposed to have been driven out by his Advaita and he denounces the Buddha and his path of renunciation. In Rao's mythical formulation the Buddha is the archetype of man's quest for truth but in his thesis Buddhism is the "near-truth." In which of these two opposed stances may we find the true Raja Rao? The answer can only be, in both and neither. The tension that such a conflict generates is never resolved in the novel.

Therefore it is perhaps inevitable that in the characterization of Madeleine and Savithri the thesis proclaims the superiority of the one while art concedes victory to the other. Ramaswamy is the centre from which both Madeleine and Savithri, as fictional entities, derive their existence. They constitute a kind of double, emanating from Rama, as both receive their metaphysics originally from him. As Madeleine tells him in regard to her own Buddhist path: "Beloved, it's you who have brought me all this." If the narrative presentation of the Ramaswamy-Madeleine relationship succeeds in such concrete details of everyday life and happenings, this is precisely because Madeleine constitutes Rama's phenomenal self, engrossed in the reality of this world. Savithri, on the other hand, is assumed to be Rama's transcendental self, hence the relationship between her and Rama is a tour de force of constant intellection. Devoid of concrete and phenomenal existence it must necessarily fill in with myth till it totally replaces reality. Since Rama finds the transcendental self to be the true identity, Rao is determined to show Savithri as the right woman for Rama, and Madeleine is destined to be left behind as a mere "woman of the marches." The question is: does Rao's respective characterization successfully establish the triumph of Savithri over Madeleine, of

Reality over Appearance, of Transcendence over Existence? Savithri appears before us as an attentive listener or docile follower in relation to Rama, no other aspect of her character gains credibility. Indeed, far from embodying womanhood in a concrete entity, Savithri is essentially an asexual figure cast only as a pupil or a disciple. One never really understands how her external life of smoking, dancing and coquetry can co-exist in harmony with her spiritual life where Rama reigns as the "Lord of this life and all lives to come." Madeleine, on the other hand, is presented in so many roles, besides that of the wife—a loving sister to Catherine whose marriage she arranges, an understanding friend to Georges whose tormented Slav soul finds in her a solace, an efficient housewife at villa St. Anne and a competent teacher in her lycée. It is Madeleine and Madeleine alone in the novel in whom the essential feminine principle operates as the creative matrix, for she has desired and borne two children to the man she loves.[37] The text provides ample evidence of the profound resemblance between Madeleine and Little Mother, despite all the apparent dissimilarity: "how like Madeleine was Little Mother, they both had the same shy presence, both rather silent and remembering everything; they love, too, more than is customary." That last sentence reveals the essential Feminine Principle that sustains the mother's selfless attachment to her child and maintains the whole creation. Indeed it is Madeleine who embodies motherhood, so Rama himself notes how "like my own mother" was Madeleine when the news of his father's illness arrived. It is only she who has the supreme feminine power to offer her whole being without being divided into isolated compartments of the physical, the emotional and the spiritual which is so palpable in Savithri. It is here necessary to realize that she does not consciously take to Buddhism as an intended rebellion against her Hindu husband who himself believes that Buddhism has given her "a conscious foothold in India." When Ramaswamy tells her that it is India that separates them her surprise is genuine: "India? But I am a Buddhist." Since Rama wants only a part of her self, his love for her being "made of the 18 aggregates" alone she can never offer her whole being which is her true self. Rama's rejection of her spiritual aspiration makes her womanhood meaningless. The tragic magnitude of her character arises out of an unconscious correspondence to a well-known archetype in Western literature, that of the Misunderstood Wife, the prototype of Tolstoy's Anna Karenina, Ibsens's Nora. The situation she is placed in is realistic enough; she is a deceived wife, a grieving mother; married to an orthodox Hindu, she is an exile among her own people. Through her inexorable *karma* she is as though fulfilling the pattern of her mythic destiny in a mimetic world. Her character stands clear and firmly enunciated, rooted in reality and going beyond it, supported by her own tragic intensity.

Despite all the elaborate and conscious mythical patterning of Savithri as Radha, Iseult, Savitri, Parvati, she remains from the beginning to the end a mere reflection of Ramaswamy, an insubstantial shadow. She is, indeed, the formula of the Great Indian Womanhood as exists only in Raja Rao's personal thesis. Madeleine, on the other hand, belongs to the multi-dimensional reality of fictional presentation. Rao's intended evaluation of Madeleine and Savithri is not adequately reflected in the literary representation of these two characters. So the urgency with which Rao tries to denounce Madeleine betrays a deeply personal concern with the thesis. Take, for example, the presentation of her Buddhism which is ostensibly her drawback as wife of Rama. Her altruism, the profusion of statues and *tanakas* Rao surrounds her with, relate her to Mahayana Buddhism. This impression gains ground, since according to Rama, the altruism of Mahayana appears dualistic. Yet strangely enough, Madeleine studies Pali, although the Mahayana texts are all in Sanskrit. Besides, her asceticism, like her Pali, as a path to *nirvana*, connects her closely to the Hinayana school of Buddhism, since Mahayana identifies *nirvana* with *samsara*. Her supernatural power, her practice of miracles, remind one again of Tantric Buddhism or Vajrayana, since such practices are strongly condemned in the Pali texts of Hinayana. Rao's Western readers, to whom the novel is primarily addressed, may not notice that as a Buddhist, Madeleine is as convincing as a hypothetical Christian who is a Roman Catholic, a Protestant and a member of the Greek Orthodox Church, all at the same time. In order to condemn her, Rao treats her renunciation with utmost cruelty. The early Buddhist ideal of renunciation, which was incidentally far less ascetic than the contemporary Vedic-brahmanic practice, is parodied heavily in the detailed description of Madeleine's physical ailments which need medical attention and therefore due cognizance of the world which is ought to be renounced. The cruellest cut is of course Madeleine's wish to retain her mother's house after becoming a

Buddhist nun. This is a totally unnecessary touch since her wish to retain the house does not play any role in this critical juncture of her relation with Ramaswamy. But it has been added intentionally to condemn her. Her renunciation of the empirical reality is sought to be presented as pretentious since she is obviously grossly attached to the material world. All this is used to justify Rama's love for her truncated self and his total denial of her spiritual aspiration. The hollowness of her renunciation would have been established beyond doubt if only it had been adequately embedded in a psychological context. Why should Madeleine wish to keep her mother's house as "a spot" to call her own, when she has renounced all, since in the whole action of the novel no emotional attachment either to the dead mother or her house or to any personal possession, has been built up or implied as an organic part of her character? In fact she has never been shown as attached to any spot of France whether in life or in death. Her mother's house never occurs in the whole presentation of Madeleine's life in narration till the author introduces it suddenly at the end, when the structure cannot assimilate an entirely new element. This improbable and technically irrelevant finishing touch, more than the incomprehensible Buddhism, betrays the personal bias of the author showing up Rao's limitation as a novelist in the problematic relation of the author to his material. The narrative technique he has employed to inter-relate the two forms of narration and intellectual anatomy reveals his shortcoming as an objective analyst who is unable to allow the independent and unique world of fiction to stand as a self-consistent, coherent and meaningful whole. In this context we may remember Francois Mauriac's brilliant analysis of the relation between the novelist and his work: "Our work is imperfect in the very measure in which it betrays the fissures in the tormented soul of its miserable writer."[38] A strong therapeutic intention disturbs the relation between Rao and his material. In actual life, both Raja Rao and Camille Rao, for a time, pursued the same path of yogic meditation geared to the supernatural, and it was Rao himself who first gained extraordinary power, strong enough to leave visible impact on the external world.[39] It was he who undertook a forty-day fast and meditation, and received in a vision the remedy of his own ailment. As for Madeleine's much-abused altruism, apparently Buddhist (and Western), Romain Rolland has noted young Raja Rao's zeal to do good to others.[40] Even Rao himself admits the profound impact of the rich humanism of the Buddhist texts on his growth as a writer. Yet in the novel he transfers the whole burden of his unusual practices, supernatural experience and Buddhist altruism onto Madeleine and Madeleine alone. It is the manifestation of Madeleine's supernatural powers, her forty-day fast, her vision of Rama's cure and above all her compassion for the suffering humanity—in fact all Rao's own past—which furnish enough justification of her rejection by the orthodox brahman husband. One part of Rao's identity is represented by Madeleine who combining some aspects of his divorced wife Camille Rao (her statuesque beauty, deep interest in Indian spirituality and above all her essentially intellectual as well as sensitively reserved personality)[41] becomes an embodiment of the West which Rao's preconceived notion of India-West polarity forces to reject.

As Roman Jakobson says: "it is the dominant which guarantees the integrity of structure."[42] It is inevitable therefore that Rao's intellectual thesis should have attempted to transform other structural components to impart an impression of unity. Yet here the aesthetic coherence is severely limited because the dominant thesis and the real-life structure which is sought to be dominated tend to fall to the same level of futility. The identity which is Ramaswamy's goal is a paradigm, a fixed logical series contained in the opening sentence of the novel. ("I was born a Brahmin—that is devoted to Truth"). The end at the feet of a preceptor, a guru, is contained in the very beginning, not as a seed waiting for temporal, biographical development into a plant, but as a cybernetic formula which is automatically operative. The very structure of the concept of identity here is syllogistic:

> A brahman is one who is devoted to Truth.
> Ramaswamy is a brahman.
> He is devoted to Truth.

Since this path to Truth can be shown only by a guru, the resolution of the novel merely records a result arrived at through an automatic process. But the whole story of Ramaswamy is a biographical, temporal progression. So is the intensely historical thesis enveloping it, using for its very structure facts of history like the extermination of the heresies or the disappearance of the Buddhist church. Hence both the components, intellectual or dialectic and the real or narrative, exist within the very same category of human experience. Both are on a level completely different from the logical paradigm of Brahmanhood. Indeed, as we have seen, History and Truth are diametrically opposed in the very assumption of the structure. If we keep the motive of approximating a paradigm in view ("Truth cannot have history"), the elaborate paraphernalia of the thesis as also its intended dominance may appear deficient in the very function of the dominant, which must constitute the focus. The dissonance between the human reality and the logical paradigm is not bridged but widened by a historical thesis which consequently highlights the fissures in the very being of the artist. In the whole design of *The Serpent and the Rope* it is an acute tension which sharpens into this crisis of the dominant. So the contrasts and contradictions can only offer a structure which is centred in an aesthetic of discord.[43]

NOTES

1. As Raja Rao himself expresses his stand in the novel: "The West is Romantic and as such historical. . . . India is classical, that is traditional." Letter to M.K. Naik quoted by the latter in "*The Serpent and the Rope:* The Indo-Anglian Novel as Epic Legend," 1968, pp. 218-19. His hero Ramaswamy repeatedly assures: "India has no history, for Truth cannot have history," p. 102; also, p. 83, p. 332.
2. Contrast this picture of a sobbing Ramaswamy, for ever haunted by his mother's death (p. 6) with the description of reaction to the death of mother as actually recorded by a modern son of India. "My brother had kept me ignorant of her death, which took place whilst I was still in England. He wanted to spare me the blow in a foreign land. The news however was none the less a severe shock to me. But I must not dwell upon it. My grief was even greater than over my father's death. Most of my cherished hopes were shattered. But I remember that I did not give myself up to any wild expression of grief. I could even check the tears, and took to life just as though nothing had happened." Mahatma Gandhi,

An Autobiography: The Story of My Experiments with Truth, 1924, 1972, p. 63.

3. Mircea Eliade, *Myths, Dreams and Mysteries: The Encounter between Contemporary Faiths and Archaic Religion,* 1957, 1966, p. 235. Also, "Anguish before Nothingness and Death seems to be specifically modern phenomenon. In all other non-European cultures, that is, in the other religions, Death is never felt as an absolute or Nothingness." (*Ibid*)
4. "In Beneras one knows death is illusory as the mist in the morning." (*SR*, p. 11) Ramaswamy can feel the truth of the above only in the death of those who are distant from him, for example Aunt Lakshamma. (p. 8) We do not find him philosophizing over the death of his own sons. Equally significant is the constant obsession with death throughout the novel, pp. 5-12, 15, 20, 33, 44, 56, 110, 133, 137, 155, 188, 206, 232-34, 236, 283-85, 356, 359-61, 377, 384.
5. For the inextricable relation between time and identity, see W.J. Harvey: *Character and the Novel*, 1966, pp. 118-20. This makes Ramaswamy's quest for identity an essentially existential theme, as Michael Wyschogrod notes: "There is no factor as closely related to the existential nature of man's situation as time. Man's existence is in time and because he must operate in and with time he cannot leave existence." *Kierkegaard and Heidegger: The Ontology of Existence,* 1954, p. 42.
6. Cf. "Consciousness is a being, such that in its being, its being is in question insofar as this being implies a being other than itself." Jean-Paul Sartre: *Being and Nothingness: A Phenomenological Essay on Ontology* (trans. Hazel E Barnes), 1956, 1966, 1977, p. 24. For the basis of the existential framework underlying the analysis of Rama's relationship with the other, please see Sartre, pp. 190, 475, 386-87, 98, 87.

   This philosophical basis of Ramaswamy's relation with the *other*, points towards man's estrangement, alienation. It is when the self is lost, that a "looking glass self" comes into being. This view of the social psychologists is maintained by Eric and Mary Josephson thus, "One acquires a self or identity through interaction with others." *Man Alone: Alienation in Modern Society*, 1962, p. 15.
7. According to Katyayana if this defect exists "before marriage

(somehow unknown) or arise(s) after it, in both cases the gift of a girl should be regarded invalid." R.B. Pandey, *Hindu Samskara,* 1949, 1969, p. 198. So the Puranas place the consumptive in the same class as the sinner, the childless and the indigent, e.g. *Siva Purana,* 1969, vol. I, p. 31, and *Markandeya Purana,* 1904, p. 91. This reality is tacitly recognized in the fictional world created by Rao, e.g. pp. 266-67.

8. See for instance the *Mahabharata, Dronaparva, Sauptikaparva, Mushalparva.* The only grieving mother in Indian literature who has accepted the untimely death of her son as an inevitable concomitant of this existence, is Kisa Gotami who becomes a Buddhist nun and hence Madeleine's attempt to be "a Vassita" (i.e. Kisa Gotami) is justified from the Indian point of view.
9. Raja Rao's own view, "a woman can only find her God through man," (letter to M.K. Naik) has nothing "Indian" about it for such subordination is to be found in every orthodoxy, sanctioned by institutionalized religion. Cf. "He for God only, she for God in him," Milton, *Paradise Lost,* Book I. "Thy desire shall be to thy husband, and he shall rule over thee." *Genesis,* 3:16. Also *I. Corinthian,* 11:7-9 and *Ephesians,* 5:22-24.
10. R.K. Veda III, lxii: 10. What Rao actually quotes as *Gayatri* is the song of a dying man from *Brhadaranyaka Upanisad,* V, XV: I. Also *Isa Upanisad,* 15.
11. Cf. A.K. Coomaraswamy, *Buddha and the Gospel of Buddhism,* 1916, 1974, p. 207.
12. "Face to Face with Raja Rao" by S.V.V, Bombay: *The Illustrated Weekly of India,* Jan. 5, 1965, pp. 44-45.
13. All around Rama is sorrow and pain. Each character is sad—his father (pp. 9, 32), sister Saroja (pp. 105, 369), Little Mother (p. 20), Georges (pp. 72, 238), Catherine (pp. 154-56), not to speak of Madeleine (pp. 12, 23), and strangely enough, the ideal Indian woman Savithri (pp. 232, 241). Rama himself emanates this sadness. (pp. 244, 252)

    Rao's "Indian" stance of spirituality and culture is hardly consistent with this pervading melancholy of the novel as is aptly noted by a French reviewer, *Et Voici, Tribune de Geneve,* 24 Juin 1959.
14. The abrupt break of Ramaswamy from this existence, and his

irretrievable height of transcendence (p. 402) implies an existential leap which Kierkegaard might have described as the capture of Eternity in time, the "Fullness of Time." Kierkegaard, *Fragments, the Point of View,* 1939, p. 13.

15. Robert Scholes and Robert Kellogg, *The Nature of Narrative,* 1966, 1968, p. 229, discuss in detail the mingling of the two plot structures--love and quest--and their recurrence in the Western literature from the medieval age to the present day.
16. Cf. Thomas Mann, *The Magic Mountain*, 1924, 1967, pp. 342-45. The thesis of Dr. Krokwoski ("Love as a force contributory to disease") underlies the human situation of Hans Castorp's relation with Clavdia Chauchat. So Hans Castorp expresses his love, identifying love with his disease: "Le corps, l'amour, la mort, ces trois ne font qu'un." *The Magic Mountain.*
17. Raja Rao himself always maintains that his whole writing is autobiographical, a chronicle of his "personal philosophical quest" e.g. Annie Brierre, "An Interview with Raja Rao," *The Illustrated Weekly of India,* March 10, 1963, p. 26. Also Elizabeth Wohl, "Raja Rao on America," *Span*, Jan. 1973, p. 37.

    Raja Rao himself, quite like his South Indian brahman hero, was deeply interested in the heresies of Southern France. However, it was not Madame Rao who was interested in Buddhism and Tantra, but Rao himself.
18. Frye, *Anatomy of Criticism,* 1957, pp. 303-14; and Malcolm Bradbury, *Possibilities: Essays on the State of the Novel,* London: OUP, 1973, pp. 3-23.
19. The inextricable relation between a hypothetical base and the form of the novel is best presented by Dorothy Van Ghent, *The English Novel: Form and Function,* 1955, p. 3.
20. J.N. Farquhar, *Modern Religious Movements in India,* 1914, 1967, the chapter on the Theosophical Society, in which the Theosophical doctrine is presented as "a blend of Buddhism, Hinduism and various forms of occultism." (p.220) Nirad C. Chaudhuri in his *Scholar Extraordinary* London, 1974, regards Madame Blavatsky founder of the Theosophical Society, as an example of "Western infatuation with Hinduism." (p. 327) Unlike the various attempts in East, North and Western India (in the forms of Brahmo Samaj, Arya Samaj,

Prarthana Samaj), the South did not formulate its reaction to the Western influence. Hence Rao's sarcastic attitude towards "theoleptic magic" in *Comrade Kirillov* as well as in *The Policeman and the Rose.*

21. Scholes and Kellogg, *The Nature of Narrative,* p. 215.
22. Frye, *Anatomy of Criticism,* p. 311. Instances of elaborate intellection may be found in *The Brothers Karamazov, The Possessed, The Magic Mountain,* not to speak of *Tristram Shandy, Moby Dick* and *Ulysses* among others.
23. The typical puranic mode does not present a dialectical confrontation between philosophical exposition and narration. Thus Prahlada's life-story, his fervent devotion, is entirely in consonance with the greatness of Lord Visnu, who succours the devotee and bestows him the greatest boon of salvation. *Visnu Purana,* 1972, Book I, Ch. XX, p. 118.
24. This "defamiliarization" offering a justification for the narrated reality derives from a romantic aesthetic. As Viktor Shklovsky points out, "habitualization devours objects, clothes, furniture, one's wife" and the main goal of art is the deautomatization, "technique of art is to make things unfamiliar." "Art as Device," *Russian Formalist Criticism,* 1965, p. 12.
25. Jonathan Culler rightly points out that it is dangerous to arrive at a homology by applying binary opposition in a complex cultural context for it may lead to serious misconceptions ignoring the essential qualitative differences. *The Structuralist Poetics,* 1975, pp. 14-16. The opposition that exists in India between non-dualism and dualism or between Vedanta and Buddhism is definitely not of the same value or quality as the conflict between orthodoxy and heresy in the West.
26. The dominance of one element is valid in theory for different elements have to be hierarchically placed. As Tynyonov holds, "A system does not mean the coexistence of components on the basis of equality, it presupposes the preeminence of one group of elements and the resulting deformation of other elements." "Arkhaistry inovatrary," quoted by Victor Erlich, *Russian Formalism,* p. 170. Erlich discusses in detail the concept of *dominata* as an essential feature of Russian formalism.
27. Shiva Niranjan, "An Interview with Raja Rao," *Indian Writing in English,* ed. Krishnanandan Sinha, 1979, p. 24.

28. As Simone Weil perceives: "A human being has roots by virtue of his real, active and natural participation in the life of a community which preserves in living shape certain particular treasures of the past and certain particular expectations of the future." *The Need for Roots,* 1949, 1952, p. 41. Madeleine's situation is not atypical of the foreign wives/companions of Indians living abroad as we find in the sensitive portrayal of Anita Desai's *Bye-Bye Blackbird,* n.d., and Kamala Markandaya's *Nowhere man,* 1979.
29. It is the use of these elements which link Graham Greene to the French Catholic writers. See David Lodge, "Graham Greene," *The Novelist at the Cross Roads and other Essays on Fiction and Criticism,* 1971, p. 108.
30. Rama has "the bearing of a young pipal tree, tall and sacred, and the serpent-stones around it. We must go round him to become sacred" (p. 9). This declaration guides the attitudes of all characters to the hero e.g. pp. 45, 91, 105, 107, 240, 329, 371. Little Mother calls him I "a prince, a god" (p. 259). Madeleine addresses him as "my liege, my lord" (p. 115). The idealization reaches its climax in Savithri's worship of Ramaswamy's feet (pp. 211-12).
31. Frye, *Anatomy of Criticism*, p. 308.
32. For details on the original Savitri's spirited personality, her freedom of intellectual power, see the *Mahabharata, Vanaparva, Patibrata-mahatmyaparvadhaya.*
33. For details please see Denis de Rougemont's *Love in the Western World,* 1956, Book I *Tristan Myth.*
34. Frye, *Fables of Identity*, p. 12.
35. Cf. de Rougemont, on the characteristics of the courtly/chivalric love. *Love in the Western World,* pp. 75-76. Also C.S. Lewis, *Allegory of Love,* 1936, p. 2.
36. The notion of supremacy of love over marriage is the centre of courtly/Platonic love. As Rougemont says, "marriage implies no more than physical union, but 'Amour'—the supreme Eros—is the transport of the soul," p. 76. But in the Hindu concept of marriage the wife being *dharmapatni* is the *sahadharmini,* the mate in the spiritual path of man, is essential in the Hindu male's performance of his duty to gods and ancestors.

    To "Indianize" the Rama-Savithri love Rao tries to borrow from Ananda K Coomaraswamy's exposition of Essence as subsisting of Being and Becoming, *Hinduism and Buddhism*, n.d, pp. 11-13. Coomaraswamy states that the non-dual Absolute is "a syzygy of conjoint principles . . . (which) become contraries only when we envisage the act of self-manifestation" in the universe of perception. These "halves" may be distinguished "as Sacerdotum and Regnum (Brahma Ksatrau)" or "Male and Female." It is because the "Regnum as a separated function is nothing but itself, relatively feminine, and subordinated to the Sacerdotum, its director," that Rao's Savithri is a female, a Kshatriya (Regnum), subordinate to Rama, a male and a Brahman (Sacerdotum). The same pattern is repeated in *The Chessmaster and His Moves* (1988).

37. The Feminine Principle "though running parallel to the male transcends it" precisely for its manifestation as mother, e.g. Ajit Mukherjee and Madhu Khanna, *The Tantric Way: Art, Science Ritual*, 1977, p. 26.
38. Francois Mauriac, *Le Romancier et Ses Personages*, 1933, pp. 142-143.
39. As Rao admitted in a detailed interview by Som P. Ranchan, "A Meeting with Raja Rao," III, *Thought*, Delhi, July 27, 1968, p. 16.
40. Romain Rolland, *Inde Journal*, 1915-1943, p. 16.
41. Camille Rao, one of the translators of Sri Aurobindo's works into French, is still remembered as "tall, well-built and very attractive" by Jean Herbert, her associate in the translation work. She was--just like Madeleine--a teacher at a lycée in Southern France. Exactly like Madeleine, she was reserved, "entirely taken up by the teachings" of a particular branch of spirituality. M. Herbert adds, "At that time she did not like to speak of her married life, which as I understood had not been a success." (Letters to the author from M. Jean Herbert, dated March 13 and April 10, 1978, Geneva).
42. Roman Jacobson, "The Dominant" in *Readings in Russian Poetics*, 1971, p. 82
43. "A work of art often expresses by means of contrast and contradictions, its levels can refer to and echo one another, but they can also realize a tension, suggest a crisis." Cesare Segre, *Semiotics and Literary Criticism*, 1973, p. 78.

The Serpent and the Rope

Part II

1. *Mimesis as the inspiration of deviance*

The language of *The Serpent and the Rope* reveals a conscious and deliberate experiment to correspond to the narrative form which tries to accommodate an abstract thesis within a realistic structure. We find, first of all, a development and flowering of linguistic realism at its broadest as well as deepest connotation. The ostensible proof of course lies in the pervasive "local colour" through borrowings from other languages, mainly French. That the reality which envelops the Hindu Ramaswamy is almost wholly Western and particularly French, remains the predominant impression left by the innumerable French items scattered throughout the novel.[1] It is quite possible to place these in an order: (a) definition of man's position in the world by profession. e.g. *notaire, madame la professeuse, huissier, vetérinaire, curé, patronne, souspréfet, garcon-de café*, etc; (b) activities in regard to state and government, e.g. *la carte d'identité, liberté suveillée, renouvellement, annulée*, etc; (c) the physicality of daily necessities like food and lodging, *e.g. boef saignant, champignon du pays, coq au vin, salle de bains, bottes de persil, cassoulets, les olives farcies aux anchois, la pissaladiere, le chevreau roti et les aubergines sautées*. etc. Even simple English *cake* is replaced by *gateau;* specialities of regional varieties are noted: *Saint-Germain, carottes de Crecy, petit pois de Clamart, romarin d'antibes, escargots de Bourgogne;* (d) Topographical peculiarities of France also occur in French, e.g. *monticule*, as well as place names in their French forms, e.g. *Iles de martiniquasises, Cambodges*. (e) French phrases: *temps modernes; les droits de l'Homme, chez Weber, Chez Madame Tissier, nous autres Francais, notre Rama, caveau de famille, chemin de cristal*. (f) Conversational bits in French: *les enfants a quatre pattes en avant, L'Archeveque Henri d'Auxerre a dit, Une Perigoadine pour le diner, Montmartre pour la nuit et les Halles pour le petit matin; mais quest ce-que vous voulez* etc. Not only family relationship *(Oncle, tante)* are in French, but also affectionate endings by French in-laws. Hence Oncle Charles ends his letter with: "Je vous embrasse tous le deux, et bien affecteusement." But the letters from Indians (e.g. from Little Mother, Saroja or Savithri) do not possess corresponding "Indian" touches in actual borrowings. It is the sensitivity to the French ethos that makes Rao preserve terms like *les philosophes, les écrivains impériaux* (e.g. even *berceuse),* with their definite connotation in French.

Such linguistic realism—to a great extent an established aspect of the realistic fictional form—goes deep into the psychological stratum. The careful choice and use of French expressions when English equivalents are available, reveals the desire to emphasize the peculiar French aspect of the reality that resides in an indefinable shade of meaning. For some French items the English equivalents clearly do not suffice; e.g. *metier, rejetéon, petit, les économies,* etc. This desire to establish a specifically "French" reality interjects into English sentences a number of French phrases and expressions peculiar to the convention of the language, *joie de vivre, l'homme moyen sensuel, faire le ménage,* etc. As an important offshoot of this French reality in the larger cultural sphere there is the repetition of words and phrases like *soutane, Marie pleine de grace* etc. A recognition, of course, of the Catholic background, makes the use of quite a few English words by the Hindu author especially meaningful, e.g. *concupiscence, fornication, tabernacle, paraclete, Assumption, Ascension* etc. It is not only the mundane everyday reality of Ramaswamy that is French, strengthened by interweaving English with French conversational habits, like exclamations *(ah la la, la vie la vie),* addresses *(m'amie, chérie, ma vielle),* phatic communion *(Bonjour, au revoir, comme il fait beau),* but even the more important cultural environs, which have decidedly impinged on his Indian identity, as revealed in innumerable quotations from French. These present an authentic French atmosphere but more significantly point towards the Indian hero's divided inner reality. It is to be noted that Ramaswamy's deepest emotion more often than not can be expressed only in French—his anguish of rootlessness, his agony of memories, even his aspiration for a harmonious self. One may not find it unnatural that the Hindu husband falls back on his knowledge of French poetry to express his relation with his French wife; but one can hardly ignore the ironic significance ingrained in the very use of French (and Italian) to confer a literary pattern on his love with Savithri—so loudly proclaimed to be wholly Indian by the thesis of the novel itself.[2] So the pilgrim hero wandering through encounters with women seems to arrive at a resolution only in the echo of a French poet. The exiled Hindu finds a portable home— "wheresoever I am is my country"—following the lead of Tristan Corbiere, "Ma patrie est ou je la plante/Terre au mer, elle est sous la plante / des mes pieds." (*Ma Patrie*)

This pervasive and profound influence of the French literary tradition which is built into the surface linguistic structure is hardly matched by a corresponding Indian. The number of directly borrowed Indian words is almost negligible, e.g. *Kusha, Sheesham, Champak,* etc. The use of some of these, being proper nouns (like Shiva, Krishna, Kailas, Nandi) or concepts peculiarly Indian (e.g. dharma, karma, maya,nirvana, lila, etc.) or spiritual (*holy, sacred, auspicious, Ganges, Benares,* etc.) may be regarded as an attempt to conform to the conventional concept of India held by a Western reader conditioned by the nineteenth-century romantic Indologists. The Indian flavour of these items is derived not so much from strictly linguistic associations as from semantics produced by a cultural background. A heavy sprinkling of such items helps to establish an authentic "Indian" atmosphere and as a formal feature belongs to the mimetic convention of the Western novel.[3]

In this connection a word about Rao's use of Sanskrit quotations in the novel is necessary, since to many of his readers this particular feature represents an absolute stamp of Indianness. Indian novelists starting with Bankimchandra, have quite often used Sanskrit verses in novels, not so much to display knowledge but to present an authentic reality, since several Sanskrit *slokas* are actually used in conversation and the daily observances of many high-caste Hindus, not only brahmans. With Rao, however, the use of Sanskrit has certain specific features, not usually to be found in novelists in Indian languages. Unlike his French (and Italian) "quotes" which are left as such, without any need of English rendering, the Sanskrit citations are always translated into English. Indeed he usually uses a few phrases as decorative pieces accompanying long English versions much of which may not be present in the original; sometimes he utilizes only translations. This brahman writer's handling of "the language of the gods" bristles however with inaccuracies already noted by critics which an Indian writer in an Indian language would perhaps never have dared to leave uncorrected. This casual use of Sanskrit not only gives the lie to Rao's lofty ambition of Sanskritizing English, but more significantly in my opinion contrasts with his impeccable French. It is curious that in sharp contrast to the smooth and appropriate use of French quotations, the application of Sanskrit to indicate deeper levels of the psyche is often fraught with problems. A long Platonic session with the Catholic Georges ends in Ramaswamy's recitation of Sankara's famous verses on the non-duality of the individual and the Absolute Consciousness, as though an identification of Plato's Universal as the non-dual Truth is automatic. But to many, conversant with philosophy, this may appear as an extrapolation. In the context of Ramaswamy's jealousy of Pratap, his Vedantic declaration, "I am Shiva," may be underlined as the mere longing of a romantic, contrasted sharply with the actuality, since in Vedanta, one who is united with the Absolute is a liberated soul (*Jivanmukta*) for ever, above all egotistic impulses. Such ironic confrontation between the quotation and the context may however be lost on an average reader. When the Hindu hero strives actually to transcend the body ("For a moment you had gone beyond the body, and oh, how sad it is to come back to bear this heavy limb"), the extended description of an ecstatic fervour is laced with two long Sanskrit quotations, each of which offers a pagan Hindu sensuous experience entirely sufficient by itself. Such dissonance lurks even in the most crucial use of the famous Vedantic lines ("Who are you and whence have you come") offered as an adequate expression of Ramaswamy's agony of loneliness after his separation from the wife and the beloved. But the inevitable impression of rootlessness, of alienation in existential terms, is bound to the temporal history of Ramaswamy, whereas the Sanskrit lyric exhorting renunciation of the world, deals not with history, but with ontology, not with personal frustration, but with a timeless question. Hence the rest of the Sanskrit text ("*ka me janani ko me tatah,*" i.e. "who is my mother, who my father?") is left untranslated, for this would come into conflict with Ramaswamy's biography, his constant harping on family heritage and reminiscence of the dead mother. The tendency to grant supremacy to the fictional framework may have even prompted the highly individual English rendering of Sanskrit verses. To convey Ramaswamy's decision to leave Madeleine, Rao offers a long passage from Bhavabhuti's *Uttararamacharitam*. The concluding lines (*"ekah samprati, . . ."*) in which Madeleine is made to read her fate, run thus in the novel: "But now alone is Rama, and faded his dearest things/Heartless would it be not to linger long looking/Or leave without deep salutation to Pancavati." It is difficult to grasp how this seemingly innocuous verse could possibly lead to the avowed result—Madeleine's momentous realization of rejection, "And now Madeleine understood,"—unless of course she had caught the original meaning which the readers are denied, for these lines actually translated are, "alone now, *after being the cause of the loss of his dear (wife)*, how should Rama, *sinful as he is*, visit that very same Pancavati, or how pass on regardless of it?"[4] It is interesting that Rao's rendering of the Sanskrit, for which he takes sole responsibility (in the Acknowledgement), absolves the ancient Rama of all the sin (*papah*) of destroying his beloved (*nasitapriyatamastam*) and fits admirably into the thesis of the modern Rama in which the beloved herself is at fault. The whole point of our discussion is not to reflect on Rao's knowledge of Sanskrit, but to suggest an invariable tendency to subordinate Sanskrit to the demands of an alien form in an alien medium perhaps at the cost of traditionally impartial Hindu scholarship.

It is therefore natural that in sharp contrast to the importance of the body and the frequency of words denoting varied sense-experiences which characterize classical Sanskrit literature, Raja Rao's "Indianness" reveals itself in an emphasis on inferiority.[5] The linguistic experiment in English to structure the specific "Indianness" which is assumed to be metaphysical, is what deserves special attention. This may, firstly, be found in the use of certain words in greater currency than is perhaps warranted by the immediate context of the realistic situation. This quantitative deviance concerns words related to man's inner world, e.g. *inward, being, self, inturned, awareness*, etc. Take for instance the use of (a) *inward:* "For once Madeleine seemed to have intuited womanhood as though the outer turning had slipped *inward*"; men are perfect "when they turn *inward*"; "The old Royalist city, with its spread, low trees and *inward* hotels"; "The Mediterranean turns *inward*";

(b) *being:* "a concord in one's *being*"; "Absorbing Paris into my *being*"; "the interstices of my *being*," "a binding at the altar of one's *being*."

The incessant repetition of *self*—360 times in a novel of 406 pages—is so pervasive that it really forms "the stylistic essence" of the whole novel as a Western critic has rightly observed.[6] But the problem is that the referent of *self* does not seem to be consistent; indeed, cannot be consistent if we have Rao's thesis in view, for Ramaswamy's goal is to realize the Vedantic concept of Absolute Consciousness in which all distinctions of *you* and *me* cease. But he seems obsessed with *self*, though a Vedantin should first of all give up his ego. It seems quite possible that the *self* in this novel may have two directly opposite referents. Consequently we may find here "the most ambiguous that can be conceived," which according to Empson, "occurs when the two meanings of the word, the two values of ambiguity, are the two opposite meanings defined by the context, so that the total effect is to show a fundamental division in the writer's mind.[7] Take for example a few random quotations, (1) "London was no longer a city for me, it was my*self*"; (2) "To act, then is to be proscribed to your*self*"; (3) "He alone acts who is a stranger to him*self*"; (4) "Krishna fought himself against *himself*, through himself and in *himself*, and what remained is ever and ever *himself*—the Truth"; (5) "*Pau*, and the solitude of the mountains, had given me back to *myself*." One does not need a more obvious proof of Rao's obsession with identity than this insistent repetition of *self*.[8] Nor is it far-fetched to deduce from this bit of linguistic evidence that there is a deep anguish in the author, overcome by the enormity of a threat to identity. What seems to me far more important is the total lack of clear patterning which alone could have established an unequivocal assertion. What exactly is the *self* in quotations (3) and (4)? The use of *self* in some instances seems to indicate a new value which is totally opposed to the English meaning of *self* as "personality," "ego," "what one is," etc. The *self* that is Truth, or knowledge, must necessarily indicate a conscious attempt to find an English equivalent for the Sanskrit *Atman* which may mean either "ego" or "the Absolute," depending on the context. The first and foremost task of a Vedantin is to extinguish the *self*, the ego, because this physico-mental personality is a *maya*, a phenomenal imposition on the Ultimate Reality. Hence Ramaswamy's agony, "How can one go from one*self*"?

Here *self* clearly indicates the ego as it normally does elsewhere in the English language. In other places however, the same connotation of *self* is hardly implied: for example, "To whom does one belong? To one*self*." Here self has to be an adequate linguistic correlative of the Sanskrit *atman* as the Absolute. As Rao clearly indicates, "You cannot go beyond your*self*, your impersonal principle."

Is it this "impersonal" principle, the Absolute, the Brahman, that Rao strives to convey through the English personal pronoun basing himself on an analogy with the dual notion of the Sanskrit *Atman*? In Sanskrit the use is related to the very ethos of which the language forms a part because Sanskrit has been understood by a dominant though small group of people in whose particular system of thought the non-difference between the individual and the absolute in the Ultimate Reality may form the very centre. The question is, can the English term *self* perform the same function as the Sanskrit *Atman*? It is not only a question of communication, which may be relegated as an "accidental" function of language, but of the fundamental semiotic nature of language that is being challenged. Can a conscious analogy turn a verbal item rooted in one particular system of signs into another sign belonging to another system altogether? What will determine the structural principle of the function of language—the relation between the signifier and the signified?[10] In order to evade precisely this problem, the scholars—both Western and Indian—have often used *Self* with a capital to denote the Absolute, thus distinguishing it from *self* with a small 's.' Rao himself has followed this well-known convention in his quotation of Yagnavalkya's famous exposition of Self, as well as in the final statement of the Vedantic position. Since in other places he has not adhered to this very fine and yet fundamental distinction, the crucial difference between solipsism and the Vedantic concept of the Self as Absolute Consciousness remains vague.[11] After Ramaswamy has repeatedly quoted Yagnavalkya's enunciation of Self as the basis of human love, he concludes in the last meeting with Madeleine: "Love, my love, is the self." This is not an accidental confusion generated by Madeleine's refusal, but the ultimate and final record of Ramaswamy's own bondage to self. He has earlier declared, "ever and always does one fall in love but with oneself" which echoes Valéry's "Et qui donc peut aimer chose/que soimeme?" (And who can love any other/Than himself?)

Indeed Rao's tendency to add the individual limitation (*one*self, *my*self, *him*self, *your*self) is in sharp contrast to the Sanskrit convention of Self (*Atman*) uncircumscribed by any personal attribute. One may risk the conclusion that Rao's stylistic model is French. This is hardly a chance coincidence, but the revelation of the hard core of egocentricity that seeks assurance from the *Fragments du narcisse*. Does this dependence on the very myth of Western subjectivity not suggest then the Indian hero's failure to embrace the Impersonal Self that is the Absolute? If the difference between personal entity and the Absolute has been consistently maintained at the lower phenomenal level of human communication, then only the non-difference in theory at the highest level could have been fruitfully suggested. But this distinction throughout the novel is repeatedly confused, so that one cannot gainsay the suspicion that the ego is being passed on as the Absolute.

This ambiguity is enhanced by Rao's use of "I" in quite a few instances, which no possible analogue in Sanskrit may justify:

> the congress of circumstances in which two beings had known a truth, which had a beginning, a middle and an end, yet had been consecrated for an instant at the edge of the "I."

This "I" cannot simply be the same "I" which is the first person singular pronominal sign in English. Rao first of all turns it into a noun—note the use of the preceding article *the*—and secondly, tries to give it an abstract value, building up with words like *being, truth, consecrated* and the unusual combination of *congress* and *circumstances*. In other words by mere contiguity, nearness of abstract words he is trying to instil a new abstract and general referent into a sign which normally indicates the concrete and the particular self. It is the same principle of contiguity that operates in the lines which follow:

> Discovery is a whisper to oneself and the night of love is an *embalmment*, a *holiness* that we place outside time, in the *knowledge* that creation is truth.

The *I* that is meant to be used as a synonym of *self* or the Absolute is sought to be established with the help of a technique that must be called realistic despite the metaphoric interplay, since contiguity is the dominant principle behind the collocation of *embalmment,* and *holiness, outside time, knowledge* and *truth.*[12] The selection of the words follows a metaphoric scale although the intention is clearly referential—to indicate "the I" as the Truth.[13] Since poetry and truth are constantly opposed in the thesis of the novel, the attempt to arrive at the Truth through poetic devices can only stand—if it can at all—by a dependence on the realistic principle, that of metonymic combination and assemblage.[14] This will be clearer in "the Presence that I am" and lastly in "eternity the 'I.' " Incidentally this use of a definite article before a pronominal reminds one of a similar French habit, for instance, *le moi* (the I/me) is perfectly valid in French but not in Sanskrit. The deviance in English is made significant by the fact that in both these examples the "I" needs explanation which is provided by the words close to it in position, *presence* and *Eternity*; and it is this contiguity which lends meaning to the "I" as also the article, even the quotation marks. The reader is clearly told by the author that this "I" cannot signify the English "I" with the help of a digressive legend, offered as a specific referral. "It was Astabakra who said, 'wonderful, wonderful am I,' he with eight deformations. Yes, one is 'wonderful—when one is not one, but the 'I.' The last clause clearly suggests that the "I" is the opposite of ego. But the main point is that the referent of "I," the meaning, so to say, can be decoded only by combining all the data presented here. This incidentally is the basic principle of realistic technique which we ourselves have found so strongly embedded in Rao's building up the atmosphere. It is therefore interesting that although Rao has an intellectual thesis along with a human situation, he usually avoids technical terms or the conventional jargon of Indian metaphysics except perhaps the term "non-duality." Take for example the lines, "truth was whenever one *is* —for there is no anywhere or any when, but all is when one is not." It should be noted that the model of such rhetoric on the *be* verb is not Sanskrit, but the English of T.S. Eliot, "and what you own is what you do not own/and where you are is where you are not" (*Four Quartets*) and of course Shakespeare's "And nothing is but what is not." (*Macbeth*, I.iii. 141 .

In the usual jargon of Indian metaphysics however Rao's line should mean that Truth is identified with the Asololute Reality which is beyond space *(anywhere)* or time *(anywhen)* and is recognized when the ego is extinguished *(one is not).* Rao's deliberate selection of items here is no doubt poetic and indicates the English literary background but the objective is to represent an experience through mainly verbal presentation, eschewing abstraction, and he can attempt to do so only by basing himself on the principle of realism—contiguity or association. It is the placing of *was* with *is*, *anywhere* with *anywhen* (which is incidentally of lower grammaticality than the former), *is* with *is not*, that have to combine to indicate the meaning. In other words we find here even in poetic selectiveness an instance of the essentially realistic nature of the linguistic function. Here positional and semantic contiguity becomes "the constitutive device of the sequence."[15] It is this realistic principle that carries the overload placed on some common English items like *self*, *I*, or *be*. (e.g. "Savithri gave one the sense that, do what you would you could only *be*, and since you could only *be*, nothing could happen to you.")

In Sanskrit, however, the ultimate *(Atman, Brahman)* is usually conceived as an abstract state and expressed as a nominal, seldom as an action in the process of realization of the Sanskrit verb *to be,* for the simple reason that the Sanskrit style habitually rests on a customary elision of this very verb. It is precisely this constant elision that makes the heavy nominalistic style in Sanskrit possible, as has been noted by Rulon Wells.[16] In sentences like the following, no Sanskrit linguistic form stimulates the obvious deviance, (a) "God is, and goodness is part of that *is-ness*," (b) "Water is not positive to water—water is positive to nothing. Water is, So something is. and since *is-ness* is the very stuff of that something, all you can say is 'Is is.'"

The very fact that there is no Sanskrit linguistic tradition that leads to such deviances draws attention to Rao's creative use of the English language. It may as well be held that in such deviation we come to a point of breakdown of language since it is quite clear, especially in "Is is," that the very principle of transformation that defines the relation between deep and superficial structures is being ignored. The syntactic structure is the observable surface which we experience directly, the deep structure we can retrieve only by a complex act of decoding. Rao is obviously set on the difficult and perhaps impossible task of simplifying this transformational process and to keep the surface and the deep structure as close as possible in order to convey the core of his own experience. Whether this strikes at the very root of language as a system, since the structure VP + VP ('Is is') is considered impossible, is of course to be considered. But my contention is that even this deviation is foregrounded against the convention of the English language because it does follow the other rules of English structure: note, for example, the consonance with number (third person singular), the use of the capital (Is) to denote subject and also the correct position of the subject and predicate, the former preceding the latter—the last two incidentally have no validity in Sanskrit. In "is-ness," the usual nominal suffix is entirely English. There cannot be any doubt that these innovations are intensely individual and belong to idiolect, Rao's personal utterance, but their low grammaticality, which is meant to be a poetic device, is motivated and controlled by a mimetic urge. The consistency and the systematic character of Rao's play with the *be* verb tends to make it a foregrounding device, which Jan Mukarovsky defines as "the aesthetically intentional distortion of linguistic component."[17] This kind of freedom with syntax may be a part of the psychological realism associated with the stream-of-consciousness novel to suggest various levels below a verbalized consciousness. But in Rao this freedom is exercised on a considerably articulate level of the psyche. In fact the sentence (a) as well as the whole passage (b) form an actual conversation, and against the background of this internal framework, the transformational deletion, the verbal invention, can hardly be justified, because the latter can be an aesthetic success only in the representation of pre-verbal consciousness by literary convention.

2. *A Baroque Stylization*

The stress on language proves that Rao's form is representational, his object is to imitate an actual experience, since it is in "realist aesthetics" that the dominant is the verbal art.[18] His linguistic inventions or deviances in lexis as well as in syntax tend to emphasize the realistic or the representational. An analysis of some of the regular characteristic features of the syntax in the novel exposes a fundamental bondage to the real which may be found particularly in the typical baroque and non-classical elements in its style. "The chief mark of a conventional, or 'classical' art," says Morris Croll, "is an approximation to evenness in the size and form of the balanced parts of a design"; the mark of a modernistic art on the other hand "is the desire to achieve an effect of balance or rhythm among parts that are obviously not alike"— "some strangeness in the proportions."[19] Take for example the following passage of *The Serpent and the Rope*, with the sentences numbered for our convenience:

> 1. Little Mother was a shy and silent person. 2. I used to say she spoke as though she were talking to the wall or to a bird on a tree. 3. She always spoke to herself as it were. 4. She spoke to me sometimes, with long silences, in simple sentences that she could not formulate, for her education was meagre. 5. But her voice was infinite in accent and tone, as though it were some primitive musical instrument, that could make noise, which having been used from age to age had learnt the meaning of sound. And sound is born of silence.

We may notice here an elaborate manipulation of literariness in the careful varying of the length of the sentences (8 + 21 + 8 + 21 + 35 + 6) with an obvious tendency to form rhythmic pattern; the exploitation of sound value in stress and syllabic length (*silences, sentences, formulate*) and the recourse to figures of speech like simile and antithesis. But the characteristic element is the last sentence which appears sudden and unconnected with the rest of the passage distinguished from the others by a change-over to the present tense and by an ostensible generic structure as though a universal truth is unearthed through a process of induction from the data of preceding sentences which describe a person. This kind of juxtaposition, of a concrete description of a real life situation in the past tense, with a generic sentence cast often as an aphorism in the present tense, shows the mix of narrative and dialectic, realistic and abstract. It is useful to remember that there is no inextricable cause-effect relation of a developmental nature involved in these two forms; they are distinct and yet the whole attempt is directed to reduce the distinction to the minimum as though these constitute a coherent organic whole. These can co-exist, not in a logical structure, but only in imaginative construct. Here the whole paragraph as unit, dealing no doubt with Little Mother's "real" picture, also builds up an undercurrent of relation between *sound* and *silence* by repetition which by the fact of verbal association alone may be found related to the concluding aphorism. This perhaps explains why many of the generic sentences occur at the end of Rao's paragraphs. Take for example the three "conclusions" terminating the three paragraphs in p. 35. It is therefore imperative that we should take a whole paragraph as a unit in studying this novel, because the generic sentence, which often appears problematic, is to be related to the whole context in which it is placed. Thus the sentence, "He who possesses Sanskrit can possess himself," may confuse the reader if he forgets the rest of the passage which has built up the connection between the Sanskrit language and the compulsive urgency of the narrator to realize his identity deemed to be "Aryan" with the help of words like *Ganges, Himalaya, Yagnavalkya, philosophy*, reaching a climax in "*noble and imperial heritage*." In syntax, the linguistic technique aims here at a *deliberate asymmetry* in order to produce, as we have seen, balance or rhythm. This asymmetry is a result of the uneven length of the members within a period which may be seen also in the paragraph. Take for example: "So Maya did not die, Maya recognized truth being truth; Maya was as such nothing but truth."

The impression of a rhythmic design is distinct, based on unequal members within a period. If we apply this principle to Rao's paragraph, we not only perceive a design but also perhaps the central focus. Take, for example, the following paragraph:

> 1. People have asked me—Georges among them—what indeed it was that happened between Savithri and me in Cambridge. 2. Nothing more had happened, in fact, than if you look deep and long at silence you perceive an orb of centripetal sound which explains why Parvati is daughter of Himalaya, and Sita born to the furrow of the field. 3. I heard myself say I heard myself. 4. Or I saw my eyes see that I saw. 5. She became the awareness behind my awareness, the leap of my understanding. 6. I lost the world and she became it.

The unusual length of the second sentence (39 words) is set off against the very next one (7 words) which increases in the succeeding two sentences (9-10 words) and ends in a short one (8 words). The shortest period (no. 3) may also be taken as the central focus, for this reveals "what happened" between Rama and Savithri,that his identity—he believes—is affirmed. Incidentally the repetitive pattern of the short sentences (nos. 3 and 4) which is a permanent recurrence in Rao echoes Valéry: *Je me voyais me voir* ("I saw me seeing myself," *La Jeune Parque).*

No doubt the passage exhibits important rhetorical features like synaesthesia, repetition or antithesis, but these are subordinate to the syntactic structure which controls, in its rhythmic pattern, the verbal universe of the novel. The very self-consciousness of such rhetoric often leads to a point of tortuosity in the absence of logical advance, in the progression of the members either in the period or in the paragraph. In other words the connections that may exist at the depth of the creative source are perhaps deliberately omitted in the expression. It is a specific stylistic form in prose which in European tradition has always expressed "the energy and labour of minds seeking the truth" and "the motions of souls" to convey as Croll puts it, "not a thought but a mind thinking." It is therefore natural to find in Rao a distinct tendency towards aphorism (or *pensée*) as in the informal and meditative style of Pascal, La Bruyere or Sir Thomas Browne, carried on later by the Romantic writers, all of whom present not so much an intellectual system as a subjective experience. It is the use of the coordinating conjunctions in a period or a paragraph that may in one sense point to the emphasis on experience. The most widely used conjunctions in Rao's work are *and, but, for*. These are the same connectives which, according to Croll, "allow the mind to move straight on from the point it has reached" and "they do not refer back to any particular point in the preceding member; nor do they commit the following member to a predetermined form. In other words, they are the loose conjunctions, and disjoin the members they join as widely as possible." The frequent use of such conjunctions, which is almost a stylistic mannerism in Rao, is a manifestation of the absence of or of the tenuous link between sentences, and mark essentially an informal discursive form geared to imitate experience. We may indeed find the model of Rao's prose in some of the French Catholic writers. Here is a sentence from Leon Bloy: "Le monde en est infiniment inconnu et indevinable; mais on peut, jusq a un certain point, contenter l'esprit par l'hypothése fort plausible d'une ascension éternelle, ascension sans fin dans la Foi, dans l'Esperance, dans l'Amour." (*Celle qui pleure*, MCMXLIX, p. 28). Compare these lines from Rao's novel: "There is a point in one, a centre, a knowledge, touching which there is no becoming; there is only the end of the quest, the desperation, the Truth."

It is clear from these examples that there is a pattern which can accommodate a lot of rhetoric in consonance with a uniform literary tradition which *Kanthapura*'s mixture of heavy rhetoric and intense colloquialism in a free paragraph construction did not achieve. Rao's language matures with his surer grasp of a literary tradition, his utilization of a specific model for his purpose.[20] In fact, it is this underlying mould that serves as an adequate vehicle for a mind, caught in the actual process of thought and results in generalizations which abound in Rao. In the English Decadents too we have the same kind of adaptation of the nonclassical prose. Here is an extract from Oscar Wilde, with sentences numbered for our analysis:

> 1. It was not till the third day that he ventured to go out. 2. There was something in the clear pine-scented air of that winter morning that seemed to bring him back his joyousness and his ardour for life. 3. But it was not merely the physical condition of environments that had caused the change. 4. His own nature had revolted against the excess of anguish that had sought to maim and mar the perfection of its calm. 5. With subtle and finely wrought temperaments it is always so. 6. Their strong passions must either bruise or bend. 7. They either stay the man or themselves die. 8. Shallow sorrows and shallow loves live on. 9. The loves and sorrows that are great are destroyed by their own plenitude.[21]

The stylistic features which may be found essentially related to the total aesthetic effect lie in the deliberate asymmetry of the sentences, creating a rhythmic pattern, an intention to emphasize "literariness" over and above the referential content in the manipulation of stress and syllabic length, the use of alliteration *(maim* and *mar, bruise* or *bend),* repetition of a word *(shallow)* and of a pattern *(either . . . or),* a hint of paradox in the last line which presents a grand finale in the obvious selection of the word "plenitude," *le mot justé*. It is impossible to miss the tendency to form generalizations with a strong aphoristic flavour characteristic of *pensées*. As we have seen, all these three elements, rhythmic pattern, rhetoric, aphorism, characterize Rao's handling of English at this stage. Indeed the resemblance between Rao and Wilde in the rhetorical exuberance should be obvious, as in the following instances, (a) "Her trust makes me faithful, her belief makes me good." (Wilde) "My courage was failure turned into strength, her laughter was fear turned into simplicity." (Rao) (b) She had marred him for a moment, if he had wounded her for an age." (Wilde) "I lost the world and she became it." (Rao)

It is however the generic sentence which in both Wilde and Rao particularly reveals the connection with the French tradition in its often brief and paradoxical stance consciously exploited for aphoristic value.[22] It is astonishing how strongly Rao's aphorisms resemble Wilde's famous paradoxes in stylistic terms. Take for example Rao's "Love, my love, is the self." "For man, woman is anonymous." "Women are great hiders of the unsayable; their gossip is only their own sorrow turned downside up." "Not achievement but self-recognition is pure significance." "To hold is to be: to love is to submit." We may place these side by side with Wilde's "To be premature is to be perfect," "To be in love is to surpass one's self." "Pleasure is nature's test, her sign of approval." "To be good is to be in harmony with one's self." "Scepticism is the beginning of faith."

One is reminded of Rao's own admission that the French language possesses an "aphoristic value." Nor is the link with the English Decadents far-fetched at the conceptual level, for Rao, like the Decadents, confesses the impact of Roman Catholicism; his Hindu hero in the novel, as we have seen, justifies the Inquisition. In other words, the only unifying element in the novel is supplied both at the narrative and the linguistic levels, by a dominant force of European tradition. To regard Rao's habit of generalization as peculiarly Indian and to read profound, even Vedic, wisdom in each *apercu* is perhaps to underscore deliberately at the cost of a whole literary heritage.[23] Besides, the presence of the generic sentence in Rao indicates, as in Wilde, a constant jump from the particular concrete human situation to an abstract generalization. It is the adaptation of *pensée* in the fictional structure that such leaps almost inevitably entail. When Ramaswamy, leaving the pregnant Madeleine in France, enters into a "wedding" ritual with Savithri, the episode ends in his generalized musing: "We seek in our progeny the incarnation of lost hopes. We fornicate on our own wives the gifts we would give our loves. We breed bastards because we lack courage." They are reminiscent of Lord Henry's generalizations when Dorian Gray falls in love with an obscure actress:

> We think that we are generous because we credit our neighbours with the possession of these virtues that are likely to benefit us. We praise the banker that we may overdraw our account, and find good qualities in the highwayman in the hope that he may spare our pocket.

Dorian's belated repentance after the actress dies for him is cut short by Lord Henry's showering of abstract precepts, many of which are as charming as "nothing makes one so vain as being told that he is a sinner." Rao's Savithri, married to Pratap, is asked to go back to her husband with this conclusion from the narrator-hero, "Love is the rejoicing in the rejoicing of the other." The final statement of Rama's break from Madeleine is also a generic sentence in the same pattern, "Love is the loving of love." In both the writers, the wisdom of the abstractions is less important than the digression these generalizations offer from the critical situation. In other words, an urge for romantic escape may have been the source and spring of the elaborate display of wisdom couched in aphoristic utterances which often draw more attention to the form of expression than to the content of meaning for sheer rhetorical emphasis.

However, a fundamental difference in motivation distinguishes Rao from Wilde although he may use the same stylistic devices found earlier in Wilde's prose. Equipped with the same kind of rhetoric, Rao appears invariably serious and often irritatingly prescriptive—in short "Indian"—whereas Wilde is so thoroughly Western and pleasantly provocative, his famous wit turning his philosophy into art. In other words, we have here a case of *stylization* which occurs when the same kind of style is reproduced for a purpose essentially different from the one which guided the original. "Stylization," as Mikhail Bakhtin points out, "presupposes style" and "forces another intention (an artistic-thematic intention) to serve its aims, its new intentions."[24] The new intention in Rao is part of his obsession to establish an "Indian" identity and thus overburdened, his first-person narrator's discourse fails in its attempt to transmute a personal experience into art. By a peculiar convention, the fictional reality of a novel is always built up and maintained by the use of the preterite or the past tense that Roland Barthes calls the cornerstone of Narration.[25] Hence the generic sentence in the present tense is considered and invariably found to be "a regular tell-tale of the intrusive, assertive, author." In the traditional novel therefore the general observations are usually blended with the fictional past under some kind of a cover which may take the form of humour in Dickens or irony in Jane Austen.[26] The witticism of Wilde is a device to intersperse the fictional art with his view of life. Lacking the cover of wit and humour, the function of the intermediary in Rao's art falls on sheer verbalization which emphasizes the subjective preoccupation so much that the distinction between life and art seems precarious.

3. *Images and motifs: Metaphor and Metonymy*

The emphasis on the subjective apprehension of reality which is revealed in Rao's informal syntax is strengthened in his use of imagery. The main principle that guides the imagery of *The Serpent and the Rope* is a constant attempt to establish a relation between the abstract and the concrete as we find in "Her movements were made of erudite silence," "Some deep absence grows in me like a coconut on a young tree." "Once again it happened last night—that same emptiness, that mango-seed like kernel that lay within me."

This mingling of the abstract and the concrete no doubt forms a necessary part of the whole design which inter-relates concrete human situation and abstract formulation, narrative and intellectual thesis. Here are more instances from Rao's novel, "Time lay like sunshine over the earth," "Far away like a truth, I thought, the sea must stretch itself," "Just as we can park motor-cars, we can park thoughts in time, and go away on our job, which is living."

We may compare these with some of Sartre's images: "precious pieces of advice which stick to your teeth like soft carmel," "convenient past, pocket-size past, little gilt-edged book full of fine maxims," "Absurdity was not an idea in my head, or the sound of a voice, but that long dead snake at my feet, that wooden snake." Graham Greene is yet another writer who revels in such yoking of abstract-concrete.

In this novel, however, the analogical compulsion assumes a very characteristic form of an apprehension of external reality by a particular mind. Everything, even an inanimate object of nature, is sought to be presented not as it is, but as experienced by an individual consciousness. The imagery thus is often a further extension of Ramaswamy's individual self. In his avowed quest for truth, he seems to find it everywhere in a constant analogy. A piece of eighteenth-century architecture has "a truth about it that" makes his "morning rich." If Madeleine is lovely, she looks "true." In fact the whole world acquires meaning as well as existence only in so far as it is grasped by his consciousness and this can be effected only with the help of analogy: "Mont St. Victoire was like myself seen in a dreamless sleep." It is clear that Mont St. Victoire has no existence as it is or as *en soi*. It derives its existence when it is translated into Ramaswamy's experience by the *pour soi*. The emphasis on a personal apprehension of the world embeds his style in the phenomenality of appearance as the reality which is intensely subjective as a result. "Life seemed as though reality and I and the mountain were points in some known awareness." In all these examples we find an essentially realistic mode centred on the actual and the concrete, trying to incorporate the abstract or the metaphysical through the device of imagery. In each the distance between the tenor and the vehicle is great enough to cause serious disturbance to the realistic illusion which is stretched to the limit. In other words, there is a very strong and insistent attempt to make use of the essentially poetic instrumentality of defamiliarization to expand the limits imposed by the realistic form. This has been expressed through various devices at each level by the sprinkling of unusual words (e.g. *ocelous, cervine, ocellate, cerulean, elocubration, rememorate, ingurgitating* etc.) or deliberate archaism (*flavoursome, leapeth, bejewelled, gladsome tidings*) in lexis and rhetorical manipulation of occasional inversion and parallelism in syntax, for example:

> The impossible is the reality, the fervent is the intropid, the passionate, the high. Fruits are made of space; grass is made of light. . . . And in between the archwayed walls are studious boys—and far away, the girls that weave into life the space of thought, the substance of sight and movements of the moon, that a better England, a better India, a better world be circumscribed.

At the same time we can perceive the irrevocable pull of the realistic form in one specific stylistic character—a marked tendency to use simile rather than metaphor. Notice for example a great prevalence of expression to denote similarity which is the structural principle of simile. We find relatively less use of metaphor in which that principle of the poetic use of language, of substitution, operates. Hence the images require connectives *(like, as though, seemed)* to relate the tenor and the vehicle which are thus found similar but not exactly equivalent, and cannot be substituted as a metaphor would demand. Northrop Frye distinguishes between metaphor and simile as models of mythical and realistic literature respectively:

> Realism, or the art of verisimilitude, evokes the response, "How like that is to what we know!" When what is written is like what is known, we have an art of extended or implied simile. And as realism is an art of implicit simile, myth is an art of implicit metaphorical identity.[27]

Take for example the following passage in Rao:

> Her hair was gold, and her skin for an Indian was like the unearthed marble with which we built our winter palaces. Cool, with the lake about one, and the peacock strutting in the garden below. the seventh-hour music would come and all the palace would see itself lit. Seeing oneself is what we always seek: the world, as the great sage Sankara said, is like a city seen in a mirror. Madeleine was like the palace of Amber seen in moonlight.

The obvious symbolist manipulation of synaesthesia is however centred on one fundamental linguistic unit—*like*. This illusion of reality which is sought to be retained in analogical relation occurs not only in the description of Madeleine who is condemned for her acceptance of the world as real, but also in the presentation of Savithri for whom ostensibly, as the "true woman" of Ramaswamy "there is no world":

> Savithri was there, not in me but *as* me; not as someone far, unreal, relegated to a country in rounded space, but *as* light which seemed never to fade, never to know where to go—*like* that constant sound that texts say which in the silence of things, the first vibration, the primary sound, the *pranayam*

> *OM* propounds itself, and from which all that is world is created. Savithri, *as it were*, was the meaning of meaning, *Sabdartha*.

The dynamics of the imagery here is controlled by the principle of association or contiguity which brings together different aspects of the same concept, the primary sound. No doubt in both the passages there lies the perception of a basic similarity between Madeleine's fair skin and marble, Savithri's presence and the eternity of the sound-principle. But the similarity is maintained or expressed verbally along the scale of contiguity. In the first it is physical, in the second intellectual. The marble is associated with the palace of Amber which is really built of marble, and actually stands in the lake, the peacocks forming a part of the same famous scene of north India's royal gardens. In the second paragraph, the contiguity would be no less obvious though it establishes a relation between a tenor and a vehicle both of which are more or less abstract. Savithri here is, as everywhere in the novel, more of an idea, a theoretical entity rather than a concrete reality. She is actually addressed by Rama as "my principle." So the image of a never-fading light as well as that of primary sound emphasizes the abstract quality in spiritual association with permanent values. In both the passages however there is a deliberate attempt at "Indianness." In the first, a reference to the great philosopher Sankara's theory of reality presents a metaphoric validity through verbal connections (*like* and *seem*) with Madeleine's beauty. At the same time it is the physical function of reflection that relates Sankara's "city seen in a mirror" and Rao's palace seen in a lake. In the second passage the "Indianness" is more pronounced through ac tual sprinkling of Sanskrit words, *pranayam Om*, *Sabdartha*. Incidentally, the idea of word as the origin of the universe is as much Christian as Hindu ("In the beginning was the word . . ." St. John, 1:1), but the combination of Sanskrit words attempts to deflect the Western association and imparts a kind of "Indian" spiritual gloss which usually sends Rao's admirers into ecstasy. The stylistic mannerism, "the meaning of meaning," drawing from the Upanishads (e.g. "the breath of breath/ the eye of the eye" etc. *Brhadaranyaka Upanishad,* 4: IV: 18), puts the final seal of Indian spirituality upon the whole description. In the Hindu literary tradition, however, especially in Sanskrit, such manipulation of the Upanishadic style to present a heroine has perhaps no precedence,[28] nor is it clear if the philosophical connotation of meaning (*Sabdartha*) is successfully established here with the notion of primary sound. One may suspect it is the proximity of the *word* which suggests the *meaning*, even *pranayam* and *Om* are actually Sanskrit equivalents of the same notion, the one being the synonym of the other. The principle which holds the whole in cohesion is that of contiguity or association which is very much a part of that "realism" which Rao often claims to have rejected.

In fact it is the principle of contiguity which is the moving force behind the peculiar development into digression that some of Rao's images characteristically display. Take for example the image comparing Pratap, Savithri's fiancé, to a lame horse or an old bull in the palace yard:

> If she talked of him with a touch of condescension it was not because of social difference, it was just because she liked being kind to something, something inevitable, unknown, such as a lame horse in the stable or it might be an old bull, fed in the palace yard till it died, but meanwhile being treated as an elder, a palace bull, given the best Bengal gram and the choicest of green grass. And when it died, for it would "die," it would be given a music-and-flower funeral and have orange trees planted over its grave. And one day some virgin would light a lamp and consecrate it, and every day from that time on, the sanctuary would be lit with an oil lamp, as dusk fell over the palace grove.

Savithri's being a princess naturally has suggested "palace" and then the vehicle takes on an independent life, describing aspects of the life of these animals in the palace—their food, funeral, consecration, memorial—all etched in vivid evocative phrases till the tenor that was Pratap is completely forgotten. But each item—*Bengal gram, green grass, music-and-flower funeral, lighting lamp* etc.—is a part of the whole life of these animals presented in a condensed context, deleting many other parts of their lives.[29] No doubt the omitted aspects might have been as essential as those which are presented, or even more essential, for example, the activities of the horse or the bull. This absence of logic in deleting one or more items from a natural combination signifies that the total presentation, the digression itself, is a rhetorical figure, not so much a preçis on the life of a lame horse or an old bull kept in a palace. A similar operation of deletion and combination is to be found in the digression starting off from the image of Tibetan *tanakas* which is the metaphor for Ramaswamy's "another world" where he wants to take Madeleine away in a frenzy of passion:

> And I take her away to a world from which there is no returning—like those Tibetan *tanakas,* with cypresses and moon and waters below, and the dragon throne in the middle. You seat him and say, "Son, sit here," and he sits, does he, the Lama; you cover him in brocade and sound the horn outside, and wave after wave of it comes echoing back to Lhasa: across mountains and deserts it incarnates and comes, for the Lama is crowned and seated in the Potala. Then all the treasuries are opened and all the windows too, and the white horse waits with decoration, sash and fife, for the summer palace and the people.

The vehicle elaborates a sensuous description of an actual scene depicted in a *tanaka* which in turn leads to a piece on the investiture of a Lama and the famous summer palace directed by the principle of contiguity or association. Indeed, much of the digressiveness of the whole form of the novel is controlled by the law of association which is one of the cardinal foundations of psychological realism. Take for example all the speculations on history and philosophy of history that the words *Albigenes* or *Cathar* has produced in the story of Ramaswamy.

Even a mythical diversion—an obvious metaphor like the tale of *budumekaye*, or a lengthy argument on kingship—is suggested by the mere physical contiguity of Savithri, round and fat like a *budumekaye* as well as a princess. The flight of poetry in the celebration of woman as "The earth, air, sound . . ." is no doubt metaphoric, but it is suggested by the actual historical event of the coronation of the English queen which incidentally supplies Savithri the immediate occasion to visit Ramaswamy with her father, a native ruler. The fact that the whole piece is a digression does by no means affect the realistic fundamental basis, for this metaphoric digression is controlled by metonymy. In discussing *Ulysses*, David

Lodge underscores the general tendency of *Ulysses* towards an encyclopaedic allembracingness,'' away from the concern with individual experience as ''typical'' of the modernist novel.[30] It is precisely because there is no contiguity in actual life between Savithri and the legend, or the coronation and the situation of Ramaswamy, that these can be combined and used as metaphors without logic in the reality of Ramaswamy's mind, through verbal association. This mixture of metaphor and metonymy is dominated by the principle of contiguity which has been identified by Roman Jakobson with the realistic mode and provides the base of the whole structure of *The Serpent and the Rope*.[31] In fact once contiguity between two items is established, the same images or variations on it are likely to recur like a Wagnerian leitmotif, whenever the author invokes an experience similar to the one which had originally established the relation. Take for example the image of a high mountain which occurs a number of times. It starts with the actual experience of Ramaswamy's pilgrimage to Haridwar and beyond, in the height of the Himalayas where he realizes the connection between ''the solitude of the snows and the identity of truth.'' Hence, on many occasions when he feels proximate to Truth, as in the confrontation with Georges, the image of the mountain reappears. It is because of the association deriving very much from an actual experience that makes him receive his ''Principle,'' Savithri, at the Quai Saint-Jacques of Provence with a recall to the mountain far away:

> It was just like going to Nainital. The air was crisp, and you felt the snow beyond. I was going to meet the Himalayas, the Ganga flowed everywhere.

There are words and phrases in the novel which by recurrence build up symbolic significance. Take for example the use of the word ''rag.'' Speaking about Georges's sincere Catholic belief, an image of Georges is presented as a municipal cleaner collecting ''rags'' which here stands for human misery since in the sorrow and suffering is to be found the proof of God's existence (''Dieu est parce que le mal est'').

> His sincerity was moving: one felt he bore the heavy history of humanity on his bent back. He carried our sorrows and our stupidities, rags that we threw on his back, as he went along

the street. The more you threw, the more he blessed.

When Madeleine is found throwing "all her rags on Georges as though she were helping someone to be himself," the symbolic meaning overtakes the literal completely. The symbol becomes a motif when we find Madeleine providing comfort to Georges losing in a game of chess with Ramaswamy, "and now it is not he who bears her rags but she bears her crown of his making." The pattern here derives an emphasis by being placed in a parallel structure as well as highlighted by antithesis *(he, her; rags, crown; her, him).* A more obvious pattern may be found in the reiteration of "bridge." It is first offered both as fact and a metaphor: "Like all melancholic people Madeleine loved bridges. She felt Truth was always on the other side." The factual, realistic aspect is elaborated in the description of Ramaswamy buying her books "which had such beautiful ivy-covered bridges built by Romans," her visits to see *this bridge* at Saint-Jean Pied-de-Port or that at Point de Valentre. In her hope that her son Krishna Pierre would grow up to "build bridges for India," the symbol assumes a concrete shape. But the tragedy that "Pierre could never cross the bridge of life" emphasizes the gulf between her and Ramaswamy who realizes, "The bridge was never crossed." Pierre's death makes Madeleine, who is supposed to be anti-cleric, come back to the Roman Catholic Church. Now her Hindu husband feels that there can be no point of contact between them: "There was no bridge, all bridges now led to Spain." Spain is not only a geographical entity they never visited, but also historically associated with the Roman Catholic Church in its most militant aspect. Hence Ramaswamy concludes: "The bridge was anyhow there, and could not be crossed, I knew I could never go to Spain." Here the image of the bridge that cannot be crossed stands as a symbol of the permanent impediment to a true marriage. Hence the life of Madeline with Ramaswamy can best be an "occasional drive over a bridge" with all the pathos of a transient, momentary contact. But the symbolic richness is derived from repetition which completely substitutes the literal referent in its late occurrence:

> The job is to build bridges—not stone or girders, for that would prove the permanence of the objective but like the rope bridges in the Himalayas you build temporary suspen-

sion over green and gurgling space.

Here *bridge* is a leap to the Absolute, but as a symbol it is embedded in a context with the help of association, the details of an analogy—the great Himalayas suggest height, rigorous pilgrimage, and silence, and even the source perhaps of the holy Ganga (*gurgling space*), all presented in metonymic association.

There are quite a number of such motifs which lend not only richness to the texture of the novel, but present actual points of correlation between the narrative and the linguistic structures. Thus "elephant" may be found to symbolize erotic frenzy, "haemoglobules" indicate physical demand or "ants" suggest non-thinking, insensitive existence. It is significant that the pattern of all these symbols is determined by the original context which seems to be causally related to its meaning. In other words none of these is offered as a "pure" symbol which has been defined as "an image which embodies a meaning with which it has no direct connection."[32] Indeed, it is neither faith nor magic which connects each of these symbols here with the meaning, but the context in which it is embedded. If "elephant" denotes erotic passion it is because of the appropriate and lengthy translation of a Sanskrit passage in which such an elephant in passionate frenzy is sought to be described in full.[33] The same principle operates in the cases of all repetitions tending to form patterns.

We must therefore conclude that despite large scale incorporation of poetic or metaphoric elements at lexical, syntactic and symbolic levels, the dominance that supplies unity to the linguistic structure is of an essentially realistic or metonymic nature. It is because the author is actually working in the realistic mode, that he uses the poetic devices as subjected "to the control of context,[34] either by elaborating literal details of the context into symbols, or by drawing analogies from a semantic field associated with the context."

4. *A crisis of the dominant*

We have seen in the preceding chapter that in the narratology, the realistic mode is not intended to be the dominant, it is in fact meant to be subordinate to the intellectual, abstract thesis. So if in the analysis of the style, we find a decided dominance of the realistic, in what way do these two, the narrative and the linguistic, then cohere? Consider for example the place of the two descriptions of Madeleine and Savithri, analyzed already as stylistic items, in the total structure of the novel. In the narrative framework, Madeleine and Savithri are the doubles of Ramaswamy, one being a reflection of his actual, phenomenal self, the other symbolizing his aspiration for the ideal, the transcendence. As such, to present Madeleine with the help of Sankara's famous simile for the phenomenal existence ("a city seen in a mirror") has an eminently aesthetic value; so too would appear Savithri's portrait as the Eternal Verbum, set against Madeleine's transient reality. To emphasize this opposition or contrast, Rao utilizes a phraseology which is strongly reminiscent of the presentation of the Brahman or the Absolute Consciousness in the Hindu texts. Therefore the semantics of this kind of expression tends to impart transcendence to Savithri who is obviously the embodiment of womanhood. But in Ramaswamy's (as well as Rao's) thesis woman is related to the phenomenon— "woman is the world." The Brahman being the transcendence, the Absolute Reality, "there is no world," and so "eternity is only for men." In the thesis, Savithri as a woman belongs to the category of relativity, of *maya*, of untruth, but in the manipulation of language, she acquires the transcendence which the so-called philosophy of the novel reserves as an exclusively male monopoly. It is one of the many ironies, yielded by a close reading of the text, that Rao's presentation of Madeleine alone is in perfect consonance with his total design. Between Rao's intellectual intention and fictional execution, comes in the Western triangular plotting which requires the elevation of the Indian Savithri who thus becomes *Aksara-lakshmi* (the Word-Goddess), the Truth, to justify the rejection of the French wife, as beautiful as *maya*, the earthly phenomenon. If the victory of India is achieved here at all, it is effected at the cost of structural harmony, because the concept of woman as the Truth or the Absolute can hardly be accommodated by the author's own rigid non-dualist (and perhaps chauvinist) stand which leaves Woman at the level of relativity. There is thus a strong though hidden contradiction between the Indian author's use of the English language and his thesis, as the former always tends to uphold the Western narrative structure.

The question is, if we find the relation between the two structures to be that of opposition, what does it all lead to? Norman

Friedman has pointed out very aptly: "Parts and devices are there in the work not just to 'relate' but to do a job, to forward a purpose, and that purpose is its end or form."[35] It is in the actual interrelation between different devices that this end or the structural principle of the form may be discovered. Take for example the presentation of Ramaswamy's reaction to the news of his second son's death in the context of his union with Savithri, which has disrupted his relation with Madeleine in such a way that the unborn child Madeleine is carrying is the only link left to bind the husband and wife. The introduction is laid in a generic sentence: "Noble is the game of life and pentathlic the works of civilization." The inversion, the parallel construction and the use of the rare word "pentathlic" give the statement a stylized and proverbial cast. It is as though a great truth, a universal observation, is placed before us, through poetic devices to be noted carefully. One may however point out that the word "pentathlic" has been suggested by the expression "game" for mere association as a word rather than of any referential function in this context, for what follows, that is, "the works of civilization" as enumerated, have very little similarity with a pentathlon unless we understand by this term a mere diversity:

> Birth and death, sowing and reaping, the communication of joys and sufferings; the subtleties of statistics, the names of loves, diplomatic determinations, subterfuges, losses, conquests; the drowning of queens (death of kings), the killing of dictators or of their fist-faced henchmen.

Most of the expressions which are placed in combination (e.g. *birth* and *death, subtleties* of *statistics*, the *crowning* of *queens* etc.) are normally found in close association in our thought. Even the "killing of dictators" may be seen as a reflection of Ramaswamy's associative thought process since he has so many times referred to the Nazis already. But the question is, why is this elaborate piece of digression guided by mere association? The purpose is to link through sheer verbal intermediaries the generic sentence of the beginning to the specific concrete situation at the end in a loose analogy, indeed so loose that it is almost non-existent in what follows:

> these follow one another, *as if* the magnificent line of ants at my feet in the Lal Bagh had any knowledge of other things than that the sun shines in between two gusts of monsoon winds, and have no premonition of the trees that wave their tops in jubilant youth, that aeroplanes hover above the earth, bearing people back and forth, and from all the lands and from *round the roundsome globe*, or that the telegraph wires which pass by me, have carried the destiny of men for decades: "Shamoo died," "Subhu succeeded exams"; "Lakshmana transferred to Dehra Dun, Military Depot"; and they will carry it for several decades more, unless more simple means dispense with wires and *conglomerate absurdities*, so that important news does not reach us on a bicycle, with a blue coat and khaki trousers, and brick-coloured envelopes do not contain the *amalgam of destiny*.

The whole passage which is one sentence—the longest in the novel—is completely guided by the principle of metonymic association; sunshine and monsoon, tree top and the hovering aeroplanes, telegraph wires and some examples of messages sent—all combine to present a very tenuous link with the opening generalization through the loose expression "as if," suggestive of analogy. The paragraph begins with an avowed assertion of the "nobility" of this existence which is clearly meant to be acceptable in its rhetorical and poetic emphasis. It ends with a discovery that the reality consists of "conglomerate absurdities" in which things as mundane as telegraph wires, a bicycle, a blue coat and khaki trousers and a brick-coloured envelope bring us "the amalgam of destiny." The life that is in theory—as the generic structure implies—so noble, is found to be, in actual experience utterly absurd. The stark discrepancy between the thesis and actual life, which forms a fundamental contradiction in Ramaswamy, is muted and blurred in the piling up of digressive detail controlled by metonymy. At the same time in the metonymic digression is incorporated metaphorical expressions sharpened by abstract-concrete juxtaposition and sound value—*conglomerate of absurdities* and *amalgam of destiny*. One can hardly miss the manipulation of the syllabic length as also of stress in the careful selection of items. There is, further, the pathetic fallacy of wondering whether ants can have any premonition of the absurdities of this existence. It is also impossible to ignore the deliberate rhetoric in the repetition and archaism of *round* and *roundsome*. Obviously the realistic mode of metonymy progressing syntagmatically is here punctured with poetic or metaphoric manipulation which relates to the other or paradigmatic aspect of language.[36] The configuration that emerges is particularly interesting since the poetic or metaphoric emphasis on life as a noble game, a *lila*, a cosmic play of the Absolute, is juxtaposed with the realistic and metonymic presentation of life as existence, an utter absurdity. The sheer volume of associative digression sets off all the strength of the opening aphorism. The two poles, metaphoric and metonymic, are here utilized for a confrontation of opposites. A pattern like this may be regarded indicative of a fundamental division in the very being of the author since the essence of an individual's personal style, centres in the interaction of these two poles. The very fact is, the news—given in the next paragraph—which means so much to Ramaswamy's life, severing the only thin and tenuous thread holding up his marriage, has absolutely no comprehensible connection with the external reality. The contingency of the existence is conveyed not only through the telegraph poles, the uniformed peon and the usual envelope, but in the very shapeless mass of the sentence which seems to resist form, order, and ultimately, meaning. In other words, the looseness of the construction itself is the reality for Ramaswamy, for it is as endless a continuum as the line of ants at his feet and as unthinking. The complexity of the novel's structure lies in its attempt to present the two poles of opposites extending in a continuous interplay of voices, because here is an instance when "two directly intentional statements converge in the same context," and form an open dialogic movement, unresolved and inconclusive.[37] Moreover it is the continuous, unresolvable presence of opposed modes which the author would not (or could not) reconcile, that renders multivalence as the inevitable structural principle of *The Serpent and the Rope*.

This absence of univalence, so to say, is so pervasive in the total structure that it appears especially at those points—as in the instance given—where the narrative and the linguistic forms coalesce and push the metaphysics into the background. Perhaps the best example of the inter-relation of different structural levels and the resultant impasse is provided by the single stylistic item—the recurrence of a particular clause from the beginning to the end of the novel: "from whence there is no returning." This is the goal of the Buddha and reiterated in the novel as such.[38] No doubt it matches perfectly the mythical leitmotif, Ramaswamy in quest of truth is a Buddha-to-be, Bodhisattva being the very archetype of man in search of the ultimate. Yet after Ramaswamy rejects Madeleine ostensibly for her Buddhism, "the near-truth," and arrives at Truth led by the guru, his supreme experience, the vision itself, is presented in the repetition of these very words of the arch heretic, the Buddha, "I have gone *whence there is no returning*." No Vedantic formula, none of the great texts of the Hindus (*mahavakyas*) here can bring the brahman to the Truth.[39] Nothing perhaps betrays the breach in the "I" more blatantly than this significant leitmotif of linguistic recurrence against the background of his thesis, condemning Buddhism.

In fact even the very exposition of Ramaswamy's so-called Indian/Vedantic standpoint is not exactly free from ambiguity. Take for example the central passage of the thesis which is obviously set for the purpose of exposition and to establish its relation with the human situation: "The world is either unreal or real—the Serpent or the Rope. There is no in between the two." It is actually not the Vedantic purport that is the guiding principle here, but a typical English syntactic construction *either/or*. Sankara, the great non-dualist philosopher, never stated this opposition. Indeed, Sankara's unique contribution to the Indian metaphysics lies in his clear assertion of the *middle status* of the world as existence in between the illusory and the absolute. Trying to fit Sankara's non-dualism into an *either/or* structure, Rao fails to maintain the fine and essential difference between the illusory and the empirical. For Sankara the world is not unreal, it is inscrutable (*anirvacaniya*), neither real nor unreal (*sadasad-vilakshana*) placed in between the complete lie and the ultimate reality. It may not be far-fetched to trace this confusion of levels in Rao to the constant syntactic pattern of *either/or* which leaves no room for the world as the middle level. As a matter of fact, this *either/or* pattern dominates the whole structure of Ramaswamy's thought, his philosophy of life as well as of his history. His mind operates constantly in sets of binary opposition which is perhaps most faithfully represented in this characteristic pattern:

> There can be only two attitudes to life, *Either* you believe the world exists and so—you. *Or* you believe that you exist—

and so the world. There is no compromise possible.

Hence Ramaswamy has to declare all other branches of even Vedanta philosophy as near-truths, and not only Buddhism. The continued opposition between orthodoxy and heresy in the intellectual construct is thus an operation of this linguistic structure, since the semantics of culture—the Indian ethos–never perhaps enunciated the concept of heresy which arises out of the *either/or* pattern. It is no less significant that the *either/ or* structure belongs essentially to the ethical category since it implies choice and freedom, but Rao's avowed "Indian" metaphysic has constantly opposed "moralism" which he terms a "biological reflex." After declaring "right and wrong are questions of a personal perspective, but *dharma* is adherence to the impersonal," he contradicts himself immediately: "The impersonal alone is right." We can hardly miss the use of the word "right" which he himself rejected as a sign of ethical value. One cannot help the conclusion that ultimately it is the English language which creates the reality for the Hindu Raja Rao. As Ronald Barthes says, "It is language which teaches the definition of man, not the reverse."[40] The complex pattern of contrasts and contradictions in the formal structure of *The Serpent and the Rope* reveals an impasse as a consequence of an acute crisis of identity in which the deep inroads made by an alien culture are crystallized in the ultimate dominance accorded to the alien medium.

This leads to a strange but inevitable conclusion—that the more Raja Rao wants to prove himself "Indian," the more Western he emerges in his connections to a linguistic system. He has posed to reject the whole Western mode of fiction for the "basic assumption that the world is real—an assumption he could not make."[41] The technique he adopts to establish his "Indian" identity as "metaphysical" is ostensibly opposed to the "realistic." To get away from "realism," his alternative is the poetic mode, the paradigmatic aspect of language. The irony of the situation arises precisely here—his exploitation of the poetic modality binds him completely to the West for the paradigmatic choice is totally dependent on the whole linguistic system of a given nation. It is not for nothing that Rao invariably has to fall back upon Eliot or echo translated Valéry. Exiles from native languages excel as novelists rather than as poets because of the fundamental inextricable relation between literary convention and a whole ethos which governs the poetic dimension. The wealth of association connecting words and forms to reality exist only in that particular language alone. Take for example Rao's frequent use of the word "home" which is replete with all the wealth of association—security, personal relationship and comfort—deriving ultimately from the Christian God who is the true "home." Coming home for a Christian signifies a return to the loving Father, after estrangement, the Fall. Since Rao's Absolute is not a personal God, his use of the word lends ambiguity to sentences like "My real home is in Travancore," "Once a person finds himself he comes home." For a Christian, "home" can never be "himself," it is only in the love of his personal God that the individual occupies fundamentally a different level. For a Hindu Vedantin, on the other hand, realization is not a coming "home," but the recognition of the non-difference between himself and the Absolute, who is hardly the loving Father carrying the eternal assurance of home for his straying sheep. The linguistic system of English, which is inextricably connected with Christianity, defines the semantics of "home" and "himself" in the personal, pluralistic context of scholasticism and encloses the Hindu monist or non-dualist, who, instead of being released into the eternity of the *Atman*, is left imprisoned into himself, into solipsism, and it is the language which acts as the chain. His Savithri, the very symbol of India, cannot even send a cable to Ramaswamy the brahman, without drawing on European literature. Her telegram, "In your joy is my freedom," hardly veils the imitation of Dante's famous line, "And in His will is our peace." Our appreciation of the image of Madeleine, looking for a spiritual path, as one lost in the forest draws on the opening lines of the *Divine Comedy* ("In the middle of the journey of our life I came to myself in a dark wood where the straight way is lost"). Even a casual phrase like "the shine of the world" derives its poetic inspiration from the well-known surrealist title "Clair de Terre" (Earth Shine). Indeed, the whole poetic discourse of *The Serpent and the Rope* is a maze of echoes from the Western literature in which the Indian writer loses himself in stylization.[42]

Even the formal aspects of Rao's rhetoric undergo a sea change and produce ambiguous effects. A poetic device like inversion, which Rao's Indian admirers often assume to be a consequence of "Sanskritization," possesses in English particular characteristics which are entirely different from those it may have in Sanskrit because Sanskrit is a highly inflected language system, with a word order that is free, not subject to that fixed pattern in English or French (subject-verb-object) which imparts a highly rhetorical flavour to Inversion in these languages, but will hardly do so in Sanskrit.[43] One is reminded of Jan Mukarovsky's perceptive analysis of poetic languages as "rooted in the system of a particular national language," since "the more the linguistic aspect asserts itself in a literary work, the more strongly it is bound to a given national language."[44] In other words, the more poetic or literary Rao is in his use of English, the more deeply is he embedded into the West. Yet strangely enough, he seems to uphold a polarized opposition between the metaphysical "India" and the poetic "West." His heroine Madeleine, Christian-turned-Buddhist, is rejected by her Indian husband in the quest for Truth because both Christ and the Buddha, being "poets," are to be summarily driven out from his "perfect civilization." Hence Rao's manipulation of the poetic dimension of English to arrive at the Truth-that-is-metaphysical, produces an elaborate exercise in ambivalence. The emphasis on linguistic structure to establish a specific "Indian" identity in English makes Raja Rao a classic example of the exile, who, despite all his talent and knowledge, must necessarily reveal himself as an eternal outsider standing at the periphery of the literary tradition of the West as well as of India.

NOTES

1. Charles Morgan's *The Voyage*, 1942, set in France with all French characters is a relevant comparison in assessing the extent of French influence on Rao's *The Serpent and the Rope.* In Morgan's novel, despite the obvious French background and some thematic preoccupation with typical French elements, the actual French influence on his style is almost negligible. This indicates two things: firstly, the very form of the novel that Morgan adopts for his purpose is far less realistic or mimetic than the form underlying Rao's novel; secondly, the extent of French influence on Morgan as an artist operates at a different level altogether; it does not by any means overpower

his non-French identity.

2. E.g. "Dieu est loge dans l'intervaile entre les hommes," p. 207. Rama's final statement of his relation with Savithri vis-a-vis Pratap, "He (Pratap) is your husband and you are mine," p. 362, is an echo of Henry V's declaration to his French wife, "Donc vostre est France et vous estes miennes," which is quoted by Rama himself, p. 204.
3. The fact that most of these Indian loans are nominals proves its relation with the stylistic norm of the 19th century realistic fiction which was according to David Lodge "generally notable for nominalization, the appropriate vehicle of its heavy freight of specificity and local colour." *The Modes of Modern Writing: Metaphor, Metonymy and the Typology of Modern Literature,* 1977, p. 148.
4. Bhavabhuti, *Uttara-Rama-Caritam,* ed. and trans. S.K. Belvalkar, 1915, p. 39. In fact, Rama's self-accusation is a recurrent theme in the drama, e.g. Act. II: XVIII.
5. Henry W. Wells, translating Sanskrit poetry, finds: "English-speaking people are by no means at home in refinements of sensations of sight and sound, and especially of touch, taste and smell, as are the ancient Indian." *A New View of Translation, Ancient Poetry from China, Japan and India.* 1968, p. 24.
6. Ray J. Robert, *The Novels of Raja Rao*, Books Abroad, 1966, vol. 40, p. 413.
7. William Empson, *Seven Types of Ambiguity*, 1930, p. 192.
8. The frequent use of certain words in a writer shows according to Valery, "un example de ces evaluations personelles, de ces grandes, valeur—pourun-seul, qui jouent certainement un tres beau role dans une production de l'esprit ou la singularite est an element de premiere importance." *Variete* V. Paris, 1944 ed., p. 318.

   The key-words used by an author, according to Ullman, "can be interpreted either psychologically or functionally: they can provide clues to the author's mind and also to the inner structure of his works." *Language and Style*, p. 129. This derives from the famous "philological circle" of Leo Spitzer who first found individual and characteristic patterns in the use of expressions "aberrant from general usage." For details, please see Leo Spitzer, *Linguistics and Literary His-*

tory: Essays in Stylistics, 1948, pp. 11-27.

9. Raja Rao follows Max Mueller's practice of translating *atman* as *self.* According to Sir Charles Eliot, Max Mueller's rendering "jars on the English ear for it inevitably suggests the individual self and selfishness, whereas *Atman* means the universal self, the universal spirit which is self, because it is the highest (or only) Reality and Being, not definable in terms of anything else." *Hinduism and Buddhism,* 1921, 1962, p. 82. Ananda K. Coomaraswamy discusses this problem and presents a solution using Self for *Atman* and self for the individual ego. *Hinduism and Buddhism,* n.d., p. 34.
10. As Saussure lays down: "Language is a system of signs that express ideas," and he calls the concept "signified" and sound image, "signifier." *Course in General Linguistics,* 1915, 1960, p. 16, pp. 66-67. One of his main contributions which brought revolution in the study of language is the arbitrary or conventional nature of relation between the signifier and the signified which having no "natural connection" is decided by the convention alone. "No individual, even if he willed it, could modify in any way at all the choice that has been made, the community itself cannot control so much as a single word, it is bound to the existing language"; and "Because the sign is arbitrary, it follows no law other than that of tradition, because it is based on tradition, it is arbitrary," p. 71, p. 74.
11. The use of *atman* to mean the Absolute is peculiar to Sanskrit and may not be found in modern Indian languages, but that does not lead to a crisis in writers who belong to these languages. In Bengali, for example, the first person singular pronominal can mean only ego as it does in English, but we never find any suspicion of crisis in Tagore's presentation of the relation between the ego and the Absolute which is never confused. When Tagore says, "It is only when my face turns from you that I rush toward myself" or, "I go round and round myself dying each moment" there is no suspicion of solipsism. But when Rao states, "I was so free within myself," or, "To be centered in oneself is to know joy" or, "Taking me into myself, I transpire as the truth as though touched by itself," the extinction of ego, the goal of the Vedantin, is not clearly enunciated. In Rao, the Absolute can

never be *you*, because it suggests for him the existential *other* and dualism which is to him "anti-Indian." The dual aspect of the Brahman, formless and formed (*Nirguna* and *Saguna*), are often found in Tagore, e.g. "Thou art the sky, thou art the nest as well," *Gitanjali*, 1911, p. 67.

12. The metaphoric and metonymic poles here refer to Roman Jakobson's influential theory that relates the paradigmatic and syntagmatic aspects of language to these rhetorical modes and further to the poetics of poetry and prose. Thus the syntagmatic aspect is empirically connected with metonymy, prose and realism. For details, please see Jakobson and Halles, *Fundamentals of Language*, 1956, pp. 76-82.
13. According to Jakobson, "a poetic work is defined as a verbal message where aesthetic function is its dominant" placing referential function in a lower rung of hierarchy. "The Dominant," *Readings in Russian Poetics*, pp. 84-85.
14. As Roman Jakobson holds, "the two basic modes of arrangement used in verbal behaviour [are] selection and combination" and "the selection is produced on the base of equivalence, similarity and dissimilarity, synonymity and anonymity, while the combination, the build-up of sequence, is based on contiguity." Linguistics and Poetics," *Style in Language*, ed. Thomas A. Sebeok, 1960, p. 358. Also Jakobson and Halle, *Fundamentals of Language*, pp. 58-61.
15. In the poetic mode the projection is of "the principle of equivalence from the axis of selection into the axis of combination." "Linguistics and Poetics," *Style in Language*, p. 358.
16. Rulon Wells, "Nominal and Verbal Style" in *Style in Language*, pp. 219-20.
17. Jan Mukarovsky, "Standard language and Poetic language" in *Linguistics and Literary Style*, ed. Donald C. Freeman, 1970, p. 42.
18. Roman Jakobson, "The Dominant," *Readings in Russian Poetics*, p. 82.
19. For details please see Morris W. Croll's authoritative analysis, "The Baroque Style in Prose," *Studies in English Philology: a miscellany in honour of Frederick Klaeber*, eds. K. Malone and M.B. Ruud, pp. 84-91.
20. "To write a poem or a novel," as Jonathan Culler aptly points

out, "is immediately to engage with a literary tradition." *Structuralist Poetics: Structuralism, Linguistics and the Study of Literature,* 1975, p. 116. Therefore "to naturalize a text is to bring it into relation with a type of discourse or model which is already in some sense, natural and legible." pp. 138-44. Also, Roland Barthes, "Style and Image," *Literary Style: A Symposium,* ed. S. Chatman.

21. Oscar Wilde, *The Picture of Dorian Gray*, 1890, *The Works of Oscar Wilde*, 1948, Rpt. 1954, p. 152. .
22. One of the decadent features of the French Catholic writers's style as represented by Huysmans, Bloy, Bernanos and Mauriac, notes David Lodge, is "its stylistic tendency to epigram, weaving Pascalian pensées into the fabric of narrative" which combines theoretical preoccupation with fictional narration. *The Novelist at the Crossroads and other essays on Fiction and Criticism,* 1971, p. 108. The great impact of some of these writers on English Decadents is a well-established fact now, e.g. Graham Hough, *The Last Romantics* 1947, 1961, discusses the influence of Huysmans," *A Rebours* on Oscar Wilde, pp. 194-202. For the central place of Huysmans' *A Rebours* on the Decadence, please see Enid Starkie, *From Gautier to Eliot; The Influence of France on English Literature 1851-1939*, 1960, 1962, pp. 82-85.
23. The West has always indulged in sententiousness right from Seneca to Balzac. Take for example the following generalizations: "Happiness is the poetry of woman as the toilette is her tinsel." "The old mythology of love is extinct, doomed to perish by modern dandyism." "It is one of the most detestable habits of Lilliputian mind to credit other people with its own malignant pettiness." "There are no such things as principles: there are only events." "There are no laws but those of expediency." Balzac, *Old Goriot*, 1963, Everyman, pp. 11, 29, 21, 94-95.
24. Mikhail Bakhtin, "Discourse Typology in Prose," L. Matejka and K. Pomoroska, eds. *Readings in Russian Poetics*, p. 181.
25. Roland Barthes, *Writing Degree Zero,* 1953, trans. 1967, 1970, pp. 36.
26. Roger Fowler finds the conscious presence of the implied author in a novelistic discourse, "in the form of aphoristic generic sentences." With examples from Fielding and Jane

Austen he shows that it is customary for the novelist to try to hide "the moralistic and authoritative connotations of this form" by disguising it with "ironic and facetious usages." *Linguistics and the Novel,* 1977, pp. 86-87.

27. Northrop Frye, *Anatomy of Criticism,* p. 136.
28. E.g. Kalidasa, *Kumarasambhavam* (I: 32-48) presents Parvati with a wealth of sensuous details, starting with her toe nails, ends with her hair. The convention of Sanskrit literature always emphasizes an apprehension of the external world especially in relation to the beauty of the heroines.
29. For details on deletion and combination as related to the syntagmatic aspect of language, please see David Lodge, *Modes of Modern Writing: Metaphor, Metonymy and the Typology of Modern Literature,* p. 76.
30. *Ibid,* p. 139.
31. The digressive aspect of Rao's novel, instead of connecting him to the ancient Indian encyclopaedic works, actually relates him to the modernist novel because the relation that exists between the digression and the narration follows the convention of the novel. As Roman Jakobson states: "Following the path of contiguous relationship, the realistic author metonymically digresses from the plot to the atmosphere and from the character to the setting in space and time. He is fond of synecdochic details." *Fundamentals of Language,* p, 78.
32. Ursula Brumm, "Symbolism and the Novel," *The Theory of the Novel,* ed. P. Stevick, 1967, p. 359.
33. In Rao's quotation, "Elephants wild with ichor frenzy" from *Uttara-Rama-Caritam* (Act II:16), the Sanskrit equivalent of ichor is not found in the original, which uses the term *gharma* ("sweat," "perspiration") and not *matta/madamatta* ("Frenzied with lust or anger"). Nor does the context suggest physical passion for the original lines are uttered by Vasanti describing the effect of heat to Atreyi, to warn her of the risk she runs venturing out in the sun. However, an elephant in ichor is a well-known image of physical passion in Sanskrit poetry e.g. Kalidasa, *Ritusamhara, Varsavarnanam:* 14. It is to be noted that the season in which frenzied elephants occur in Sanskrit poetry is not summer as in Rao but in the rains. In fact the summer heat makes the elephant, not amorous, but quarrelsome and destructive, e.g. Kalidasa, *Ibid, Grismavarnanam:*

18)

34. Cf. Lodge, *Modes of Modern Writing*, p. 113.
35. Norman Friedman, "Forms of the Plot," 1954, *The Theory of the Novel*, ed. P. Stevick, 1967, p. 148.
36. Roman Jakobson, "Linguistics and Poetics," *Style in Language*, ed. T.A. Sebeok, 1960, p. 356.
37. Mikhail Bakhtin, "Discourse Typology in Prose," *Readings in Russian Poetics*, p. 180. Further, "Two directly intentional utterances of equal rank within a single context cannot occur together without interacting as a dialogue" producing "the weakening or destruction of monologic context."
38. Release from the cycle of existence is in fact the common goal of both Hinduism and Buddhism, e.g. the *Bhagavad Gita*, "Yad gatava na nivartante/tad dharma paramama mama" (That is my supreme abode going whither they return not). But the concept of non-return finds an emphasis in Buddhism which is amply proved in elaborate formulation of different levels of spiritual realization. Thus a sage is "paragato" (one who has gone over), the next is "anagami" (non-returner), then there is "skad-gami" (once returner), and so on. *Vinaya-pitaka, culla-Vagga*, ix. 1.4 trans. and ed. J.G. Jennings, *The Vedantic Buddhism of the Buddha. A Collection of Historical Texts translated from the original Pali*. 1947, 1949.
39. Traditionally the great texts or *Mahavakyas* are the following: (1) Rg-Veda consciousness is brahman, *Aitareya Upanisad*, III, 3; (2) *Yajur Veda*, "I am Brahman," *Brhadaranyak Upanisad* I. iv. 20; (3) *Sama Veda*, That thou art *Chandogy Upanisad*, VI: X: 3. (4) *Atharva Veda*, This self is Brahman *Mandukya Upanisad*, 2. Significantly Raja Rao has used none.
40. Roland Barthes, "To Write, an Intransitive Verb," *The Structuralist Controversy*, eds. R. Macksey and E. Donato, 1970 and 1972, p. 135 .
41. Raja Rao, "The Search for Form," lecture at Long Beach State College, Dec. 11, 1967, reported by Som P. Ranchan, "A Meeting with Raja Rao"— I, *Thought*, Delhi: July 13, 1968, p. 13.
42. As Mikhail Bakhtin points out, "What is uppermost for the stylizer is another person's set of devices precisely as the expression of a special point of view. He operates with this other point of view." "Discourse Typology in Prose," *Read-*

ings in Russian Poetics, p. 181. Since Rao's viewpoint is supposed to be uniquely Indian, the pervasive echoes from European literature are invested with profound ambiguity.

43. Strictly speaking, in higly-inflected languages like Sanskrit and classical Latin, there is no Inversion, simply because the word-order is governed by style, not by syntax. Not being a deviation, Inversion is not a foregrounding device in highly-inflected languages.
44. Jan Mukarovsky, *The Word and Verbal Art*, 1977, p. 11.

The Cat and Shakespeare: *A Tale of Modern India*

1. *An Act of Reconciliation*

The Cat and Shakespeare: A Tale of Modern India (1965), Raja Rao's third novel, admittedly a sequel to *The Serpent and the Rope*, takes up the theme of the metaphysical quest from the point at which Ramaswamy's story has carried it, and shows the next step in this quest.[1] After the confusion and groping in *Kanthapura*, and the agony of crisis in *The Serpent and the Rope*, Rao's quest for form at last arrives at the destination in *The Cat and Shakespeare*, where Rao comes nearest to a synthesis to embody his metaphysics in a literary form, without that pronounced conflict which upset the structural balance in *Kanthapura* and rent the fictional fabric of *The Serpent and the Rope*. His intellectual position may be found crystallized in the words of Ramaswamy, his hero: "I am, therefore, the world is." The central problem of Rao as a creative writer lies in the relationship between this essentially monistic standpoint and the adaptation of the novel to its literary expression, which most of Rao's critics usually miss.[2] The novel as a literary genre has evolved out of a fundamentally pluralist state of mind associated with liberal humanism.[3] This pluralistic view is basically Christian in its candid acceptance of the individual existence as real. So the suffering, the misery, of man also possesses intrinsic reality, to be redeemed by the Son of Man. But for Raja Rao, the only reality is the Absolute, "there is no world" and individual existence is completely illusory. His rigid non-dualist point of view is essentially monist and his hero Ramaswamy therefore argues that Madeleine's humanism, Christian and Buddhist, in accepting the reality of the individual and of the world, is opposed to his "Indian" metaphysics:

> To have compassion, remember, presupposes the *existence of the world*. You must have compassion towards some suffering *thing*, so suffering exists and compassion as well.

But the world does not exist as an independent reality in his philosophy, so his "India" is a concept which does not recognize human suffering and offers rather cruel comfort: "India is *impitoyable*" (i.e. without pity). The question then is, for what did Christ die on the Cross? It is the story of the Passion of Christ that underlies the development of the novel as a typical literary form of the West. In the evolution of Raja Rao as a novelist, the rejection of Madeleine symbolizes the rejection of humanism, Buddhist as well as Christian, while the representational form of the novel is based on the humanist/Christian assumption which is pluralistic. The plurality of existence stubbornly refuses to be contained in the theoretical paradigm of rigid non-duality, nor can a representational living mode be subjected to a pre-fabricated mould. In the evolution as an artist therefore both the philosophic point of view as well as the representational mode have to undergo transformation.

The tension in the form of the earlier novel was generated by the author's problematic relation with reality which caused a marked oscillation between a complete surrender to the chaos of contingency or a total distancing from even the fictional reality. In the crisis of violent action in *Kanthapura*, the narrative technique almost collapsed in a vain attempt to retain the distinction from life which is however totally given up in the resolution of *The Serpent and the Rope* when we find Trivandrum, without any rhyme or reason in the fictional world so far depicted, becomes the end of Ramaswamy's agonized quest. On the other hand, the last lingering impression of the grandmother and the aged in *Kanthapura* fades away in a fantasy, Ramaswamy and Savithri in *The Serpent and the Rope* cease to be fictional characters and are substituted by mythical prototypes consciously by themselves. In both cases, the linear progression of the traditional form based on an assumption of causal development finds the resolution particularly problematic. In *The Cat and Shakespeare* the narration itself appears to be a series of "non-happenings" which may be summarized in the following order:

1. Ramakrishna Pai, a brahman clerk in the Revenue Department at

Trivandrum, in Kerala, lives estranged from his wife, Saroja, who is always busy looking after parental property and their children. At Trivandrum, Pai's life revolves round his neighbour Govindan Nair, a clever resourceful clerk who works in the Ration Office and talks about Vedanta in an English flavoured with Shakespearean turns and phrases, and his mistress, Shantha.

2. Nair, with true neighbourly concern, attends upon Pai when he is afflicted with dreadful bubos and points out the desirability of having a house of one's own since his mistress Shantha is pregnant.

3. The mystery of multiplication of ration cards is set forth in the ration office. With Velayudhan Nair, an expert in such jugglery, Govindan Nair goes to a "Doctor's clinic" and meets a young whore "with necklace, black hair and rich bosom," to whom he expounds Vedanta and leaves a ration shop licence no. 9181.

4. Nair pays for Pai's house acquired in his daughter Usha's name.

5. Nair's son Shridhar, playmate of Usha, dies and Shantha comes to live with Pai and Usha.

6. Nair is arrested on a charge of having taken bribe from an old woman, whose son, the owner of a ration shop, has suddenly become rich.

7. No. 6 is actually a consequence of no. 7, in which John presents a cat to Nair in the office because everybody has heard repeatedly Nair's philosophy of life, "Learn the way of the kitten, then you're saved. Allow the mother cat carry you." While Nair and his colleagues indulge in a mock-Hamlet scene, expatiating on to-be or not-to-be, the cat jumps on the boss Bhoothalinga Iyer's head and he dies of heart failure.

8. The cat, left to Pai and Shantha, is taken to the court during Nair's trial and it points out the incriminating file. A ray of light from above reveals Bhoothalinga Iyer's signature and Nair is set free.

9. The cat, now permanently with Pai, leads him to a garden, just outside the wall, where he finds "truth not as fact but as ignition."

10. Govindan Nair, transferred from Trivandrum, leaves Pai who continues to live with Shantha and play at house building.

It is evident from this brief summary that the focus of *The Cat and Shakespeare* does not lie in the narration of a story of life, unfolded chronologically. The diminution of the narrative has to be made up with an alternative aesthetic ordering. It will be of course drastic to suggest that the story has disappeared completely; rather, it may be found "automatized," that is, its function has changed from the main or referential to the auxiliary, which is in this novel, symbolic. This change in the function of the plot is not however as erratic as some readers have found, because it does possess a literary background. As Jurij Tynjanov holds:

> In a work in which the so-called plot is effaced, the story carries out different functions than in a work, in which it is not effaced. The story might be used merely to motivate style or as a strategy for developing the material.[4]

We must however remember that there are some vividly "realistic" patches in *The Cat and Shakespeare*, which have been noticed by critics. For example, the social context of Kerala's unique Brahman-Nair extramarital relation renders to the unconventional man-woman situation a semblance of verisimilitude which would have been difficult to effect in any other Hindu community of the Indian sub-continent where a similar union would have created a great deal of social and psychological problems.[5] The historical background of the Second World War throws up the rationing system which supplies the appropriate milieu for the guru Govindan Nair's roguish philosophy. The pervasive corruption, an offshoot of rationing, leads to determine the "action" of the novel in two ways. Firstly, it makes Nair's arrest and trial possible and his precept of Cat-and-Kitten is literally translated into reality. He has followed the way of the Kitten and has been saved by the mother Cat in flesh and blood. Secondly, Pai's purchase of the house depends to a large extent on Nair's financial assistance which seems to stem from a mysterious unspecified source of income. Yet the realism of *The Cat and Shakespeare*, despite the vividness of isolated scenes and manipulation of historical background, is not motivated towards the traditional representational mode as it has been in Rao's former novels. Here, as in Kafka's novels, the realistic details are utilized for a distinct transcendental significance. The situations in Rao's work are all banal, indeed no less than Kafka's lawcourt or the castle as the source of realistic descriptions. But these are subsumed under assessments which are not at all guided by the realistic interest of social and historical import, for, through the chinks of the fictional world in its mundane appearance, lurk the invisible forces of the transcendental which is not so much emphasized as embodied in the very banality. Ordinary items of human experience are charged with a meaning and value which transcend all normal realistic possibilities. The mode in which *The Cat and Shakespeare* is presented is more illustrative than imitative, more symbolic than realistic.

In *The Serpent and the Rope* too we have seen Rao's attempt at manipulation of symbols. But there the form is realistic and as such, symbols are embedded, as we have seen, in the immediate context, in the semantics of the situation alone. The repetition of *bridge, mountain, ant, elephant* are motifs of decorative rhetoric in the traditional structure. The *bridge* may have stood for the distance between the phenomenon and the noumenon, *mountain* for the vertical ascent towards spiritual realization, *ants* for the unthinking animal existence or *elephants* for erotic frenzy; but these do not control the story of Ramaswamy in his journey to the Absolute through his encounters with women. At no critical stage do these symbols lead to the development of the narrative. Their function, largely, is to lend richness to the narrative texture through poetic approximation.

But in *The Cat and Shakespeare* symbols control the total form because it purports to be a "metaphysical comedy." In the Christian sense, the term "comedy" implies the formulation of salvation, the great prototype of which is offered at the end of Dante's *Divine Comedy*.[6] The epithet "metaphysical" particularly insists on this aspect to be distinguished from the social and secular varieties which are more common. Ramakrishna Pai, the narrator-hero, is just an average human male, an Everyman, as he says, "I am not particularly tall or fair or good or bad. I am just a man." His aspiration is mundane, he just wants a house of his own where he can live with his woman and child. But this house is also a tabernacle, the symbol of earthly existence of a soul that fundamentally belongs to the Divine. So his small white house has "an ochre band on it—almost as on a temple" for the colour ochre is traditionally associated with spirituality in India. Pai constantly thinks of extending the house upwards, adding more storeys, since the vertical progress is a well-known pattern of transcendence. As the house is like a temple, the temporary abode of a soul whose home is the Lord Himself, it displays some deities in the form of windows: these all open towards the sea—the infinite expanse of water, the very symbol of primordial creation. "A window on the sea is a window on God." Pai's little house continually echoes with the sound of the waves from the sea as if a continual reminder of the divine creation. Pai's mistress Shantha is allied to the divine creator in her role as a mother. So Shantha, carrying four months, has a mysterious affinity with the sea ("the sea knows me," says Shantha). It is to the swelling crest of the waves that her motherhood supplicates for a child. So, like the sea, her connection with Pai's house is inextricable. She represents, in human form, this existence, the creative aspect of the Supreme. So she is constantly occupied with house and land. She is referred to as "Vazhavankad-house" by Govindan Nair as though she could be equated with stone or mortar. "In fact her house is she." She imparts security to Pai's life as the wall which encloses the house does by delimiting it. Pai, safe and certain with his woman and children, lives in the spot on the earth given to him—his life rotating in the eternal groove of man's existence on this earth since time immemorial. But beyond this cycle of time lies the Apocalypse, the garden which embodies redemption.[7] It is the journey of the Everyman Ramakrishna Pai from the house to the garden that constitutes the significance of the pilgrim's progress from Time into Eternity.

This Christian pattern presents "rosy" as a qualifier of the garden. In Rao's story, *The Policeman and the Rose*, the narrator-hero is "arrested" as soon as he is born into existence, he is finally redeemed by a rose, for the rose, an apocalyptic flower, stands for Grace.[8] No less significant is the entirely gratuitous nature of the Grace that Pai often hopes for. He does not exactly search for it or undergo any spiritual effort or *sadhana* which plays such a dominant role in all systems of Indian religion, Hindu, Buddhist and Jain.[9] Pai, led by the mother cat, arrives at the garden and is blessed with the vision of the Supreme. He has done nothing to deserve grace which is here completely free.[10] One finds the efforts of Govindan Nair, maybe, though perhaps inexplicably, related to Pai's salvation which seems a kind of windfall. It is Nair who "does" things for Pai out of his love for a neighbour. The importance of grace and compassion for the Other in this novel by Rao can be properly understood only against the background of Rao's own previous "Indian" stand in *The Serpent and the Rope*, that stems from an uncompromising non-dualism which the author himself often reveals in interviews:

> Indian civilization is based on the idea that every person must seek his spiritual guide. *Among the Hindus you will not find the cult of Christian charity.* The Hindu conception of *Dharma* is quite different. In doing your *dharma* you also express your love. In the Christ and in the Buddha there is a special form of compassion for your neighbour.

In the original French of this interview, Rao presents an illustration of this basic difference:

> Ainsi en 1943 lors de la grand famine du Bengale il y a euun énorme exode sur Calcutta, et trois millions d'etres sont morts dans les rues de la ville tandis que d'autres festoyaient dans les restaurants; et il n'y eut pas à signaler la moindre revolte. Cela illustre bien les différences entre les attitudes hindoue et catholique.[8]

Surprisingly, in the novel where he admits to have concluded his Indian/Hindu pilgrimage, Govindan Nair, the prime mover of action, overflows with the milk of human kindness for the Other, his neighbour Pai. It is precisely the compassion for the neighbour that is revealed in Nair's uncalled-for service to Pai lying unconscious with dreadful bubos. This compassionate behaviour is certainly non-Hindu, if the acquiescence to the fact of three million starving people dying without rebellion in front of Calcutta restaurants feasting with food during the great Bengal famine, is the yardstick of Rao's Hindu *dharma*. No bond of Hindu *dharma* impels Nair to arrange for the purchase of Pai's house or to slip in money through the window whenever a child cries. His role as a guru does by no stretch of logic go beyond his expounding Brahman to the brahman. No doubt, it is as a guru that he points to Pai the right way to salvation—not through wisdom (which Rao so incessantly equates with Indian civilization as does his hero Ramaswamy in *The Serpent and the Rope)* but through a complete resignation to faith, with that total surrender without any stain of doubt or effort which we find in a kitten as it is so securely carried in the mouth of the mother cat. For Nair, the way of the kitten is the road to salvation, because man is redeemed by grace. The question is, does the Absolute Consciousness or Brahman of Raja Rao who seems to equate "India" with non-dualism bestow grace? The passage of grace is always downwards as Simone Weil observes, "La Grace, c'est la loi du mouvement descendant."[12] Hence the falling of sacred leaves indicates in this novel the blessings of the Lord. It presupposes a fundamental qualitative difference between man and God—a difference which Rao's non-dualism can never accept, nor can it have a personal God who out of His love for humanity bestows grace freely. Hence the place of *sadhana* or spiritual endeavour is of supreme importance. In Christianity, on the other hand, the Cross of Christ seems to bear the whole burden of human sin and constitute the basis of grace which is naturally gratuitous. If a Christian, being a sinner is saved by his God, it does not indicate arbitrariness on the part of God, for the price has been paid by the Son of God Himself: "But God commendeth his love toward us, in that, while we were yet sinners, Christ died for us." (*Romans* 5:8). So when we find Ramakrishna Pai, a Hindu without any *sadhana* to his credit, blessed with the vision of Beatitude, the strength of the gratuitous grace perhaps lies in the fundamental dogma of Christianity in which it is always a free gift.

Rao's comedy has therefore to strive for synthesis in the concept of the neighbour, to love whom has been so far the duty of the Christian (or the Buddhist) alone. "I sing of man," says Ramkrishna Pai," because he is my neighbour. After all, one's big neighbour is oneself. The neighbour's neighbour is always the Self."[13]

The rejection of Christ and humanism in *The Serpent and the Rope* is atoned for here in this acceptance of man and neighbour. Govindan Nair the guru goes to prison, as though in atonement for the whole corrupt life going on in the ration shop, as well as for the "extramarital propensities" of his boss. Whether this affair is a cock-and-bull story or whether Nair is really innocent of the charge against him we are not sure. But this temporary bondage of Nair makes the redemption of Pai, his neighbour, possible, for Nair's cat is left with Shantha to teach Pai the kitten's way to salvation. One may even simplistically formulate that Nair dies a temporary death so that Pai, the Everyman, may be redeemed.

This underlying Christian pattern comes to the forefront in the mystic experience of Pai which is the high watermark of this novel and is worth considering. The journey he undertakes from the existence of the house to the essence in the garden is but a graded progress in space, and the passage from one to the other needs no vertical leap. Pai, after toying with the idea of building three storeys, stops at only two: "I will never build a house three storeys high. Have you ever seen a house so high, no, not in Trivandrum." Raja Rao himself ended his spiritual quest at the feet of a guru in Trivandrum. "When you come to Trivandrum," writes Rao, "you feel you've come home. For Trivandrum is the home of the homeless. Everybody is born homeless."[14] Trivandrum, therefore, is a macrocosm in relation to Pai's house, and a microcosm in the background of the whole creation, just as the tree that stands by the wall is a form of the Apocalyptic garden, a descendant of the Cosmic Tree, the source of the twin trees of knowledge and life. Its leaves are trefoil, indicative of the Divine Trinity. Pai's predecessor Ramaswamy also was aware of the symbolism of the tree, particularly because of the Buddha's enlightenment under the Bodhi tree and concluded, "all men are but pilgrims of the Tree." Rao's Shaivite bias makes it a *bilva* tree, sacred to Shiva, and elevates it to the position of the cosmic tree with a multiplicity of symbolic functions.[15] This tree is the symbol of birth, growth and death as also of regeneration. So Shantha, big with child, is seen under the tree: Nair's son Sridhar plays here with Usha and once here in the rain catches pneumonia to die. At the same time the falling of its leaves presents salvation to Pai who constantly looks at the tree as though the scraggy stump holds the mystery of resurrection, the twice-born will somehow emerge from its thorny bark. Indeed, there seems to be little doubt that this tree is an earthly existence of a Divine import, to remind him constantly of the possibility of the descent of the grace. His guru Nair promises: "Your three storeys will go high. Your leaves will have fallen on Shiva." But Pai listens to Shantha's advice, "why be so ambitious," and so decides that the vertical leap is not for him. This decision itself binds him closer to the Christian existentialism which accepts this spacio-temporal reality.[16] Hence steps appear—the Jacob's ladder—to guide his journey. Such steps constitute the most earthly form of Transfiguration.[17] In the movement from one world to the other, we find Pai at the point of epiphany. That the vision itself is a mixture of Hindu and Christian metaphysics should not only be inevitable, but completely in keeping with the total design of reconciliation:

> I saw nose (not *the* nose) and eyes seeing eyes seeing, I saw ears curved to make sound visible, and face and limbs rising

> in perfection of perfection, for form was it.

The true Reality therefore lies in the universal, not so much as the Platonic concept, but as the form which alone is the "perfection of perfection."[18] It is this Aristotelian revision of the Platonic concept of reality that Saint Thomas Aquinas offered as the substratum of the whole Christian theology. The very concept of reality as the scene of man's ethical action starts here and Rao's Vedantin hero clearly accepts it, although in strict non-dualism the universe of form (as well as of name) is only a phenomenon like a city seen in a mirror; or as in a dream.[19] Thus there is probably no very logical common ground for a meeting of the two opposed modes, one declaring the Reality as Form the other as "not this, not this."[20] But Rao, in my opinion, approaches here to mystic faith rather than to any rigorous and intellectually viable system of Indian thought. For only in a spiritual mystique, contradictions may be dissolved. Indeed the vital function of religious symbolism is its capacity to express paradoxical situations or certain patterns of ultimate reality that can be expressed in no other way."[21] So Pai's Christian epiphany mingles with Hindu Brahmaprapti (realization of the Absolute) for there is no personal God in this mystic communion. "I saw truth not as a fact but as ignition. I could walk into fire and be cool, I could sing and be silent." The emphasis is on the reconciliation of all opposites so that the phenomenal perspective of time, the great terror, lies at last vanquished. What a Catholic poet is assured of— "Death, thou shalt die"—a brahman seems to realize in life:

> I woke up and found death had passed by, telling me I had no business to be there. Then where was I? Death said, it had died. I had killed death. When you see death as death, you killed it.

If "Death is swallowed up in victory" (I Corinthians 15:34), this is precisely because the sting of sin, which for the Hindu Vedantin resides in the sense of ego, the personal self is at last removed. "I remain over, having killed myself." The obsession with self, with identity, is a proof of the bondage to time, the victory of death. So the Hindu reaches that plane where there is no death, for there is no more the illusion of ego; he has passed from non-being to being, from death to immortality. The brahman at last realizes his native heritage through accepting the Christian existence—perhaps in spite of himself.

If Rao is seen in exclusively Indian terms, then in this novel he is left with two symbols, mother cat and dream, which cannot be presented in a coherent whole of thought because these derive from mutually exclusive sub-systems of philosophy, the cat from the Southern school of modified non-dualism, and the dream from non-dualism itself. The cat indicates that the world is, the dream decrees that it is not, it is *maya*.[22] If the world is a dream, a *maya*, how does it matter if one resigns like the kitten carried by the mother cat, or exerts individual effort clinging like a monkey cub to its mother as the rejected wife Saroja ("a tremendous worker") does? We are indeed expected to recognize the world as dream and this can be done only through meditation and renunciation as the great Sankara illustrated in his Own life and work. The non-dual path is through knowledge whereas the Southern school of modified dualism favours *Prapatti* or resignation to faith. How can these two exclusive traditions be synthesized in a novel in English and why is such an attempt made at all? The urge for such reconciliation does not arise from an academic interest, but from Rao's own encounter with Western civilization which accepts the reality of the existence. In other words, his adoption of the cat symbol and the particular variant of an Indian philosophical subgenre is a means to absorb the ethical essence of Christianity—the compassion for the other and gratuitous grace. Seen in this perspective, his selection of the Cat school *marjaranyaya* is eminently justifiable, for many Indian philosophers trace in this particular subgenre a recognizable impact of Christianity.[23]

Indeed, the whole background of *The Cat and Shakespeare* is homogeneous only in so far as it is Western, for the *house, tree, garden* and the *cat*, a domestic animal can be understood as elements in a harmonious design which is fundamentally Christian.[24] If we accept Rao's implicit notion of the world as an equation of *maya* or *vyavahara* of non-dualism and the Platonic illusion, then the whole Western movement of a metaphysical approach to reality is harmonized, for the neo-platonic modification of the universal as form connects Christianity with Plato and saves the Hindu Raja Rao from a laceration of being. Hence the cat is presented to Nair by John, a Christian. Rao himself regards Plato "a companion of all pilgrimages," and admits that through St.

Thomas Aquinas he arrives at the Gangotri, the origin of the holy Ganga.[25]

It is therefore natural that for the existential portion of the novel, Rao has a strong Christian tradition to embed his symbols like *house, tree* and *garden* in. But for his Hindu aspiration he has to offer a private set of symbols which are originally derived from the representational mode for they lack the sanction of tradition. He wishes to indicate the non-dual concept of the phenomenality of this world through an image which has the principle of relativity translated in perception—the ration shop ruled by the great scales. This human world, being relative, is subjected to evaluation, to moral judgement according to our action which again is our *karma* predestined from previous births. At a ration shop everybody gets his quota according to the colour of his card, the world offers everyone rewards and punishment according to one's *karma*, the ration apportioned in this earth. So "we all live on ration," and "life is a ration shop." The scale weighs everything according to the ration card, "Where is your card, Sir? Green, red or blue?" The symbol is vivid and catching no doubt, but cannot be taken as a "pure" symbol, for it is rooted in the immediate historical and semantic context, it has no permanent religious sanction of the kind *house, tree, steps* or *garden* are invested with. There is thus a sharp qualitative difference between the two sets of symbols, religious and private. So in establishing a relation between Pai's house that is a tabernacle and the ration shop that is so secular, Rao has to bring in another private symbol, *Shakespeare*. Clinging to the dramatic situation of Hamlet's to-be or not-to-be, Rao infuses ontology into what Shakespeare perhaps meant only as an expression of indecision at a particular moment of the hero's crisis, and presents the Kingdom of Denmark as a ration shop that is the replica of this world of relativity. For Rao, Shakespeare—being perhaps the creator—is beyond duality.[26] So Govindan Nair, the guru, is full of Shakespeare, and holds his sway over both the ration shop-office complex and Pai's house-wall-tree. In fact, Shakespeare as a symbol of non-duality is rooted in an associative process; didn't the Bard take his farewell in those famous words: "We are such stuff/ As dreams are made on and our little life/ is rounded with a sleep"? So Rao's Trivandrum, the microcosm of the universe, is "like a place you live in your sleep" as it is also "the city of enlightenment."[27] This kind of reconciliation finds waking and sleeping not as opposed modes but alternate events truly inter-changeable like André Breton's two communicating vessels—so much so that Pai returns from the garden into the house and goes on with his normal life here, on this plane of mundane reality, unlike the predecessor Ramaswamy who is lost in the height ("I will not return"). This harmony of opposites can be offered only by a mystic faith through expression in art, not in a codified rational philosophy. *Shakespeare* is Rao's vehicle for non-duality and as such to the readers who are prepared to accept a private symbol, presents the victory of the artist over the metaphysician. The quest of Raja Rao, an Indian writer in English, ends in a comedy, in an act of reconciliation, and as such the title *The Cat and Shakespeare* is justified, because it offers a concentrated mystique of the personal faith of an artist astride two cultures. It is a deeply personal correlative for the meeting of opposites, striving towards an objective formulation:

> I hear the clock chime at night from my house.
> Thus I live a bit of eternity.

2. *Towards the Poetics of anti-novel*

In the theme of *The Cat and Shakespeare* we have seen how urgent the need is for a reconciliation of antithetical views, of "to-be or not to-be." Such antipodal points in human experience can co-exist—as we have already stated—only in a subjective structure of imagination sustained by a mystic faith, but not in the rigorous rationale of an intellectually consistent system. The literary form in which such a theme may find its habitation has to disregard the logical mode of narrative development, the cause and effect relation—the basis on which rests the traditional realistic novel. The conventional novel starts with the data of a few selected items, from our experience which through evolution leads to the conclusion as a chain of cause and effect, building up an interaction of plot and character in a linear progressive development. In *The Cat and Shakespeare* on the other hand the form extends—we cannot say it progresses—through a series of "happenings" which happen as "non-happenings," gratuitous encounters juxtaposed by chance.[28] Thus Govindan Nair goes to consult a child specialist ostensibly for his sick son Shridhar, and is found philosophizing before a young whore. That this meeting is nothing but casual is only one aspect of the matter. In the details of description of the girl and Nair's action, this episode strongly resembles the story he later writes in jail, about his boss's extra-marital affair, which, to complicate the issue further, "came true as he wrote it." The question is: what is the relation between the episode presumably happening earlier with the fiction-that-is-real which comes later? Past, present and future are all mixed up and the lack of linearity confounds fiction with reality, leaving the reader in total uncertainty as to what precisely happens and when, if anything happens at all.[29] This episode may be seen as an example of the microstructure of the novel, which reflects the macrostructure of the whole in its mysterious dynamics of interaction in the relationship between Pai and Nair. Indeed between Pai's placid life with Shantha—not strictly unconventional in Kerala's typical brahman-nair tangle—and the adventures of his roguish neighbour Govindan Nair, there seems hardly any logical interaction. How does Nair's arrest logically lead to Pai's salvation in the garden? Here is an instance of the more modern form sometimes associated with the anti-novel which in spatial terms may be found circular, concentric or even mosaic. Against such a developing tradition, the structure of *The Cat and Shakespeare* may be perceived as a whole which consists of a non-logical transformation in the relationship of the characters, Ramakrishna Pai and Govindan Nair. From the very beginning, Pai is cast in the role of an object. Things happen to him, he is affected by them just as the British bubos find his body an easy prey. Govindan Nair appears as the agent, the active character, the subject, who fetches some strong evil-smelling native medicine to drive out the British bubo. It is he who always talks about Vedanta, schemes how to acquire a house, leaps this side or that side of the barrier of the wall. Pai is always at the receiving end of his efforts. Indeed, if Nair is very much a nominative, Pai seems destined to be the accusative. Yet at the end it is in his vision that the manifestation of the Supreme takes place, his mode of life the novel sets as its resolution. Clearly he is to be an agent, a subject. The arrest and trial of Nair constitute the watershed demarcating the two roles of Pai, objective and subjective, the one with which he begins, the other with which he ends. Out of the absurd imprisonment of Nair emerges the new role of Pai as agent, for he takes charge of the cat and he succeeds in reaching his goal. As soon as this happens, Nair is withdrawn from the fictional reality, for it is clear that, though an agent in action, his purpose is to be instrumental in the story of Pai's salvation. We now realize that the role of Nair is actually equivocal, for, although he is presented as an aggressively active and philosophizing rascal, all his efforts are directed, not towards himself, but to facilitate Pai's journey across the wall. As Pai admits, he would never have gone to the other side of reality but for Govindan Nair who finally transpires to be an instrument. If one applies a grammatical analogy one may sum up the structure of *The Cat and Shakespeare* as an exercise in the passive voice with a long subordinate clause in the active, crystallized in a core sentence like the following: Ramakrishna Pai is led to his salvation by his neighbour Govindan Nair who plays the role of guru and ultimately proves the efficacy of his teaching in the life of his disciple.

This structure is created with the help of a mixed form—narration and intellectual digression. In the previous novels the components of the mixed modes are constantly at conflict with each other, one questioning the other, in one case resulting in violent disjunction, and in acute ambivalence in the other. Further the function of intellection in *The Serpent and the Rope* is romantic, raising the shabby reality of a hackneyed triangular love defamiliarizing it with high-pitched intellectual discussions and a crowd of mythical parallels. In *The Cat and Shakespeare*, the intellectual analysis without the sharpness of an invisible encounter, assumes a more meditative and mystic aspect, and what is of primary importance, it offers a perennial source of humour which is perhaps the characteristic mark of this novel. This leads to a mixture of the sublime and the grotesque as the fundamental operative principle to effect which the novelist has to adopt a unique technique from surrealism. By "surreal" one need not be confined to the much publicized paraphernalia of early surrealism like automatism, dream-transcription, mediumistic trance and certain spectacular exhibitionist oddities in behaviour. The surreal in *The Cat and Shakespeare* resides in the consistent denial of rationality with the help of intelligent digression manifested in a special kind of humour[30] which alone sustains the structure, operating in symbols from disparate sources which are held firmly in cohesion. It is to be noted that critics are usually baffled or annoyed with Rao's humour in this novel and even his admirers fail to account for it in the total design.[31] Yet humour is as pervasive in *The Cat and Shakespeare* as melancholy is in *The Serpent and the Rope*. Indeed it is the very antipode of its predecessor in which everything is enveloped with sorrow—marriage, childbirth and of course death. In *The Cat and Shakespeare* on the other hand, everything is an object of gentle laughter, not the vindictive satiric demonism, but the quiet humour which indicates distance as well as involvement. Everything is subject for a joke, whether it is a disgusting disease like an attack of bubos, or the pathetic death of a child, not to speak of the arrest and trial which assume an absurd dimension as Govindan Nair spins a "hen-and-heifer story" about his pious brahman boss's fondness for women, while the judge goes round and round his table in search of truth. The humour here almost always tends to arise out of what is normally regarded as painful for human beings—death, disease or conflict with the law. In each instance, it is the function of the humour to absorb the content of human suffering, and present it as a form of universal divested of the individual and the particular which is the human condition. The death of Shridhar, Govindan Nair's son, is presented thus:

> The bamboos were already in the courtyard. Death had come. It spoiled a nice courtyard, with flower beds of roses. I never went across the wall. How could I? I could hear Tangamma weep, then, Govindan Nair said something. Dr. N.C. Pillai is such an able man. He walked out of the house efficiently. It was a bad case, he said. His Gladstone bag was so knowledgeable. It contained mysterious instruments that spoke. Death is such speech?

The immediate situation in which Shridhar's young life of seven years is consecrated to flames is completely distanced through the help of humour that pays a disproportionate attention to the spoiling of the courtyard and the pretension of the doctor which seems to have spread to his Gladstone bag—all these details tend to deflate the human sorrow by introducing inconsequential diversion. A later reference to Shridhar's death effectively ejects the issue out of the human feeling of pain: "That is why Shridhar died. Usha spoke over the wall and the cat carried him away. Funny, Sir, that a child is carried away by a cat." This "funny" aspect arises, not from the narrative of a human life but from a constant intellectual frame of reference in which death may be seen as untrue or unreal. This framework is supplied by Rao's metaphysics which takes the human situation completely under control. Thus the description of Shridhar's death is followed by a dialogue between Pai and Usha, on generalities like life, death, marriage, in which the father teaches the daughter the Vedantic truth that real life is "where no flames can burn," beyond this phenomenal existence. This is the narrative pattern characteristic of *The Cat and Shakespeare* in which a human situation in fictional reality is presented and immediately rendered unreal through humorous distanciation based on a witty play with metaphysics.[32] In fact, Shakespeare's to-be or not-to-be supplies the principle of organization of narrative and meditative components and the function of the latter is to modify the former by prolonging the creative process, by lengthening the form.

This distanciation through humour deriving from philosophy can be better appreciated if seen as a deviation, a foregrounded device against Rao's whole previous work in which human suffering and his metaphysics clash so violently. In *The Serpent and the Rope,* the agony of Ramaswamy and Madeleine is presented within the serious and tragic formulae of the traditional-modern form of the novel which conflicts at sensitive points with Rao's metaphysics that rejects suffering as the proof of dualism, of the independent existence of the world which in his view cannot be real. The only way to escape from the impasse, suggests *The Cat and Shakespeare*, is to treat suffering itself as unreal and it seems that only a special brand of humour can shake the irrevocable reality of human misery. So Rao's humour is of that particular variety which André Breton following Freud defines as a process permitting "to refuse to admit that the trauma of the external world can touch one."[33] But the rational response to the physical suffering of bubo, the death of a son, the ignominy of a charge of corruption cannot but be fraught with pain. To break the inextricable bond with rationality Rao utilizes a higher intelligence that the surrealists term as distinterested play of thought which enables humour to channel the desired liberation.[34] Pai's unconscious body covered with dreadful eruptions, laden with pus, is an object of laughter when Shridhar mistakes it for death, because his father finds in it an opportunity to play with the concept of reality as true awakening:

When you fall unconscious they say you are dead. In fact

> where were you, brother, when Shridhar thought you were dead? Were you dead to yourself, my friend? You purge to live. You sleep to die. When sleep is life, where is death? Ha, ha, ha.

Here is what Breton would characterize as a typical element of *humour noir*—the comic as the sublime.[35] This grave tomfoolery stems from intelligence which in the form of play of thought performs a surreal function, that of breaking down the barrier erected by rationality between the two states, conscious and unconscious—to-be and not-to-be—representing different realities. This play releases humour by distancing the immediate concern of pain. Moreover, a relationship is established between a concept of Vedanta ("sleep is life") and Pai's diseased body which would be denied by a rational philosopher, but may be found acceptable as bizarre, as grotesque through the operation of humour. In other words, metaphysics becomes a structural component through humour in a surreal technique.[36]

Not only humour, but the very extension of the narrative itself is propelled with the help of a surreal emphasis on irrationality. The basic condition of form that it may have a coherence is centred on the satisfaction of the reader's anticipation aroused in the beginning of the novel, and *The Cat and Shakespeare* fully satisfies this requirement. Pai desires to receive grace—like the absent-minded hunter who throwing leaves on the sunken image of Shiva becomes blessed with the manifestation of the Lord himself. This desire is fulfilled not by rational and traditional character development in accord with the realistic formula, but by allowing the marvellous, the fabular, to dominate.[37] Pai's house, like the typical surreal retreat, is a privileged locale where everything is possible, the wishful fantasy is real, a cat can take man to the Beatitude. The motif of the kitten being carried by the mother cat is introduced as a metaphor of complete resignation and through constant repetition becomes the central symbol. Then the mother cat appears in flesh and blood and proceeds to prove the validity of Govindan Nair's philosophy by practice, frees Nair from prison and leads Pai to the garden. The technique here is distinctly surreal in the extension of reality where symbol ceases to remain a symbol. So the vision of Pai is mystic and marvellous in nature, and refuses to be rationally analyzed according to one particular system. What Pai is blessed with is not the Vedantic wisdom ("Jnanam is India," as Ramaswamy has held) but an illumination. The technique registers a revolt against rationality to reach this goal through a confluence of humour and intelligence that transforms the material circumstances of an average clerk in a banal extramarital alliance, living on the generosity of an unscrupulous friend, into an allegory of salvation, a metaphysical comedy.

To allow the surreal technique to operate, other components in the structure undergo transformation. Since a denial of rationality is a blow at the very form of the traditional novel, in *The Cat and Shakespeare* we find a caricature of the compositional principle of the novel.[38] Take for example the triangular plotting which is the most convenient peg for a Western author to hang his story on. In *The Cat and Shakespeare*, the triangle consists of Ramakrishna Pai, his mistress Shantha who is in reality as domesticated as a conventional wife, and his neighbour Govindan Nair who is a combination of a guru and a rogue, and as such the whole plan thoroughly upsets the romantic tradition of extramarital passion which serves as a theme in several novels including Rao's *The Serpent and the Rope*. Of course Shantha is not married to Pai, but the complications in the plot do not arise out of Pai's love for his mistress Shantha and aversion to wife Saroja. Her relation with Pai is a caricature of the grand romantic passion patterned by the Tristan-Iseult legend—the very prototype of the man-woman encounter in the fictional tradition, because she has become the mistress of Pai not from a passionate love for an individual man or for his particular qualities, but from the admiration for Govindan Nair's philosophizing. It is because Nair's son Shridhar dies, that she comes to live with Pai. She looks after the cat for the animal belongs to Nair. Although she is still the Other, a residue of the existential role of woman in *The Serpent and the Rope*, she is not wholly an object here. Unlike Savithri, Rao's grand formula of Indian womanhood, Shantha, is never seen as a docile disciple of Pai in an asexual role. Indeed, she seems to understand Nair's riddles better than Pai and hence has a semblance of individual independence. It is she who repeats Yagnavalkya's exposition of the Self (which was done by Ramaswamy in *The Serpent and the Rope)* and befuddles Pai showing that she proves his existence ("only I say you. And you say I"). Unlike his proud predecessor, Pai readily admits his own limitation and finds her equivocation ("she always says two things at the same time") nearer to Govindan Nair's roundabout way of talking. So, like Madeleine, she has an independent profession as a teacher, the responsibility of a family to think about (her widowed mother and brother, not to speak of the landed property). As Madeleine "had never touched any one," Shantha too has "never touched any man before," and stands in sharp contrast to Savithri's coquetry. So Madeleine's dead son Krishna Pierre is momentarily resurrected in Shantha's lovely child, Krishna. At the same time, Shantha is not a three-dimensional character who inhabits a fictional reality in flesh and blood which Madeleine does in her tragic rejection. This is because Shantha is presented completely on the surface, more of a Platonic universal of womanhood than a particular woman. She "is not a woman, she is woman," as the narrator states. This recalls Ramaswamy's journey to Plato proving "Georges is not Georges—Georges is man." But in the preceding novel, this is only a temporary intellectual victory for Ramaswamy, since throughout the novel Georges is presented as an individual typical no doubt of the tormented Slav emigré, but at the same time a particular person enclosed by time, with his battered arm and Catholic fervour. The reality of *The Serpent and the Rope* is peopled by characters very much like Georges, who are individuals as well as types, but never pure abstract universals. Most of them bear the distinguishing traits of character in a traditional novel, what Iris Murdoch would describe as "a dynamic merging of the idea of a person with the idea of class."[39] In Shantha we find no such depth in which different layers coexist. She is sufficient entirely on the surface, "I am no Panchali or Damayanthi. I am just a woman. Lord, may I just be woman." She is almost a one-dimensional character, the illustration of womanhood as Form, she is not representative of a class. In other words the very principle of characterization is laid bare by extolling her as form and denying her individual roundness in concrete situations. Her function is to feed the cat which eventually takes Pai across this existence. It is never clear if she herself has achieved any spiritual goal or if she longs for it. She seems to be sufficient by herself, playing with the house-building. At best, she is close to being a mediatrix, but she never represents the independent Feminine Principle or *s akti* to be worshipped as such.[40] Since she is an illustration of an abstraction, she may not excite the hero into an obsessive desire for dominance which marks the arrogant Ramaswamy's relation with women. Besides, Pai too is reduced to the bare essentials of manhood, without the romantic idealized content of his predecessor—he is "just a man." He is not so much a modern anti-hero as the illustration of abstract manhood, for he seems to have no background, no parents, no country, no relatives—so very unlike his predecessor Ramaswamy. We know more about his wife Saroja, presented only in glimpses, than the milieu in which Pai may be embedded. His only claim at being the hero of the novel is the fact that when Shantha goes to the Revenue Office with her problem about her land and Pai stands against the filing ladder, she knows him immediately "to be her man." If she has decided to worship him, it is from the natural order of things in the world and has nothing to do with Pai's qualities. This presents a caricature of the love-at-first-sight convention and also of the intensely personal love with spiritual pretensions, both of which are followed in *The Serpent and the Rope*.

If Pai is a subject in relation to Shantha, he is clearly an object in relation to Govindan Nair, a guru-cum-rogue who builds his disciple a house, explains Brahman to the brahman and of course provides him with the mother cat. In fact it is this unusual combination that enables him to take care of Pai's two worlds, the here and the hereafter. It is this mixture of irreverence and the sublime that marks the satire on the conventional preceptor, the grave father figure whose glimpse we caught for a moment in *The Serpent and the Rope*. Moreover, the very presentation of a character consistently from outside points towards the technique of the anti-novel. Although a lot of things happen which normally should cause great internal disturbance—the premature death of a child, imprisonment and trial—we have little knowledge of what goes on in his devious mind. Like Shantha, he also exists strictly on the surface, as though the author admits the impenetrability of characters in his own fictional creation. Since the presentation of psychology led to a problematic of narrative technique in delving the souls of Ramaswamy and Savithri, here the author seems to abjure the omniscience of the creator, and evades the authorial responsibility altogether. To try to understand them with reference to actual situations pertaining to social and phenomenal reality, as some critics have done and reached a state of exasperation, is fundamentally a wrong approach, because in this novel, it is not authenticity that is sought for in those fictional personages, but an intensity which links them to their creator, not to the external reality. Like surreal characters they have a function similar to that of a lightning conductor. [41] A minimum of particularities seem adequate to define them because they are embodiments of desire and personify the aspirations of their creator. Although we know so little about Pai, Nair or Shantha, none of their actions, nor their behaviour in any of the situations they happen to be placed in, surprise us. In other words they seem to fulfil André Breton's hope, acting "in an altogether foreseeable way in view of an unforeseen result."[42]

The absence of interiorization which explains motivation and supplies justification, indicates a rejection of psychology, which is however a part of the larger revolt against logic, the main prop of the novel form. It is the assumption of a stable logical relationship between cause and effect that constitutes the very basis of the hypothetical reality of fiction.[43] As we have seen, *The Cat and Shakespeare* does fulfil the expectation aroused in the beginning, not as a causal progress through character development, but through the operation of the marvellous, through the denial of commonsense rationality. This principle itself is built into the work to show the actual rejection of logic in the process of composition. When Shridhar is fatally ill, his father Govindan Nair's obsession with non-logic takes precedence over his paternal concern to play with the idea of the cause of Shridhar's illness— "Since you want a cause, anything is the cause. The more innocent a thing, the more mysterious its cause"—and concludes, "Usha is the cause of Shridhar's illness."

Apart from the obvious satire at causality revealing the technique of the novel which is "a system of no logic, and that is the story"—the passage is a pointer in the direction of the new fiction in which the novelist-at-work is to be exposed.[44] In the little pastiche, the mock-Hamlet scene which may have irritated readers accustomed to traditional-modernist fiction, the organizing principle of the novel is intentionally exposed to the reader. It attracts attention to the fictionality of the fiction, as Hamlet's play-within-the play is to function "tropically," "to hold, as 'twere, the mirror up to nature," and suggest the innermost meaning through characters as symbols. We know from the pastiche that the fictional world that has been created is an artifact which imitates the relative nature of our reality. An action committed in the play (as the murder of Polonius) is like a killing done in dream. So the mother cat with the full impunity of Vedantic *maya* kills Bhoothalinga Iyer because the death of the boss is necessary in the novel. A live Bhoothalinga Iyer would have been a real nuisance in the trial of Nair, especially in effecting the miracle of his signature, not to speak of the "sheer pornography" that Nair ladles out on the pretext of giving an account of his boss's promiscuous habits. It is through the Shakespearean interlude that we are prepared to take the whole fictional world as a piece of fiction whose purpose is "tropical," to illustrate an abstract idea of phenomenality, a relative world beyond which lies the Absolute Reality. So the title is not a mere surrealist stunt, but a pointer to the new technique that the novel has adopted in its post-modernist leaning towards the anti-novel. As a novelist, Rao seems to have solved for once the problems that he has confronted in his attempt to adopt the traditional representational mode of the novel by evolving a symbolic variant of the anti-novel that draws his experience and his view of life into a harmony.[45] If the organic wholeness of a work of art has any bearing on an inter-cultural encounter, the utilization of sophisticated Western poetics in "a tale of modern India" points towards a desperate artistic attempt to bridge the rift in the very self of the brahman novelist astride two modes, the archaic and the modern.

3. *The break-through: a zero degree writing*

"A new form appears not in order to express a new content," writes Victor Shklovsky, "but in order to replace an old form, which has already lost its artistic value."[46] In our analysis of the narrative form of *The Cat and Shakespeare* we have noticed the replacement of traditional-modernist realism by an illustrative, symbolic form effected by a technique which is associated with surrealism and as such anticipates the anti-novel. It is therefore our task to see how the form is actually realized in style, for it is the use of language that constitutes the final test, especially in the type of fiction to which Rao seems to direct his talent—the fiction in which the narrative is gradually foreshortened to emphasize an alternative aesthetic.

The language of *The Cat and Shakespeare* has not attracted much critical attention presumably for its simplicity and lack of that luxuriant and heavy rhetoric which characterize Rao's earlier works. However, it is this apparent simplicity, the restricted and severely mundane vocabulary, the acceptance of the normal state of the English language that by itself constitutes the aesthetic device, for it is to be seen as a deviance foregrounded against Rao's previous works which set the standard. In other words, by the time Rao comes to write his third novel, his stylistic inventiveness has become more or less automatized. His rhetorical manipulation of elegant inversion, antitheses, parallelism, archaic flavour, has become so habitual that he seems to have developed a highly idiosyncratic, personal standard of normal language.

In *The Cat and Shakespeare*, it is against his own standard language that the de-automatization has to proceed, for without de-automatization, the drawing away of the veil of habituality, the aesthetic use of language is hardly possible. This explains an interesting and perhaps paradoxical fact—that in *The Cat and Shakespeare* linguistic form holds the narrative structure in cohesion, since story has undergone diminution, and at the same time there is no obvious, immediately striking experiment in verbal art, something that marks his other works. At every level, vocabulary, syntax and imagery, we find an operation of the principle of contraction rather than of expansion, because it is meant to de-automatize the standard already set by his own baroque expansion and luxuriant inventiveness.

In *Kanthapura* the mingling of colloquial speech with literary devices of rhetoric bears the stamp of the traditional, realistic and modern form whose very essence, according to Eric Auerbach, lies in the mixture of high and low.[47] Its sophisticated development in *The Serpent and the Rope* emphasizes that minute craftsmanship which constitutes the very equipment of the realistic mode, characterized by Roland Barthes as "a combination of the formal signs of literature (preterite, indirect speech, the rhythm of written language) and of the no less formal signs of realism (incongruous snippets of popular speech, strong language or dialect words etc.)."[48] In the careful use of rhetorical devices, the style of *The Serpent and the Rope* hovers on preciosity in its syntactic manoeuvres and artificial stretching of the vocabulary, not to speak of the conscious craftsmanship evident in the imagery. Its very eclecticism ties it to history, to Time which is for the Vedantin in Rao, only phenomenal. His eloquent inversions, memorable antitheses and stimulating epigrams may, from a certain point of view, be considered as spectacular signs of the fabrication which the traditional form of novel invariably demands. So a mutation in form must be accompanied by a drastic change in language. Consider the opening lines of *The Cat and Shakespeare:*

> I have a small white house here, with a courtyard. from the back I look over coconut trees, and huts, and somewhere there's the sound of the sea. I was appointed a divisional clerk, Trivandrum, some two years ago. I left my wife and two children at Pattanur. My eldest was five years of age, my youngest three. It's not easy to change schools, you know, and then it was monsoon time.

This is fundamentally a different use of language from the stylization evident in Rao's other works. *Kanthapura*, as we have found in the first chapter, starts with an inversion for emphasis ("*Kanthapura* is its name"), goes to another elaborate one ("High on the Ghats . . . sugarcane"), which presents the scene in an impressionistic liveliness. This is focused further throughout the passage with repetition, alliteration and conventional poetic diction, specific defamiliarization for effectiveness using rhetorical figures. In *The Serpent and the Rope* the exploitation of literary tradition is even more elaborate as well as subtle in the opening paragraph, replete with irony, rhetorical interrogations, paradoxes, unusual placing of attributes:

> I was born a Brahmin—that is *devoted to Truth and all that.* . . . But how many of my ancestors since the excellent Yagnyavalkya, my legendary and Upanishadic ancestor, have really known the Truth excepting the sage Madhava, who founded an empire or, rather, helped to build an empire, and wrote some of the most profound of Vedantic texts since Shri Sankara? There were others, *so I'm told*, who left *hearth and riverside fields*, and wandered to *mountains distant* and hermitages "to see God face to face." And some of them did see God face to face and built temples. But when they died, for indeed they did "die"—they too *must have been* burnt by tank or grove or meeting of two rivers, and they too *must have* known they did not die.

The aim of such concentration of heavy rhetoric is a serious representation of fictional reality as a solid world entirely plausible in its particular emphasis on romantic idealization whereas in the first work the stress was on a poetic distance approximating to the legendary.

In contrast to this seriousness in fictional representation, the language of *The Cat and Shakespeare* does not seem to use the traditional tools of literariness so customary in building up fictive reality. We may find in its very simplicity, without colloquial snippets or literary manipulation of artifice, a tendency towards a neutral style, since it does not utilize these conventional opposites—either of the language of everyday speech or that of literariness. A passage like the following may indeed be felt to possess what Roland Barthes would call an "amodal form" of indicative mood or of the "zero degree writing."

> 1. Shantha lives with her mother and two brothers round near the Poolimmod. 2. The brothers go to school. 3. The mother cooks. 4. Shantha earns (they have some property too, in North Travancore). 5. Shantha also loves. 6. Her house is not far. 7. Only in the monsoon are the roads very difficult. Even so we somehow manage with each other.

The unusual brevity of construction, especially in 3, 4 and 5, reminds, one almost of the first lessons in a children's language primer. The effect is an intentional dissociation from the literary convention of the traditional novel form which has so far been Rao's own as well. In the preceding work, Rao strives to find his own style by enhancing the existing mode with the help of customary weapons—archaism, conceits, purple patches—usually quoted by his admirers—which merely led to the same kind of solidity erected by craftsmanship that one finds, for example, in André Gide or Oscar Wilde. Here his intention is primarily to break through his own wall of art. It is therefore significant that the residue of *The Serpent and the Rope* is often utilized almost as a satire on its own literariness. Take for example the inversion in the passage just quoted which in contrast to the similar constructions in *The Serpent and the Rope* meant to be so elegant and serious, here emphasizes the mundane reality of the mud and slush of monsoon. In fact the few inversions that occur in this novel are mostly satiric in extending rhetorical elegance to the very prosaic. Take other examples like "Invisible are the ways of Destiny," to explain Shridhar's French leave from school to carry Pai's food; or "Notorious are the Nairs for the mess they live in," which needs no explanation. Even in "wonderful is man" gravity is not the focus, since it is followed by "he needs to be told he is" as an elaboration, and so seems facetious on the face of it. One of the few instances where inversion performs the customary function of rhetoric—as we find amply in the other two novels—is in the single note of sadness from Shantha ("white is the foam " since it sings of "despair"), which affects by sheer proximity the succeeding description of Nair: "Like a pirate on the high seas is Govindan Nair"; the other is "form was it," conveying the spiritual essence of Pai's enlightenment with an aesthetic finality.

The studied simplicity of construction which so pointedly avoids the usual rhetoric of deviation and foregrounding that characterize Rao's preceding works may be perceived no less in the careful restraint on the vocabulary. One may apparently find the vocabulary marked by a negative treatment. The words which are repeated are ordinary nouns—*sea, tree, house, cat, kitten. wall*—and common verbs like *be, have, sleep, awake, love, build, live, weigh* etc. The emphasis on monosyllables by itself is a refusal to enter into elaborate literariness which the lengthy words in *The Serpent and the Rope* so often suggest. One is immediately reminded of the surreal practice of emphasizing common verbs.[49] More important however is the inextricable connection of the repetition of these very words with the symbolism of the whole novel. Yet all these words belong to the daily humdrum life of man anywhere on this earth. None of them primarily connotes any abstract idea. Yet through the device of repetition these often reveal a symbolic value which is embedded in the whole narrative structure. In other words, in this novel the unusual currency of the common items is to be regarded as aesthetically motivated to control the whole design. If each of these has double referents, these seem to be guided, at least the majority of them, as much by personal predilection as by Christian and Vedantin background. Each is fully accounted for in the whole narrative of Ramkrishna Pai as the illustration of an idea so much so that it is perhaps not possible to distinguish the two forms, linguistic and narrative, as independent elements. Indeed one may even say, that in *The Cat and Shakespeare*, style is the form. Take for example the conscious persistence of the word *house* for which the substitute *home* is never used. This selection is a proof that the house of Pai is only the earthly existence, a tabernacle, not his true *home* which is one with the Lord Himself; or the repetition of *dream* related to the non-dual concept of the empirical existence—a product of *maya* which is like a dream, the Absolute being the Supreme Reality. For the surrealist incidentally, it is the state of dream that constitutes "the superior reality."[50] In Rao's use of the word "dream" as a symbolic motif of this empirical existence, we find therefore a foregrounding of the "Indian" intellectual content as a contrast against the background of the literary association of the word that surrealism has brought in vogue.

However, the aesthetically-oriented deviance which happens to be perhaps the only noticeable departure from the norms of standard English, is a particular syntactic pattern which lays bare the compositional principle of Rao's allegorical mode, namely, a fusion of the particular with the universal: (1) "And Shantha is not just a woman, she is woman" (2) "She (Usha) is my child. She is not merely that. She is child." It is by the simple omission of the particularizing article (or possessive adjective/pronoun) that Rao suggests the symbolic universal nature of the individual characters who therefore inhabit a fictional world which is not imitative of contingency but illustrative of the true Reality. Indeed, the subtlety of the device may appear concealed unless we compare the French rendering: "Shantha est pas simplement une femme, elle est la femme," "elle est mon enfant, mais elle, n'est pas simplement cela, elle est l'enfant." In the French version, the particular and the universal are distinguished by antithesis, between *une* and *la*, *mon* and *la*: this construction by the virtue of the distinction seems to retain, as though, an implied opposition. But in the original English, the absence of the definite article and the possessive by itself presents, so to say, the universal concretely, withdrawing the emphasis on the difference. This may be seen as the linguistic embodiment of the metaphysic of the Universal as Form.[51] Of course the meaning does not change fundamentally in the French version but the fine shade of Rao's significance which lies in the embodiment of a complete identity between the particular (Shantha, Usha) and the universal (woman, child) is perhaps missed. In English it is embedded in the syntax. So the construction becomes clearly an intentional foregrounding in "I am cause." In the epiphany it is pointedly emphasized, "I saw nose (not *the* nose)." The last instance decidedly establishes the author's conscious deviation. It is interesting that in the French translation these two sentences have literal rendering, "je suis cause" and "je vis nez (non *le* nez)" and are therefore closer to the original, though the pattern is indistinct in French because in the other two instances the definite article (*la*) has been used. In Rao's English, on the other hand, the omission of the article constitutes by its uniform absence in specific occasions of Platonic overtones, a crucial structural image which has a dual function. It indicates the Platonic background as well as the whole allegorical mode of the novel in which the particular story of Ramkrishna Pai reflects the universal human condition.

This fundamental concept of identity leads to an expert mingling of tenses in the novel. In the preceding work, the use of the present tense seems to have been concerned solely with generic truths and universal abstractions whereas the fictional world of Ramaswamy-Madeleine-Savithri carried on in the past tense, the conventional narrative preterite. So it has appeared as though the fictional reality built on the past tense is being constantly punctured by authorial intrusion in the form of the present tense. The demarcation between past and present seems to emphasize the distinction between the particular human life presented as fiction and the universal idea which is a general truth. The tension that is generated from such continual opposition is to a great extent resolved in *The Cat and Shakespeare*. There are doubtless plenty of abstract generalizations that are cast in the present as we find in such random instances: "What is a doctor? One who knows diseases is the simplest definition." "Knowledge alone knows." "Malabar is truth."

What lends special value to the use of the present tense in this novel is its considerable extension to build up the fictional world which in the conventional novel, as in Rao's own previous work, is carried on in the past. The traditional form of the novel is inextricably bound to the past tense as a curious convention of fictionality. Roland Barthes has therefore, called the preterite "the corner-stone of Narration" for "it signifies a creation"— "the presence of Art."[52] So, Rao's frequent use of the present tense in the narration of the events happening in a fictional reality may be seen as a decisive breakaway from the traditional. Compare, for example, the introduction of Shantha in the present simple with that of

Madeleine in the conventional past. One may find in it the fusion of theme and language, for Shantha's being a universal is embodied in the language itself as the present tense is often the indicator of generic truths, whereas Madeleine is an individual, particular character cast in the past which denotes fictionality.

Since the use of the past tense suggests a solid and separate world which the readers accept suspending disbelief, its repeated substitution by the present disturbs the conventional reality which now becomes fluid and extends in a surreal manner.[53] So not only are states, conditions and descriptions in the present, but also innumerable actions that are cast not in the fictional reality of the past but outside the assurance of this solidity:

1. Shantha is carrying four months.
2. There are very few interesting faces in the ration shop.
3. Tangamma sends Shridhar with some coffee to console me. Then Govindan Nair . . . jumps across the wall.
4. The doctor knows the temperature is measured with a glass instrument that speaks, Modhu . . . cleans the thermometer and the temperature has gone up to 105 degrees.
5. Mother cat sits in a cage between the office table and the almirah.

This use of the present tense has another very important function in describing actions—to indicate the dream nature of the sensible world, for the use of the present tense is often associated with dream in literature. So the extension of reality may be conveyed, as it is actually done in some of the French nouveaux romans by banishing the past tense which is associated with the literary convention of a narrow and fixed reality. This also explains why in *Kanthapura* Rao's switchover to the present tense in all violent actions happening in a realistic presentation registers collapse of technique because Rao's form was geared to the traditional. In *The Cat and Shakespeare* on the other hand the form is not realistic but symbolic and the technique is surreal successfully endowing the fictional reality with a dream-like provisional existence where "happenings" happen as "non-happenings."

Further, the present tense is also the tense of "an experience we want to make immediate for somebody" when we use it in writing.[54] This is so because the reality is so complex that it cannot perhaps be contained or conveyed in a rigid convention of the linguistic habit of past tense. The present tense dramatizes the creative process itself. The work, instead of being presented to the reader as a product which may be examined at an aesthetic distance, calls for the participation of the reader in the process of creation itself. So the short dramatic interlude, a parody of *Hamlet*, is justified for it blends with the whole linguistic structure which dramatizes the composition of the novel. When the narrator of the novel presents the fictional happenings as "now," time becomes a flux, indivisible into sharply demarcated past, present and future. This perhaps leads to the incorporation of mental attitudes logical only in the post-independent India in a fiction the action of which is supposed to take place during the Second World War. Consider the following observations as typical examples of the fluidity of time: " in the new India plans were never so difficult, the new is made with plans" "Two is the limit—but then if you have three—on forty-seven rupees, how can you feed a third child?" British India had neither plans for development nor for population control. Rao's actual time of writing is here mixed with the fictional time which is maintained in the scales of pay his hero draws, plausible during the Second World War and not in the sixties. This brings to our mind Marc Chagall's surreal painting, *Time is a river without banks*.

This fluidity runs through the imagery of *The Cat and Shakespeare*. The wall, so solid and tangible *(tile-covered, burging, obstreperous)* is at the same time so elusive *(will-o'-the wisp)*. It is so concrete in its blunt and shabby three-dimensional existence, at the same time an abstract, "going from nowhere to nowhere," "like the sound heard and not the word understood." Here the sensory and the spiritual, the abstract and the concrete are woven into each other whereas in the *The Serpent and the Rope* the same opposites are so violently yoked together that these are juxtaposed and the difference predominates. Indeed, it is the imagery of *The Cat and Shakespeare* that records a synthesis of different modes of language—literary and metaphysical, in an *écriture unique* which is the hallmark of surreal writing. The central image, suggested again and again, is a comparison between Govindan Nair and the cat. His preaching of the philosophy of Cat is very concretely embodied in his being almost a sort of feline figure, so that Pai in his subordination to him is a kind of kitten being carried by the mother cat. Nair is "round and tall," he continually "leaps across the wall" or "jumps across the wall," he would "open his paw" to bring out some betel leaf and tobacco. The way he massages his limbs and plays with toe-nails does indeed remind one of a cat's toilette. Above all he "*meowmews* the dictionary" as he declares: "All my language can be reduced to that—meow, meow, meowoow." Anyone acquainted with surreal aesthetics and aware of the recurrent motif of the cat in surreal art (e.g. Leonora Carrington's *les chats*) is particularly reminded of that half-cat half-human figure of Victor Brauner's *Woman into Cat* which is at the same time so elusive and real.

It is because Nair is the mover of action as we have seen in our study of the structure, so the lion's share is given to Nair in imagery too. Since he is admittedly Pai's guru ("Govindan Nair is my guide"), the sacred tree "spreads like a holy umbrella above him," the sea being the manifestation of God's creative power, Nair is the "mighty pirate" who looks "indeed as if he had ploughed the seas." The single luxuriant piece exploiting symbolist devices—a residue of *The Serpent and the Rope*'s symbolist imagery—compares the devious intricacies of Govindan Nair's thought to an elaborate jungle scene. It is Nair's constant jokes about the Absolute that make the surreal fusion of the sublime and the ludicrous so natural in images like "God is a ledgerkeeper" interested not in the morality of profit and loss, but in Truth—"in the correct maintenance of the accounts." Death is the "clock tower of the Secretariat, it chimes time," "like the office peon carrying a slip from some visitor to the boss, destiny brings the British bubo to Pai." In all these instances the emphasis is on the ordinary, the mundane, without that elaborate literary effectiveness as the aim which dominates the previous works of Rao. Yet transcendence lurks through the chinks of banality.

It is true that in the realistic patches, presenting "a tale of modern India," there are colloquial bits, samples of "Indian" English, occasionally obvious rhetoric-like archaisms which have been noted by critics and do link the language with the style of Rao's previous work. But the point that needs emphasis is that all these traditional stylistic devices that Rao exploited to its farthest limits in previous works appear here not as foregrounded aesthetic devices but as background, and the unusually simple constructions, prevalence of common monosyllabic words, imagery from familiar fields constitute the foregrounding. In other words, in *The Cat and Shakespeare*, compared to Rao's previous works, the role of background and foreground registers a complete reversal.

Besides, another marked difference from the earlier works lies in an almost rigorous subordination of the rhetoric to the structural function of symbolism so that the differences between the traditional and the subjective are carefully maintained. Thus the connection between Nair and the Cat is supported by faith whereas the relationships between death and clock, life and ration-shop, ledger-keeper and God draw from the immediate context of social and contemporary reality. In the fusion of the real and the ideal, the mundane and the sublime, the linguistic structure of *The Cat and Shakespeare* presents the very essence of an allegorical mode which in literary tradition is both symbolic and mimetic.[55]

NOTES

1. Shiva Niranjan, "An Interview with Raja Rao," *Indian Writing in English*, ed. K.N. Sinha, p. 22. Also "Raja Rao on America," Elizabeth Wohl, *Span*, Jan. 1973, p. 37.
2. David McCutchion, however, realizes the "paradox" of a "brahminical novel." *Indian Writing in English*, p. 31.
3. W.J. Harvey, *Character and the Novel*, 1966, pp. 24-26 for details.
4. Jurij Tynjanov, "On Literary Evolution," 1927, *Readings in Russian Poetics*, p. 70.
5. Kerala, perhaps unique in the Hindu communities of India, had till recently a partially matrilinear society where the non-brahman nayar women could keep brahman lovers. The children born out of such unions belong to the nayar community of their mother.

   The traditional Hindu patriarchal society elsewhere in India enjoins that to satisfy the ancestors—one of the primary duties of a Hindu male—one has to produce a son by his wife joined to him by *dharma*, sastric sanction. A "polluted" progeny born out of a mixed marriage cannot offer rice-ball and water to the famished ancestors and leads the family to hell, e.g. *Bhagavad Gita*, I: 41-43.

6. Northrop Frye, *Anatomy of Criticism*, p. 43
7. Deriving from Christianity, garden is the traditional place for redemption in Western literature (e.g. St. John, 19:41). Cf. Mikhail Bulgakov, *Master and Margarita,* 1938, 1967, 1974. He presents a series of calamities unleashed by the Devil and his companions including a Cat in Moscow which ends in Margarita's compassion for the condemned and the Master's granting freedom to Pontius Pilate in the Biblical garden. In the Hindu tradition, on the other hand , the redemptive association rests on the river Ganga, the purifier of all sins (*patitapavani*).
8. For details on rose as the apocalyptic flower in Christianity and its use as a redemptive symbol associated with garden in Western literature, see Northrop Frye, *Anatomy of Criticism,* p. 144. Also, Harry Levin; *Symbolism and Fiction*, 1956, p. 14. Rao's acceptance of this very important and essentially Western symbol is fully substantiated in his story *The Policeman and the Rose*, 1978. A major part of the story describes: "The Rose of Travancore is the story of a pilgrimage." In the Indian tradition, however, the apocalyptic flower is lotus.
9. For example Haripada Chakravarty amply proves the essential requirement of the Indian systems of religion to be ascetic discipline or effort, *Asceticism in Ancient India: In Brahmanical, Buddhist, Jaina and Ajivika Societies*, 1973. He maintains: "The West stresses on God's grace and not on monk-life for liberation, whereas the East insists in individual efforts of a monk for the grace of God which ushers in liberation." Introduction, p. xxxviii.
10. The concept of gratuitous Grace is fundamental to Christianity as Sabapathy Kulandran makes it clear. He also quotes St. Augustine: "Grace is something received from God. It is a favour of God." *Grace: A Comparative Study of the Doctrine in Christianity and Hinduism,* 1964, pp. 27-28.
11. Raja Rao, Interview with Annie Brierre, *Illustrated Weekly of India*, French original, "Le serpent et la metaphysique," *Nouvelles Littéraires*, 28 fevrier, 1963.
12. Simone Weil, *La pesanteur et la grace*, 1948, p. 5.
13. From the point of view of philosophy one may feel acutely uncomfortable here. Christianity is a moral religion because it accepts individual's existence and hence "Love thy neigh-

bour" forms the base of Christian humanism for it recognizes plurality as valid. The idea of Self (*Atman*) as the only Reality forms the essence of monist thought and is fundamentally opposed to the Christian pluralism in so far as it is expressed in the concept of the "neighbour."

14. Raja Rao, "Trivandrum," *The Illustrated Weekly of India*, Feb. 25, 1962, p. 12. Also, *The Serpent and the Rope*, pp. 404-6.
15. As Mircea Eliade presents, "It is because Cosmic Tree symbolizes the mystery of a world in perpetual regeneration that it can symbolize—simultaneously or successively—the pillar of the universe and the cradle of humankind, the cosmic renovation and the lunar rhythms, the centre of the world and the path by which man goes from Earth to Heaven etc." *The Two and the One*, 1962, p. 198.
16. It is because Christianity accepts man's existence on earth as real, it is predominantly a religion of ethics, concerned with man's actions here and now. According to Rao, India, which he equates with non-dualism, a branch of monist thought, is beyond questions of morality. Hence the opposition between Christian Madeleine and Hindu Ramaswamy is basically this: "We Europeans believe in being good."/ "We Indians in being wise." (*The Serpent and the Rope*, p. 338) And "Truth is the only substance India can offer and that Truth is metaphysical and not moral." (p. 350)
17. Frye, *Anatomy of Criticism*, p. 203. "Its most common settings are the mountain-top, the island, the tower, the light house, and the ladder or staircase." The ladder or staircase, according to Mircea Eliade, "gives plastic expression to the break through the planes necessitated by the passage from one mode of being to another." *Images and Symbols: Studies in Religious Symbolism*, 1952, 1961, p. 50.
18. On Thomas Acquinas's adaptation of the modified Platonism of Aristotle, see Maurice de Wulf, *History of Medieval Philosophy*, 1926, Vol. II, p. 11.
19. Sankara, *Sri Dakshinamurty Stotra*, 1:5.
20. This revelation of the Absolute as the unity of form however clashes with the Upanisadic presentation of the Absolute as traditionally formless and attributeless (*nirakara* and *nirguna*), the only fitting description being "not this, not this"

(*neti, neti*). On the other hand, the Absolute when revealed as personal God or *Isvara* manifests thus in the *Bhagavadgita*: "Behold O Son of Partha, by hundreds and thousands, my different forms celestial, of various colours and shapes." XI: 11:5. In other words the vision of Ramkrishna Pai fits in neither the concept of formless Absolute nor the view of *Isvara* with infinite forms—the two major Hindu attitudes.

21. Eliade, *The Two and the One*, p. 205.
22. Ramanuja's modification of non-dualism is based on a rejection of Sankara's concept of *maya*, the world as dream. As Thibaut comments, analyzing the two commentaries on Vedanta Sutra by Sankara and Ramanuja, that the word *maya* seldom appears in Upanisads and he accepts Ramanuja's criticism of *maya*. George Thibaut, Intr., *The Vedanta Sutra, The Sacred Books of the East, ed.* Max Mueller, Oxford, 1890, vol. xxxiv, pp. cxvii-cxx. Also, P.N. Srinivasachari, *The Philosophy of Visistadvaita*, 1943, pp. 52-59, 257-58, 225-27.
23. Indeed R.G. Bhandarkar is explicit on the impact of Christianity on this particular Hindu branch of thought. *Collected Works of R.G. Bhandarkar*, ed. N.B. Utgikar, 1929, Vol. 4, *Vaishnavism and Shaivism* , pp. 80-81.
24. Cf. Northrop Frye's presentation of the Christian design:

    divine world = society of gods = One God
    human world = society of men = One Man

    animal world = sheep fold = One Lamb
    vegetable world = garden or park = One Tree
    mineral world = City = One Building, Temple, stone.
    Anatomy of Criticism, p. 141.

    This pattern is embedded in *The Cat and Shakespeare* which only substitutes God by guru and Lamb by cat.
25. Raja Rao, "Books which have Influenced me," *The Illustrated Weekly of India*, Feb. 10, 1963.
26. Raja Rao's letter to M.K. Naik quoted in "The Kingdom of God is within a 'mew'," p. 143. "Shakespeare is, as it seems to me, someone who has gone beyond duality, and as such he is a universal symbol."
27. Cf. Raja Rao, "In Trivandrum you always live at two levels."

"Trivandrum," *The Illustrated Weekly of India,* Feb. 25, 1962, p 12.

28. For this feature of the New Fiction see Philip Stevick, "Scherezade runs out of plots, goes on talking, the King puzzled listens an essay on New Fiction," *Triquarterly,* 1973. Rpt. *The Novel To-Day,* ed. Malcolm Bradbury, pp. 200-13.
29. The same uncertainty is often the impression left by a nouveau roman like Alain Robbe-Grillet's *Le Voyeur* which led John Weightman to conclude: "It is impossible to be sure what "really" happens and what is imaginary," "Alain Robbe-Grillet," *The Novelist as Philosopher: Studies in French Fiction,* 1935-60, p. 243.
30. Raja Rao's abrogation of causality with the help of intelligent play of thought is neither abstruse nor peculiarly Indian. For the role of intelligence and humour in surreal poetics, see J.H. Matthews, *Towards the Poetics of Surrealism* 1976, p. 91. S.C. Harrex correctly notes: "The comedy (in *The Cat and Shakespeare*) is often the result of a dream-like surrealistic chain of associations." "Raja Rao: Companion of Pilgrimage," *The Fire and the Offering: The English Language Novel of India,* 1935-70, Vol 2, 1978, p. 196.
31. E.g. Meenakshi Mukherjee, "Raja Rao's Shorter Fiction," *Indian Literature,* 1967, X, 3, p. 74 and. Naik, "The Kingdom of God etc." and C.D. Narasimhaiah, *Raja Rao*, pp. 132-66.
32. For the typical surreal function of "distanciation," see Matthews, *Towards the Poetic of Surrealism,* p. 92.
33. André Breton, "Le moi se refuse a se laisser entamer, a se laisser imposer la souffrance par les réalities extérieures, il se refuse a admettre que les traumatismes du monde extérieur puissent le toucher," Preface, Anthologie de l'humour noir, 1939, 1950, p. 14.
34. Matthews, *Towards the Poetics of Surrealism,* p. 93.
35. Breton, "L'humour a non-seulment quelque chose de libérateur, analogue en cela a l'ésprit et au comique, mais encore quelque chose de sublime et d'élevé." Preface, *Anthologie de l'humour noir*, p. 14.
36. This combination of humour and spirituality instead of being grounded in Indian aesthetics in which it may not have any precedent, is actually the characteristic stamp of surrealism. As Ihab Hassan observes, "an orphic, an erotic and comic

vision" often converge in surreal writing. *The Dismemberment of Orpheus: Toward a Post-Modern Literature,* p. 73.

37. "The marvelous is always beautiful, anything marvelous is beautiful, in fact only the marvelous is beautiful." *Ibid,* p. 14. So Malcolm Bradbury recognizes the "surreal and fabulous dimension" of the new fiction, *The Novel To-Day,* Introduction, p. 10.
38. This is a part of post-modernist aesthetics in which surrealism has played a prominent role. J.H. Matthews observes that a surrealist "will orient his novel away from established form" and in the process "will reject many of the techniques the conventional novelists have brought as nearly as possible to perfection or, inverting them, he will turn them to ridicule." *Surrealism and the Novel,* 1969, p. 4.
39. Iris Murdoch, "Against Dryness," *Encounter,* Jan.1961, Rpt. *The Novel Today,* p. 27.
40. Shantha's creative power is a reflection of God's creation, she is not the universal, creative matrix of Tantra. Raja Rao follows here the Southern School of modified non-dualism, a deviation from the original theistic insistence of Ramanuja on the consort as having equal ontological status with God.
41. For surreal characters, see Matthews, *Surrealism and the Novel,* p. 20.
42. André Breton, "What is Surrealism?," trans. David Gascogne.Rpt. *What is Surrealism. Selected Writings,* ed. Franklin Rosemont, 1978, p. 135.
43. The novel, as Dorothy Van Ghent points out, proceeds by hypothesis. It says implicitly, "given such and such conditions, then such and such would take place." *The English Novel: Form and Function,* p. 3.
44. "The common property to all nouveaux romans is that they embody the creative activity of the novelist—they display the novelist at work." John Sturrock, *The French New Novel,* 1969, p. 4. Stevick points out the tendency of the new fiction "to allow the compositional act of a self-conscious prominence" and "to represent, explicitly or implicitly, the act of writing as an act of play." "Scherezade runs. . . ," *The Novel Today,* pp. 215-16.
45. Since for Rao the world is both a dream and a reality, at different ontological levels, to present an experience of this

world faithfully will have to combine somehow oppositions. Hence the obvious relevance of the surreal aesthetics. "I believe in the future resolution of these two states, dream and reality, which are seemingly so contradictory, into a kind of absolute reality, a surreality." André Breton, *Manifestoes of Surrealism*, p. 14.

46. Viktor Shklovsky, "The connection between devices of *syuzet* construction and general stylistic devices," 1919, trans. Jane Knox, *Russian Formalism*, Stephen Bann and John E.Bowlt, ed., 1973, p. 53.
47. Eric Auerbach, *Mimesis: The Representation of Reality in Western Literature*, p. 322.
48. Roland Barthes, *Writing Degree Zero*, 1953, 1967, 1970, p. 73.
49. This distinct characteristic of surreal writing is discussed in detail by Anna Balakien, *Surrealism: The Road to Absolute*, 1959, 1972, p. 164.
50. André Breton, *Manifestoes of Surrealism*, p. 26.
51. Since the very theme of the novel is the human situation seen as a symbol of transcendence, this construct may be considered a "syntactic imagery" which M.A.K. Halliday defines as "the foregrounding of certain patterns in syntax as the expression of an underlying theme." "Linguistic Function and Literary Style," *Literary Style*, ed. S. Chatman, p. 347.
52. Roland Barthes, *Writing Degree Zero*, pp. 36-39.
53. In surreal writing, as Anna Balakien points out, "The tense most often used is the present." *The Road to Absolute*, p. 164.
54. J. Sturrock, *The French New Novel*, p. 34.
55. For details on the allegorical mode as combination of the representational and the illustrative, see Robert Scholes and Robert Kellogg, *The Nature of Narrative*, pp. 108-9.

Comrade Kirillov

1. *A conclusion that is not*

From a detailed analysis of narrative and language, it is clear that in *The Cat and Shakespeare*, Raja Rao concludes his quest as a philosoper-novelist, having at last evolved an individual and distinctive correlative in an allegorical form which mixes representation and illustration within a surreal aesthetics. But for the reader, the experience of *The Cat and Shakespeare* may present a few disconcerting aspects because the rigorous symmetry of the structure itself will appear somewhat of a suspect. Its hermetically sealed neatness is open to the criticism of a gathering obsession with technique which leads to subordination of theme to language. One is of course free to follow a strict structuralist like Roland Barthes who has declared that content is non-existent because "subject is a level in the hierarchy of interpretation," the text being "an onion, a construction of layers, whose body contains, finally no heart, no kernel, no secret, no irreducible principle, nothing except the infinity of its own surfaces.[1] Regarded as such an "onion"—a construct of layers—Rao's novel may satisfy a structuralist, especially in the dominance accorded to language. But in Rao's evolution this predominance of language raises, as I have already mentioned, a peculiar paradox because, according to Roman Jakobson, the widely acknowledged guru of structuralism in literary criticism, it is "in the Realist aesthetics that the verbal art assumes dominance"[2] and it is precisely against this very aesthetics, equating it with Western/alien tradition, that Rao's "Indian" identity has waged a lifelong crusade. As a consequence, he is forced to give up linguistic experimentation and gradually confine himself more and more to the limited sphere of syntactic variation which in any case offers an artist much less freedom than imagery and even lexis. So the language that evolves is transparent in simplicity but at the same time possesses the concentrated layers of thought in a crystal as evident in a passage like this:

> Birth is instantaneous with time. Who is born where? Time is born in time. And that is Shantha. To be a wife is not to be wed. To be a wife is to worship your man. Then you are born. And you give birth to what is born in being born. You annihilate time and you become a wife. Wifehood, of all states in the world, seems the most holy. It stops work. It creates. It lives on even when time dies. Suppose you broke the clock, would the garden go? Suppose the garden were burned, where will the sky go? Such is woman.

It is not exactly impossible to understand the passage referring to the opposition between Time and Eternity that underlies Rao's intellectual view, to his concept of man-woman relationship, of marriage, the traditional symbolism of the garden, his personal symbol of the clock and so on. The abrupt transitions from one sentence to another can be explained as a particular stylistic feature, a continuation of the non-logical paragraph construction of *The Serpent and the Rope*, and close to the idiom of modern poetry. We may also, if we like, appreciate the neutrality of the carefully evolved simple style dominated by monosyllables. But the problem is unless we are unusually conscious of these features all the time, we may find the language too lightweight to convey what it intends to convey, because it is loaded beyond its potential and tends to turn on itself desperately in a permanent pattern of involutes. Even if one may not expect a one-to-one correspondence, one may not be prepared to accept an allegory rooted in subjectivity alone. Consider for example, Rao's individual, highly unconventional use of the Cat symbol from a school of modified non-dualism which accepts a personal god, hence the hunter is blessed with the vision of Lord Shiva himself. But in the vision of Rao's hero there is no God; because here Rao's rigid non-dualism which denies a personal god takes over. So Pai's godless epiphany remains suspended in the void of a personal mystique. He does not appear to have realized the non-difference between the individual and the Absolute Consciousness in an unequivocal declaration that one expects from a

Vedantin for whom the reality is." "I am Brahman." On the other hand though Pai is led to salvation by his faith, never do we get that absolute gesture of surrender to the will of a divine father, which springs from the belief that "We are of God" and "God is love" (I John 4:6,8). If the fundamental core of difference between the impersonal, metaphysical "India" and the ethical, poetic West of Christ which Rao himself so vehemently brought out as opposite poles in *The Serpent and the Rope*, gives in to an ordered hierarchy in *The Cat and Shakespeare,* the structure is based almost entirely on an individual apprehension of Truth. Such an obsession with the subjective may utterly confuse a reader who may be acquainted with the Indian tradition of philosophy as well as with the Christian background of Western literature. He is condemned to a prison of language where time *must* be illusory, death *must* be unreal, the world *is* at one moment and *is not* at the next depending completely on the author's own level of interpretation. Even if the grand finale is "I remain over, having killed myself," the paradox is meaningful if only one understands the "I" as the Brahman, the "impersonal," not as the personal pronoun of the English language. The whole manoeuvre aimed at the destruction of the materialist view of the world purported to be Western, turns on itself and ultimately establishes the supremacy of the external form. One wonders if we do not find here an example of "the symbolic annulment of language by producing aberrant meanings," which is, according to Sartre, the tragedy of surreal aesthetics and leads to "the realization of nothingness by too much fullness of being."[3] In *The Serpent and the Rope* the language provokes reactions favourable and unfavourable. But the danger of the style in *The Cat and Shakespeare* is that it may not evoke any response at all because it tends to relinquish the function of language by a constant dislocation of relationship between the signifier and the signified. What is missing here is the deep involvement of language in a human context which marks the previous novels. Contrast the uniform, smooth and slippery exterior of *The Cat and Shakespeare* with the jagged ups and downs of *The Serpent and the Rope:*

> I composed several letters to Savithri. What could I tell her? "To him," says the Upanishads, "who is earnest, to the Atman comes the Atman. It was not land and rivers that separated us. It was Time itself. It was myself. When the

> becoming stopped I would wed Savithri. If the becoming stopped would there be a wedding? Where would the pandal be, where uncle Seetharamu and the elephant?

The metaphysics that underlies this passage is not fundamentally different from the conceptual base of the passage quoted from *The Cat and Shakespeare*—the relation between Time/Existence and Eternity/*Atman*. But the language here, as distinguished from the other, is rooted deeply in the human context, in the choice before Ramaswamy, whether he should accept the offer of Savithri. One may even point out that the realistic background of Saroja's wedding with the details of the setting up of a festive pandal and the invariable presence of uncle Seetharamu, the busybody that every ceremony needs, supplies the content of meaning—the dichotomy between Being and Becoming, the human longing for timelessness and the equally human bondage to time. Hence the shortest sentence by its length, so it seems, may convey the deepest anguish ("It was myself"). Even the elephant, reminiscent of the erotic frenzy described in detail earlier in the novel seems near to the human condition. The world of *The Cat and Shakespeare* appears almost totally dehumanized in comparison. If the dichotomy is attempted to be solved, the harmony that has emerged appears as unearthly as the bright, uniformly-lit surface of the moon, so distant from the various shades that envelop the human experience and constitute the mystery that is man. The humour of Govindan Nair sounds desperate as he runs a commentary on the Vedanta to accompany Pai's scatological event even as Alfred Jarry's Dr. Faustroll babbles on God which his donkey Bosse-de-Nage interrupts by excremental function.[4] If the sublime and the vulgar are fused here, the fusion is carried with a reductive rage.

This rage is directed at the very complexity of human relationships which is constantly sought to be negated. The three major characters, Pai, Govindan Nair and Shantha, are held together not by the personal bond of love and affection that carries the whole creation, but by a disinterested attachment which may appear paradoxical. The discontinuity from experience is indicated in the very structure of their mutual relationship—in the insistence on an unalloyed sweetness that is rather cloying. There is nothing, absolutely nothing, to jar the perfect worship of Pai by Shantha or the perfect guidance of Pai by Nair. The whole complexity of the human condition that must find a place for death, for misery, for human shortcomings, is totally evaded as in the example of Shantha's perfect motherhood:

> Usha is a grown up child, and she loves her mother, who is Shantha, for Shantha is kind, and will not talk of the Dutch. She who does not talk of the Dutch is Mother. So Mother is Shantha.

If Usha's own mother Saroja has used the bogey of the Dutch invaders to throw an occasional scare to her children, she joins a host of mothers of all ages and lands in her supposed contrariness. That motherhood is only affection and nothing but sweetness is an abstract concept which denies the whole experience of a mother. One cannot resist the suspicion that in this insistence on the perfection of the abstract form of motherhood devoid of the content of actual imperfection, we find the symptom of the author's inability to face the reality. His whole presentation of humanity as a form of the universal might bear as a motto a structural precept like this, "To reach reality one has first to reject experience."[5] This denial or evasion of human experience lies at the base of Rao's mechanistic conception of causality which is satirized in the whole novel. The example that Nair the guru offers to prove the assumed absurdity of causal relation is indicative of a fundamental disjunction:

> You wear a Gandhi cap—a two-anna piece of one-foot cloth that any man can put on his pate, and not even what his irreverent bladder empties could be held in the cap's depth, such its size—yet you could get arrested for anti-British activity.

Wearing a Gandhi cap results in persecution by the British Government not for any physical quality of the cap or the quantitative value of its material which Nair emphasizes, but because of its significance in the context of reality which lies in its habitual use by those engaged in the movement of Indian Independence. When Rao satirizes the cause and effect relationship in terms of the Gandhi cap as the cause and imprisonment as the result, he treats the Gandhi cap as mere physical form bereft of human content. The cap is a sign, with a semiotic function which is its theme that is totally denied by the author.[6] The whole attempt to break through the positivist conception of a stable reality therefore defeats itself and presents the external universe alone as the human condition. Life is defined ultimately in terms of a building construction or of the body of a woman, for, it is an existence where the only problem is the evacuating habits of a child.

The metamorphosis of appearance and reality sustains a non-human perfection of form as harmony. One worders if the price that Rao pays to arrive at a synthetic form as the resolution of a crisis of identity does not prove to be exorbitant. If literature has any insight into life or any relation to human import, it can hardly afford to be content with the vanishing shadow of man. C.D. Narasimaiah claims that Raja Rao has found in *The Cat and Shakespeare* "the most adequate concrete equivalent of a profound vision of life, which has its validity not only for the contemporary Indian situation, but for our entire fragmentary civilization."[7] The vision is more a dream than a realization for it arises not out of life, but of an autistic consciousness which is imperial in its isolation from humanity. As Rao himself declares: "I can say that all I write is for myself."[8] The corresponding language strives in the elaborate art of selfdestruction and questions the very function of language itself. Its validity for the "fragmentary civilization" lies in its ultimate emphasis on the depth of the fissures, in its total dissociation from human suffering. One suspects that the form itself has become a temptation and turns the literary work into a crystalline symbol, dazzling in the brightness of perfect execution, but so dry and so hard—the last refuge of the romantic escape into a dream which offers the only consolation from the unbearable contingency so real in *The Serpent and the Rope*.

2. *Ambiguity: the axis of an anti-novel*

Since Raja Rao, according to his own admission as well as our analysis, arrives at the end of his journey as philosopher-novelist in *The Cat and Shakespeare*, a book on Rao's quest for form too should reach here its normal conclusion. But Rao seems to have arrived at a point where the seeming contradictions cease to be opposed only by denying the whole human experience. Such a summit of self-transcendence may at the same time indicate the precipice of autodestruction. In fact, the whole avant-gardist movement strives to some kind of self-annihilation. "Suicide, symbolic or actual," says Ihab Hassan, "becomes the consummation of the avant-garde."[9] Therefore Raja Rao's next work, successor to the avant-gardist *The Cat and Shakespeare*, may present a kind of dramatic finality in its very title—*Comrade Kirillov* (1976), since in Dostoevsky's original, the Western literary tradition has found the very embodiment of self-annihilation as a metaphysical problem.

Raja Rao's *Comrade Kirillov*, to begin with, is an annihilation as a narrative insofar as it presents a non-plot in its flat succession of events without a perceptible rise into climax to be followed by purgation in emotional release. It may better be seen as a structure in which different segments are organized as parallels to the same thematic axis. In spatial terms this could mean the form of a prism, but in a verbal construct, the different units are to be unfolded, not simultaneously but in succession. So, unlike Rao's other novels which emphasize a continuous flow *Comrade Kirillov* is perceptibly marked into different blocks, separated from each other.

The first two sections are exact parallels, each narrates the biography of Padmanabha Iyer, a South Indian brahman (like Rao and all his heroes) in the third person. The narrator is one Rama ("a Gandhian and a Vedantin and an Indian" like Rao). In each, the narration leads to a focus on an ideological crisis presented as a dialogue between Padmanabha called Kirillov and Rama. First, we learn about Padmanabha's noble birth, Westernized education, disgust with modern India as well as with Hindu orthodoxy, a temporary frustrating experience with theosophy and his final choice of Communism. Rama meets him during the notorious purges of Stalin when he wants Padmanabha, as an Indian, to join in the protest against the Moscow trial. Padmanabha refuses and justifies the Party's stand.

In the second section we find Padmanabha's slow and painstaking growth to his emergence as a good communist standing firmly behind the Party's policy to oppose Gandhi's call for nationalist agitation in 1942 against the British. Even after the Gandhian move seems to win, Padmanabha continues to be a communist. However, we learn that his life style has always remained orthodox, South Indian and brahmanic, despite his marriage to Irene, a Czech communist who dies in childbirth leaving a son, Kamal.

The third section presents Padmanabha from a different perspective, that of his wife Irene, whose entries in diary reveal the subterranean "Indianness" of P. (Padmanabha), ensconced not only in an orthodox life style or a sentimental illogical adoration of Gandhi, but in a brahmanic knowledge of the Sanskrit philosophical grammar. This Indianness which forms the main attraction of P. to Irene, spells however the doom of the marriage, remaining a permanent incomprehensible element. Her death in childbirth seems inevitable following the entry, "I shall never go to India." In the last section, Padmanabha has disappeared behind the impenetrable communist curtains, first iron and then bamboo. But India wins, for his son Kamal, growing up with Indian grandparents, is placed by the narrator Rama in the temple of Kanyakumari and finds India embodied in Parvati, as an eternal virgin waiting for her bridegroom Shiva.

It is evident that in this novel a linear progression of events in causal order is subordinate to a structure which emanates from a concept of India as the matrix. By calling Padmanabha Kirillov, it is made quite obvious that communism can mean only suicide for an Indian. Hence Padmanabha's pen with which he writes his communist thesis is compared to a revolver. In Dostoevsky's Kirillov we can trace a literary prototype which is used here by Rao as though for mythical prefiguration.[10] Kirillov stands as an archetype of the modern logical man of the West whose communist dialectic must end in selfannihilation.[11] The interesting point in Rao's use however is the constant reference to Shatov, the other member of Dostoevsky's famous "double". One may suppose that Padmanabha in his innate love for India and a certain kind of orthodox externalism (like the mechanical repetition of Sanskrit slokas, vegetarianism etc.) approximates Shatov's fervent love of Russia and orthodoxy. Being both Kirillov and Shatov, the communist atheist and the nationalist orthodox, Padmanabha remains a soul for ever held between the cleft of "India" and Marx—a symbol of perpetual crisis.[12]

The problem in *Comrade Kirillov* does not reside in Rao's presentation of the Indian communists which may appear justified to a Gandhian, malicious to a communist and inadequate to a student of history.[13] Admittedly, Rao is being no more objective to the Indian communists than Dostoevsky is toward his contemporary radicals in *The Possessed*. In fact, the question of impartiality to the opponent is simply irrelevant in a study of Raja Rao. Our main concern is with the concept of India for a number of reasons. Critics, bóth Indian and Western, not only recognize that Rao has such a definite concept of his own but also regard it—at least some of them—as a vital factor in a favourable aesthetic evaluation of his work. Rao himself regards the realization of "Indianness" as the focal point of all his creative effort. Since this concept happens to be, as we have seen, the thematic axis in *Comrade Kirillov*, we cannot proceed without first analyzing it, carrying threads from all his previous works.

It is imperative to realize first of all that Rao's concept of India has some remarkable resemblance with Dostoevsky's idea of Russia, which is to be emphasized since in the mainstream of the Indian literary tradition of the past, such a concept of national identity is virtually non-existent. In Dostoevsky, Russia and orthodoxy and Christianity are conceived as a composite as absolute as the Holy Trinity. This indissoluble bond is the great theme of Dostoevsky's whole literary inspiration, revealed especially in *The Possessed.* The following conversation between Stavrogin and Shatov presents a clue to Dostoevsky's concept of Russia:

> Stavrogin: "Christianity saves the world, and it alone can save it—that's the conclusion we have come to and that's what we believe. That is one thing. Next: Christianity exists only, in Russia, in the form of orthodoxy. That's two.
>
> Shatov: (Interrupting) And so Russia will save and regenerate the world through orthodoxy.[14]

Hence the irrevocable conclusion is: "An atheist cannot love Russia, or be a Russian." So, for Dostoevsky, Russia is not a political or historical entity, but rather a question of perspective of abstraction: "Russia is not a republic, it is not Jacobinism or Communism. Russia is no more or no less than the embodiment of Orthodoxy."

It is impossible to miss a very clear echo in Rao's famous metaphysic of nationality, "India is not a country like France is, or like England; India is an idea, a metaphysic." *(The Serpent and the Rope)* Since for him, the Indian identity is inextricably bound with orthodoxy and a particular branch of Hindu philosophy namely Advaita Vedanta, one may find the trinity of India-Orthodoxy-Vedanta, as the hypostasis of Rao's whole creative effort. Besides,

Rao's India has a destiny, like Dostoevsky's Russia, to be apprehended with a missionary fervour. For his hero Ramaswamy. "India is the Guru to the world." Indeed one is left in no doubt of the author's firm conviction, "India is culture.[15]

This romantic and aggressive view, often applauded by Rao's admirers, has however another facet, usually ignored by them, in providing a so-called metaphysical justification for a socio-economic order which brahmanism has continued to uphold in this country. The Absolute Consciousness, the Ultimate Truth, attainable through obliteration or "sacrifice" of mind and senses, logically so it seems, demands as "right living," a continuous sacrifice of the individual. Rao himself states in his article *Meaning of India:*

> Since there are gradations in man, and since man makes society— through gradations of social conditions, sometimes called castes, we daily make offering in sacrifice to the One (or The-One-Without-another) to whom everything flows as the rivers go to the ocean.[16]

From an essentially brahmanic point of view, Rao justifies the traditionally rigid caste hierarchy of Hindu society, adding the gloss of a noble metaphysics, a palatable coat for a bitter pill. The political form of such a hierarchial tradition can hardly be democracy, so Rao's autobiographical projection declares himself a Royalist without compunction. The problem lies in the relation between this "India"—orthodox, brahmanic, monarchist—and the historical context of Indian nationalism. If "gradations of man" are just, then the gradation between the conqueror and the conquered should logically be deemed equally just; indeed, the humiliation and exploitation of the ruled may appear a veritable offering to Rao's Vedantic Absolute. So, in *Kanthapura,* Rao's first novel, the brahmanic orthodoxy sides with British imperialism. Gandhi's socio-political ideology, urging uprising against a king, questioning the inhuman treatment of the Untouchables as the lowest in the Hindu hierarchy, is rightly seen as a threat essentially directed towards the destruction of brahmanism. So Gandhi, cast as an *avatar* who should always be victorious, ends in the novel as the god that fails. Rao's brahmanic orthodoxy which is opposed by the Gandhian socio-political ideology, ultimately has to condone

Gandhi's assassination. "Godse, who killed Mahatma Gandhi, was like Saint Dominic." *(The Serpent and the Rope)* The comparison of an assassin with a revered name in the Catholic Church, Saint Dominic, cannot but indicate Rao's evaluation of the most tragic incident in modern Indian history. For the Roman Catholic Church, St. Dominic's stand against Albigensian and Cathar heresies is both necessary and just. As a great Catholic poet describes Dominic's role:

> Then, with both learning and zeal and with the apostolic office he went forth like a torrent driven from a high spring; and on the heretical thickets his force struck with most vigour where the resistance was stubbornest. From him there sprung the various streams by which the Catholic garden is watered, so that its saplings have new life.[17]

If for Rao, Gandhi's assassin Godse is "like St. Dominic," the assassination is but an execution performed to save the brahmanic orthodoxy which is Rao's "India."

In *Comrade Kirillov,* however, the same Gandhi, by some strange inexplicable magic, is transformed into the very embodiment of true India, "The Communist party backed Britain, and lost their 1917. Mahatma Gandhi won. He would always win, for he knew India." One of the main channels in which Padmanabha's "Indian-hood" breaks through every communist chain "is his adoration of Gandhi." As Irene writes in her diary, "he cannot bear any European, bourgeois, or even communist, speak against the Congress or Gandhi," and he is also "so truly and inescapably orthodox." The straight opposition between these two attitudes should make one feel that both these cannot possibly be valid at the same time. In one, Gandhi is almost a heretic, pure and noble no doubt (even as the Cathar) yet essentially a diseased branch to be ruthlessly cut-off by Godse-Dominic to preserve the health of main brahmanic "Indian" tree. In the other, it is Gandhi that is true "India." The obvious opposition between the two poles, both presented presumably with the same authorial sincerity, raises the inevitable question: in which may we find the true Raja Rao?

It is this fundamental ambiguity that constitutes the axis of the very structure of *Comrade Kirillov* which therefore turns out to be a problematic novel embodying in its very form the crisis of the novelist. The impasse that results from the opposition between brahmanic orthodoxy and Indian nationalism makes mimesis an impossible task for Rao. His whole attention as a novelist turns on the act of composition, of writing itself. The novel whether traditional or modernist, holds to a tacit convention of suspension of disbelief and accords a hypothetical reality to the fictional representation created by the powerful writer god.[18] So the reader consents to accept this fictive world as imitative of God's creation. In *Comrade Kirillov*, it is precisely this tacit and fundamental agreement between the reader and the writer that disappears. Since the novelist can no longer face the reality which for Rao is fraught with an unresolved problem, he can no longer imitate it even as a hypothetical reality, nor can he possibly possess that god-like omniscience into the souls of his characters which is the prerogative exercised by the traditional novelist. All he can do is to suggest other literary characters as possible prototypes—a caricature of the traditional modernist prefiguration of characters by mythical personages. In Rao's own *Kanthapura* Gandhi is an avatar like Krishna, in *The Serpent and the Rope,* numerous mythical figures—Tristan-Iseult, Krishna-Radha, Satyavan-Savitri—prefigure Ramaswamy-Savithri in the fictional reality. Even in *The Cat and Shakespeare* the author persuades the reader to accept a surreality in which Govindan Nair is a veritable mother cat. But in *Comrade Kirillov* the novelist is *not certain* if his hero Padmanabha is really like the Kirillov of Dostoevsky facing logical suicide, for he cannot possibly know what goes on inside his own hero, "a soul so ambivalent."

Only that reality which is directly observable as Padmanabha's behaviour and action, is acceptable in fiction. But his mind remains beyond authorial decisiveness and so any presentation of the inner state of Padmanabha is only speculative and merely fictive. Whereas in the traditional novel this fictiveness constitutes temporal reality, in *Comrade Kirillov* the emphasis falls on fiction *as* fiction. The novelist bares the whole process of composition in which the reader is asked to participate, he can no longer remain at the receiving end.[19] His stability in the reading experience is unsettled for he has to cease being a passive spectator transported into a provisionally solid fictional presentation because he has to come in aid of the author for whom the external reality is beyond comprehension, an absurd universe. This problematic essence is effected with the help of a unique linguistic device—protracted use of the conditional as a grammatical fiction:

> One could *almost* see our Kirillov, a pistol in his pocket, going round and round his shouting wife's (other man's) child, like Shatov, and *if* our Kirillov *were smitten* with dialectical despair, *no doubt* he too *would go* round and round his Wakefield Square flat, now to the dim kitchen, now to the empty hall, with only the big picture of Lenin on its rose-coloured paper, and rushing up to set some unfinished sentence of the translation right, he *might* stop a while, look into the dictionary for the favoured word, and with pen on his forehead remember each act of sin committed in angry solitude, and rushing to the telephone, he *might* ask his labour friend's pardon for every mistake in party prognostics, and dialling some innocent like me, *might* ask me for the final favour of a quick departure to the other world.

We may find in this paragraph, some classic linguistic signs of the author's deliberate dissociation[20] from the character's consciousness—the verbal constructs that control the meaning are all indicative of chance, of sheer contingency as though beyond authorial control—might (3 times), *could,* the construction—*if . . . were . . . would*—suggests even deeper hesitation; the qualifiers (*almost, no doubt*) emphasize interpretative effort rather than surety of factual reports.[21] In the traditional. modernist fiction, the superimposition of mythical prototypes of fictional characters is carried out in good faith according to the convention binding the reader and the novelist. But here that convention does not operate any more. The continued use of such uncertainty in verbal constructions in *Comrade Kirillov* emphasizing the alienation of the author from his creation, affects the stability of the reader's stance towards the experience of the novel. If Padmanabha *might* have been a Kirillov, *would* behave like a Shatv, it is never clear to the readers what Padmanabha now actually is in the fictional reality. This lack of stability is carried to the extreme in the *probable* end of Padmanabha *if* he embraces Buddhism:

> The Communist and the Sadhu have spiritual equivalences

> which made me often feel that *were* Kirillov *capable* of free thinking and not tied to a dogma, *would not* his sensibility *have* found radiance in the Buddhist Path of Non-Becoming, or *would not* his dialectical coldness, his razor-edge honesty, lead him, like Mayakovsky or Essenine, to an intellectual death.

One may wonder if the Buddhist yellow-robe, the alternative to a Marxist "intellectual death," is an equally disastrous end for an Indian or the very hope of redemption. The use of the word *radiance* may suggest a positive connotation which is later confirmed in the last glimpse that is left of Padmanabha—a hypothetical Buddha defeating the deadly Tempter, now embodied as Marxism. Here is Rao's Kirillov who, firm in his "Indian decision," sits in meditation to attain the ultimate, and "Mara himself appears in fearful fascination" tempting with Communist trinkets:

> "Go, go, Mara, Kirillov would say, "I know of your doings. I know the dialectic of Feurbach, and the State and the Revolution of Lenin. Marx has been suppressed by hagiography, and Lenin is in his tomb. Go, you many-mouthed, many-armed, you multiple-monster, Mara."

The novelist persuades himself desperately to believe that here at last is the lone stable point of fictional reality which is therefore conveyed in the conventional narrative past, "And there out of the burst of light Kirillov *recovered* his native Kingdom." This decisive stance is however momentary, to be immediately unsettled:

> In the Deer-park of intelligence he *set* his wheel-of-law a-turning and *wandered* over the vast and wondersome land of Hindusthan, working the Law of non-becoming. The wheel turns like a temple chariot's and Mahatma Gandhi himself *pulls* the ultimate cord.

That the redemption of Padmanabha/Kirillov is only mythical, more a wish-fulfilment than a reality is revealed in the use of the present tense which is psychologically, the tense of dream. In the deliberate archaism (*a-turning, wondersome*) the whole picture of reality is further distanced. That it is only an illusion and nothing but speculation is emphasized in the short paragraph which follows informing with sharp finality as well as the authority of the novelist conveyed in the traditional past tense, "Kirillov, indefatigable left for Moscow."

As a matter of fact, Buddha can be accepted as a part of the Indian reality only in a dream, for hasn't the orthodox brahman in *The Serpent and the Rope* so elaborately rejected Buddha? Buddha's logic and compassion open the road to liberation for *all* mankind irrespective of caste, which Rao's own rigid brahmanical hierarchy can never consent to. So both Christ and Buddha being compassionate are banished from Rao's "perfect" civilization which is Indian/orthodox/ brahmanic, called Vedantic.[22] Buddha, therefore, can never be a part of Rao's India. How can then Padmanabha the communist regain his "Indianness" through Buddhism since Buddha himself is to be cast out from the brahmanic orthodoxy equated with Indianness? Rao never answers this question. But we can attempt to explain the impasse referring to the historical context. The Indian nationalism in order to minimize the Western components which are historically valid has to place Buddha over and above brahmanic orthodoxy, for the ideals of Indian nationalists—anti-racism, democracy, non-violence etc.—cannot be traced to the brahmanic caste hierarchy or authoritarianism nor to the paramount importance placed on force and absence of humanism that characterize brahmanic political ethics.[23] It is only by emphasizing the Buddhist non-violence and the Buddhist insistence on ethics that Indian nationalism can find its distinctive identity, distinguished from the concept of Western nationalism from which it springs. If communism is to be condemned as a specifically *alien* creed, which fails to find roots in the Indian soil, its use of violence and its subordination of means to the end can be fought not with brahmanic but with Buddhist weapons alone. The communist Padmanabha can redeem himself only by putting on the Buddhist yellow-robe.

3. *A parody of the self*

For Raja Rao's orthodox brahmanic stand, there is no justification for the resuscitation of Buddha whom he has buried with open denunciation in *The Serpent and the Rope*. He has to remain silent therefore over the crucial question, the relation between his uncompromising and exclusive brahmanic orthodoxy proclaimed as a metaphysic of India and the broad Indian Nationalism which seems at least in theory to harmonize the diverse elements in the culture of this sub-continent. Nothing is more significant or more absolute than Rao's total silence over this fundamental issue at this mature stage of his life as a writer. The emphasis on a highly exaggerated opposition between the Indian nationalism of the Gandhians and the internationalism of the Indian communists, presumed to be "false" because of "alien" roots, seems inspired by an urgent need for a diversionary tactic which overrides the artist's genuine involvement in the reality of India where the static authority of the brahman is being challenged by a dynamic and modern consciousness. The tone of an incessant chatter which predominates the first two sections of the novel—often rising to a feverish peak in the long speeches of Padmanabha the communist and Rama, the Gandhian—is an indication of the desperate urge for a cover to hide the basic truth which the author is unable to face. The weight of complete silence makes the novel essentially an essay in the negative particularly because Raja Rao himself was—at one point of time—an ardent admirer of socialism, if not of Marxism. He even confided, "un fort mouvement socialiste, ou prosocialiste travaille, 'Inde nouvelle et 'emportera, un depit de 'la bigoterie' (sous-entendu du Mahatma) et de la faiblesse de Jawaharlal Nehru, qui est le plus conscient, pourtant de ce mouvement."[24] One can hardly fail to note the association of bigotry with the Mahatma. So the savage satire on the Indian communists who slavishly "toe the British" since Hitler's attack of Russia, is illumined by a ferocious glare which turns on the self in caricature. The author manipulates the speech-act of another—here that of an Indian Communist—with a deliberate intention of opposing it. Take for example the following passage:

> And by some peculiar *perfect* psychological transference his *perfect* un-Darwinian enemy was this Mahatma Gandhi, *friend and fool* of the poor, the *Sadhu reactionary* who *still believed in caste and creed* and such categories, and whose birth in this world had set history many centuries backwards. Marx had *indeed* built in his theory of revolution for the British working classes revolting against their masters, heralded by the rising in the vast dominion of the British crown

> called India—and *Mahatma Gandhi came* and upset Marx. If Marx were alive *no doubt* Mahatma Gandhi would have received, under the *truculent pen* of the *great master*, the destiny he deserved. Gandhi was *somewhat of an oriental Mazzini*, with Indian mysticism *to boot*.

The linguistic features underlined, present a curious juxtaposition of two voices. the speech ostensibly belongs to an Indian communist yet the attitude of the Gandhian opponent determines the semantics for Gandhi is ultimately declared invincible. Further Gandhi's acquiescence to caste, creed and what the author terms "Indian mysticism" are mentioned not so much because these provide the Marxists their conventional weapons for attack against Gandhi but actually because these elements express the orthodox author's own point of approval. As a contrast one may remember an eminent Marxist intellectual's evaluation of Gandhi as "one of the great social reformers of history" for the jolt he gave to untouchability and his final assessment of the Mahatma as a paradox: "Gandhi was at the same time conservative and revolutionary."[25] Rao's Marxist hero evades the fundamental question—the specific definition of the Gandhian ideal, his concept of Swaraj and Ramrajya which was raised by Moorthy at the end of *Kanthapura*. So Rao's deliberate distortion of the Marxist attitude leads to facetious features in style—repetition (*perfect*), alliteration (*friend and fool*), use of unnecessary qualifiers (*indeed, no doubt great, truculent, somewhat)*, facile juxtaposition (*and Gandhi came* with *and upset Marx* as though a causal relation between the two is naturally established)—and enhance the polemical shading of the discourse. Its characteristic mark however lies in the *concealed* nature of the polemics. Through Padmanabha, Rao apparently represents the typical communist viewpoint with which he himself once sympathized, but at the same time as an orthodox brahman—which he later became—he reacts to it and this reaction seeks to determine the tone of the text. "The second voice," as Mikhail Bakhtin analyzes parody, "having lodged in another speech, clashes antagonistically with the original host voice and forces it to serve directly opposite aims.[26] In *Comrade Kirillov*, both the voices having belonged to the different selves of the author, offer constant self-parody.

The victory of Gandhi in achieving Indian independence over

the Communist prognosis of proletariat revolution, may be seen as a crushing reply to Rao's own hero Moorthy who left Gandhi for socialism. Padmanabha's Marxist stand itself is a devastating parody of Gandhi's own words to Moorthy, those very words which led Moorthy to break from the brahmanic shackles:

> There is but one force in life and that is Truth, and there is but one love in life and that is the love of mankind, and there is but one God in life and that is the God of all.

Compare Padmanabha's declaration:

> I know only one God, and that is the common man, I know only one worship and that is the Party meeting. I know only one morality, and that is a classless society.

In Padmanabha's defence of Stalin's notorious purges, there is a violent attack on the Marxist dialectic of history. What is more important from the literary point of view is the deliberate parody of Rao's own serious fictional presentation in defence of the same Stalin and the same purges in *The Serpent and the Rope* not once or casually, but again and again with full involvement. Ramaswamy elaborates the "Indian" justification of Stalin's blood-thirst:

> The King can do no wrong: comes from the idea that *the principle can do no wrong* just as the communists say: "The party can do no wrong." Talking of the communists the other day in Cambridge, I forgot to say that communism must succeed; happily for us, to be followed by Kingship. Look at the difference between Hitler and Stalin. Stalin, the man of iron, the mystery behind the Kremlin, *the impersonal being, to whom torture, growth or death are essentials of an abstract arithmetic.* As the Catholics looked for omens in the Bible, Stalin looked to *impersonal history* for guidance.

Since Rao, like his hero Ramaswamy supports the Roman Catholic Church, he admires Stalin as the embodiment of orthodoxy, "the new Catholicism"and so Trotsky is a heretic, "anther Cathar"[27] It is natural that "Stalin who is history, had to kill Trotsky, the anti-history. The pure, the human, the vainglorious leader's personal magic was an unholy impediment to the movement of history." The emphasis on negatives (*anti-history, vainglorious, unholy*), indicates the tonal evaluation—condemnation of Trotsky—from presumably an "Indian" standpoint. In *Comrade Kirillov.* it is precisely in the same view—the same condemnation of Trotsky as an impediment to the historical process—that Padmanabha seems to annihilate this "Indianness":

> Trotsky is a traitor, I say. A traitor for me is not my moral enemy, but my historical opponent. I know simpletons write that Trotsky has sold out to the capitalists. I know, as far as I can, that Trotsky is not the one to be bribed by capitalists into their golden dens. Trotsky, like Zinoviev and Kameniev, was an instrument in a great historical process. For that matter, so is Stalin. If Stalin went against history, history would not spare him because he is Stalin. History is the respector of no individual. . . .I am a communist because I understand history.

Thus Padmanabha as Kirillov repeats all the arguments of Ramaswamy, Rao's frank autobiographical projection and stands condemned for his alienation from "Indianness." The sharp difference in tone, from authorial approbation in the first to denunciation in the second is conveyed through language and language alone since the theme remains the same. The tone here reveals how the concept of Indianness has simply jumped to the opposite pole. The narrator Rama asks for Padmanabha's signature to a demand for fair trial of Stalin's victims on the following "Indian" ground:

> The cause is good. You know politics is something I do not fully understand. Human suffering, life, birth, death, sickness, marriage and love, God, I understand. I hate violence of all sorts especially political violence.

The position here is conveyed imperceptibly but decisively with the use of the word *good, understand*, indicative of positive values. Violence, which is deemed impersonal and essential in the first, is considered evil, a moral judgement which forms the basis of "hate," for, India that is impersonal in *The Serpent and the Rope* becomes personal and moral in *Comrade Kirillov*. It resides in a due recognition of *human suffering* and *God* both of which were particularly rejected earlier. For Rao, as for his hero Ramaswamy the uncompromising Vedantin, the world being a *maya* neither suffering nor God can exist. Hence the "Indian" quest seems to arrive at the Truth and not at faith in God, as Ramaswamy clearly states "Do I long for God? God is an object and I cannot long for Him." The novel has ended, not in the resignation to faith in God, but in a refuge at the feet of a preceptor of Truth. Even in the epiphany of his humble successor Ramkrishna Pai, the hero of *The Cat and Shakespeare*, there is no God.

Yet in *Comrade Kirillov*, the full volley of "Indian" attack is directed at the absence of God in Communism. As Padmanabha in his destructive "spider web," "prison-cell" logic expounds, "Metaphysical enquiry, I now say, is due to rachitism—it is like a disease caused by vitamin deficiency. God is the fiction of the lazy." The cynicism is conveyed through the violent grouping of utter dissimilarities, especially mundane and spiritual, by words of negative connotation—*disease, deficiency, fiction* (in the sense of mere untruth) and *lazy*. For the communist, as it suggests, God is negation. For the Indian on the other hand it is Communism that is annihilation. The narrator puts it thus:

> And once you have fed the Indian millions and given them nice houses *to live in,* and railways *for their monthly holidays,* and sanatoria *for their sick*, and maternity care *for their mothers*, and the Dniperstock *for the electric illumination of India*—what then, brother, is to become of your despair, your emotional upheavals, your metaphysical yearning, your God-ward beckonings?

That the communist hope of future India is only a dream, as distant from reality as a myth, is indicated especially by an absurd rhythmic regularity, a parody of Rao's own fabular presentation of India, created by Brahma in *Kanthapura:*

> You gave her the sage-loved Himalayas *on the north* and the seven surging seas *to the south.* and you gave her the Ganges *to meditate* on the Godavery, *to live by*, and the pure Cauvery *to drink in.*

If the material comfort promised by the communists seems a poor and shabby substitute for the rich, poetic and mystic Hindu heritage, it is because of the linguistic parody that is evident in this comparison. Besides the very elaboration of material comfort leads ultimately to negation—*despair, emotional upheaval*, for *God* is forgotten.

Such persistent and unabashed self-contradiction can arise only out of a deep and overwhelming urge for self-negation. The novel therefore stages a solipsistic drama of self and anti-self. Since Rao himself, after a bout of socialist infection caught in the epidemic of the thirties was duly restored to the health and security of brahmanic orthodoxy, Padmanabha, the South Indian brahman communist, might very well be Rao's alter ego. The narrator Rama (Vedantin, Indian etc.) is of course the official self of the author that has come to be established before the public eye. But there is another self hidden in Padmanabha, indicated by his probable likeness to Shatov which may indeed hold a true resemblance to Rao himself. In fact, the reference to Shatov has a dual function. Besides suggesting Padmanabha's subterranean love for India, it may very well stand as the symbol of Rao's own ambivalence to the very concept of India. Shatov professes to believe in Russia, orthodoxy and Christianity, the Holy Trinity of Dostoevsky. But, like Raja Rao, he had a stint of revolutionary association, although later on he desperately desires to cut himself away from it. The corruption generated by the "noble socialist ideal" however has left its indelible mark on his orthodox self. So when Stavrogin, the black guru of the double, mercilessly challenges his faith in God, Shatov is plunged into a wild fury:

> "I believe in Russia. . . . I believe in the Greek orthodox church. I—I believe in the body of Christ. . . .I believe that second coming will take place in Russia. . . . I believe . . ." Shatov murmured in a frenzy. "But in God? In God?"
>
> "I shall believe in God."

This desperate hesitancy, enshrined as the very epigraph of Rao's novel, belongs as much to Padmanabha/Kirillov as to the creator himself. Hence obsessive tendency to refer to Shatov again and again in the narrative although there is no resemblance between the action of Padmanabha's story and Shatov's. Dostoevsky presents

Shatov's jubilation at his wife's return to give birth to the child of another man, as an act of profound redemption, fervent with true Christian charity. This incident, with little logic, is alluded to by Rao to mark some mysterious resemblance with Padmanabha's "dialectical despair" or his running for a nurse during his wife's confinement. The line of similarity which lies in a common love for country, orthodoxy and a particular religion, all mixed together, is never quite brought out. It is precisely due to this eloquent silence that the spectre of Dostoevsky's classic figure of ambivalence tends in Rao's novel to dwarf Kirillov's logical suicide. If Shatov is evoked by Rao to redeem Padmanabha, the device certainly produces a strange effect by straining the demarcation between art and life which constitutes the conventional aesthetic distance. In fact the reader is uncomfortably aware of some secret bond extending beyond fiction between Padmanabha and the narrator Rama, who meets him only twice during the whole action for there are often allusions of a continuous association not only with Padmanabha, but even with Irene. He meets Irene only once yet mysteriously he seems to "owe" her a great duty.[28] With the actual entrance of R.R. explained in the footnote as "Raja Rao (the author)" the distance is further reduced, since we come to know of R.R.'s aesthetic sensibility (which Rao's interviewers have noted), his English as a combination of the Bible and Shakespeare (which we have already analyzed as such) his romantic propensities— "Some Tristan" which explains Rao's autobiographical hero Ramaswamy. In the narrative of Padmanabha, R.R. has absolutely no role to play and is in fact an addition in the definitive English edition alone. His function, therefore, is entirely formal— to lessen the customary distance between art and life just as it is being done in the new drama to expose the theatricality of the traditional theatre. So the consciousness in focus is a perpetual shift—Kirillov-Padmanabha-Shatov-Rama-R.R—which constitutes such a fusion and confusion of identities revolving on the axis of ambiguity that no stable self seems to emerge even as a residue.[29] One may find this confusion or the subtle intermingling, in the linguistic characteristic of a constant shift of the authorial focus in the personal pronoun. Apart from the three clear divisions—third person-outsider in the first two sections, first-person in Irene's journal holding dual focus "I" (Irene) and "he" (P.) third-person omniscient narrator in the concluding section, there is a constant mixing up of *he*, *you* and even *I* in the first two sections relating Padmanabha's life. For many, including Roland Barthes, the use of persons in narrator's focus indicates an attitude towards the whole writing process. Traditionally, *I* or *you* is the opposite of *he* or *it* which is called "the sign of absence"[30] The use of all the persons to focus the same consciousness in the same discourse may therefore indicate a constant self-contradiction and consequently an unstable attitude towards the writing process. Take for example the following passages, when the focus of each is Padmanabha and the narrator is the same Rama:

> a) So Kirillov learnt German in order to read Marx and Engels, French to read Fourier and Saint Simon, and little by little he was pushed into Lenin and the holy Russian tongue. Engels seemed a very machine of monumental and systematized thought, and as for Marx one does not talk about that greater Master.
>
> b) This colour problem in England is terrible—you always know what you *are* through others' eyes. You cannot walk a mile without discovering yourself over and again a hundred times, and even thick eyeglasses are no protection to you. You seemed small in comparison with the sturdy English, and your colour was chocolate, when it was not terribly coffee. Sometimes the umbrella saved your neighbourly discomfort, and in the parks a newspaper. But if you chanced on a negro in the parks, he told you more woeful tales than any heard in New York, and you took a superior sympathy on his darkened skin. With Indian independence not far off, you felt the protective elder, and a sure friend.
>
> c) All men in Marxism have anonymous names, and death—this last biological act—is an act of sheer surgery against betrayal. I will not betray my ideas—I am hungry. I die. The messiah will rise of my blood, and the colours of the communist land are the blue of meditations. Come, comrade death, I am yours.

In passage (a), the narrator presumes to be completely detached and satirical, in (b) this sarcasm is tempered with the feeling that the situation in hand ("the colour problem in England") is after all somewhat general which may be shared by the author as by the readers, in , (c), there is, for the moment, a complete identification and full involvement. There is a perpetual, almost mercurial restlessness that characterizes the whole tone of discourse shifting from heavy sarcasm to light irony, then to sympathy arriving at last to adoration. If savage criticism marks most of the passages in the first two sections strong, admiration counterbalances in the following:

> He was so *like a child*, was Kirillov, when it came to simple things; he *loved India* with a noble, *delicate un-reasoned love*. He loved her poetry as few among the so-called educated ones in India had—he loved the intricacies, the permutations, the magnitude of the *Sanskrit* verse. To hear him recite *Sanskrit* verse was like listening to a Pandit from Tanjore. His *sincerity*, his *enthusiasm*, his *learning*, were all alike—of one *sovereign made*.

The tone of approval almost always mingles with the author's own identification with the character. Hasn't Rao again and again glorified Sanskrit? "Je suis obsedé par le sanskrit," declares Rao proudly; for him Sanskrit is not a language but a means to arrive at *connaissance*, "qui, fonde sur la métaphysique et la grammaire, permét d'atteindre la libération spirituelle."[31]

4. *The Prison of Language*

Since the Marxist Padmanabha evokes alienation and satire and the brahman Padmanabha (in possession of self in Sanskrit) marks total identification and eulogy, it is significant that when these two confront each other in Sanskrit philosophy of word and Marxist science of language—the consequence is a riddle and a total defeat of language. As the blurb in the French edition states, Rao's Padmanabha, the communist brahman, attempts to use "la grammaire Sanskrit au service du matérialisme dialectique." So he applies the abstruse theory of *Sphota* "the central word-principle" to assess a '"Marxist classic" namely Stalin's congratulatory telegram to Hitler on the conquest of Poland which is set down thus:

1) the word reduced to its sound-value, then to its vibratory

> value, then finally to its etheric (akashic is the Sanskrit for it) structural value, is reduced to exact nothingness. 2) It is this universal nothingness that makes all permutations possible. 3) *In modern language we would say* all objects are ultimately reducible to the electromagnetic field and sound and object being one, they can be interpreted in terms of the wave equivalents, etc. 4) Marxism is a science. 5) A set of human, vocal vibrations—and in this case teleprinter—probably only produced the required physico-chemical transformation of the auditive and cerebral mechanisms, and produced a recognizable sound effect. 6) Then the word is born. 7) Stalin's congratulatory letter could be reduced to sheer scientific computation to form some seventeen hundred wave-components. 8) Hitler is pleased. 9) Stalin gets his time. 10) That is Marxism. 11) Hitler's message is physicochemical vibration in ether.

From the standpoint of sheer content, the passage strikes one as a violent and irrational forcing together of concepts belonging to different spheres and different levels of human knowledge—a metaphysical theory and a physical concept directed towards *word*, a linguistic unit.[32] The underlying assumptions of such juxtaposition are questionable, especially the facile equation between the metaphysical "nothingness" of the structure of word and the so-called physico-chemical reduction to vibration in "modern language." No less disconcerting is the simplistic conclusion that such a physical view must necessarily be the Marxist concept of word.[33] (Since "Marxism is a science.") The failure at the conceptual level to construct a well-integrated and developed structure reveals itself in the stylistic features—an unusual predominance of over-simple constructions (nos. 4, 6, 8, 9, 10 and 11) especially when expressing serious and decisive stages of thought. "Complex sentences combining numbers of deep structures in a variety of ways," says Roger Fowler, "suggest, rightly or wrongly logical sophistication, precision, mental flexibility."[34] It is therefore significant that Rao can be "logical" and "flexible" only in reproducing the idea that is already accepted—enunciation of the physical theory of sound (no. 3 and 5) because all the sentences that have some complexity in structure belong to this one category. Rao's *own* conclusions are almost invariably cast in the simplest structures, and so betray nearly authoritarian rigidity and total absence of logic culminating in "that is Marxism." Also, to be noted is the relative absence of connectives which mark logical development of thought so much so that Rao's style often, as here, tends to be paratectic. The paucity of syntactic elaboration cannot but be seen as indicative of the author's refusal to analyze and explore an idea, and makes one feel that he wants to impose his private views, arrived at without logic, on his readers rather than to persuade through analysis. One may wonder if a deliberate and persistent shrinking away from syntactic elaboration in the surface structure whenever there is a private conclusion or view involved, does not suggest a disjunction of a fundamental nature, which strains the relation between the signifier and the signified to a point of total meaninglessness. Can we accept the contention that Stalin's congratulatory telegram to Hitler is a "Marxist classic" because it is "a physico-chemical vibration in ether" composed of "17 hundred wave-components"? How would the "classic" character be affected, if the number of components had been 16 hundred 99 or 17 hundred and one? Does the physico-chemical vibration lead to the reaction mentioned in nos. (8) and (9)? or in the "sheer scientific computation" or in their "combination"? Besides if vibrations produce sound (no.8) then the *Sphota* theory has to be abandoned for the latter postulates the vibrations as "one of the numerous *results of* sound and not, *as it is commonly held*, its cause."[35]

The most important consequence of this so-called brahman-Marxist presentation of language is an utter silence as to the *meaning* of the telegram in the human context of history—that a Communist power has upheld an imperialist aggression. The whole emphasis of the irrational combination of *Sphota* and Physics is directed towards a virtual murder of language, for it is reduced to a lifeless structure of formal components entirely devoid of human content, which is bound to the ideological, social and ultimately to the living reality or phenomenon. Not all the profundity of the *Sphota* theory, nor the immaculate perfection of physical science can fill in the gaping void that overcomes the whole meaningful attitude of the author to the telegram of Stalin. A linguistic expression stretches through the "interindividual territory"[36] which is sought to be irrevocably suppressed. As a result the reader is left in complete confusion as to the author's evaluation of the character in specific situation. Does this Marxist-brahmanic interpretation represent a secret synthesis in the fragmented soul of the hero, or the absurdity of an attempt at such synthesis? The total withdrawal of authorial stance marks the deepest abyss of negation—the defeat of language.[37] If a statement in language embedded at a certain point of historical reality is nothing but some physico-chemical vibrations, the author who builds up his fictional world with words must be an absurd creator, for his verbal universe cannot but be unintelligible to himself.

The basic alienation that informs such incomprehensibility manifests itself in spectacular devices of dehumanization. The revolt against reason which takes the form of surreal fullness of fantasy in Rao's previous novel, here reveals the obverse—the void. The attack against logic as a particular Marxist stronghold ultimately betrays a separation from nature, from the vital process of life. Take for example the description of the wife of Padmanabha, Irene, whose womanhood seems to reside in "specific reflexes, glandular and neurotic":

> Kirillov really loved Irene. She had the red blood, the red hair, the passionate index finger, and dialectics had drained her lust into irate channels.

If we remember the glory of sensuous detail in the presentation of Madeleine who is a woman in *The Serpent and the Rope*, even of Shantha who is womanhood in *The Cat and Shakespeare*, we perhaps feel something frightening in the presentation of Irene, in such deliberately pathological terms, which precludes not only poetry but also the reality of human body as a whole. If physical colour is mentioned at all, its origin lies in the abstract—the Party—for it is red. She no longer possesses even the biological entity of woman, reduced to "the index finger," since it is she who seems to be the bringer of "this new world" or Communism to a brahman. The creation of a new life for Irene and Padmanabha has therefore no emotional background, no sensual acceptance of the body, but a dehydrated victory of India in abstraction:

> Kirillov even meditated, in expiation, upon the birth of a child—he would now have a child, they would have a boy, and he would be an Indian.

Objects and abstractions therefore dominate over human characters in *Comrade Kirillov*. The bare surroundings of Padmanabha—the spare kitchen without even a glass, the lone piece of cheese, receive detailed attention. It is impossible to miss the emphasis on the lifeless items—like Kirillov's dress, his pants, trousers, shirts, coat, shoes, socks—all receive a kind of authorial notice usually due to human beings.[38] Kirillov's necktie may present the very essence of dehumanization in the novel. An extreme pathetic fallacy enhances the desiccation of humanity since it blandly assumes a total interchangeability of man and object. From the length and also the kind of emphasis that the tie receives from the author, there is no doubt that in Kirillov's emotional life it has not only an "absurd inevitability" but even an inexplicable static value denied to any human being. The narrator Rama arrives with a purpose and Padmanabha adjusts "the curve of his slightly distended necktie, it was as though he were turning to his wife and saying, 'Hello, dear, what is this?'" When he victoriously expounds the Communist standpoint, he does not look to Irene, wife and comrade, but seeks assurance in the necktie which "received its pattings and it hissed and curled in ritual approval." This object is Padmanabha's "boon companion, his poetry, his sole possession," the focus of his nightly meditation which is to match the Communist activity of the day. The necktie indeed is the most valuable key to the presentation of reality in the novel:

> Kirillov's real name was Padmanabha Iyer, but his necktie had such *praterplusparenthetical* curve, as though much concrete philosophy had gone into its making, and it revealed a soul so ambivalent that I could not gaze on its self-aware turpitudes without human compassion.

If one presumes "human compassion" as antithesis to the lifeless object's "turpitude," the first belonging to the "Indian" narrator, the latter a characteristic of the Communist alter ego, the certainty of meaning will be immediately unsettled by a reality in which the object is not only "self-aware" but reveals "a soul" and contains "some concrete philosophy." The absurd verbal coinage (*praterplusparenthetical*), a Joycean imitation, leaves the lasting impression of a reality which has become meaningless.

So the novelist can suggest a meaning only by a total escape from life, in surrender to the pre-literary category of myth. The axis of the novel's structure—Indiannness—is ultimately bared to the readers as the legend of the Eternal Virgin which Kamal, the son of Irene and Padmanabha, finds in the temple of Kanyakumari. Incidentally, Kamal, born either in 1942 or before 1939 is now, "during the present split in the C.P.I." (Communist Party of India) which happened in 1964, still a child playing with a toy-horse carried on the shoulder by the narrator Rama. This licence with time fits no doubt the fabular end and may be found in consonance with the high-handed atemporality of the new fiction. The legend that Rama recounts to Kamal indicates the last testament of a crisis which has manifested itself in complicated involutions, in cunning equivocation analyzed in each preceding section. We are told that India is like Parvati, who in love with life goes to the South to immerse herself in the enjoyment of this phenomenal reality, "beautiful fruits, flowers, perfumes, medicinal herbs, precious stones, sweet water" which she refuses to renounce in a travel up the cold Himalayas to meet her consort Shiva who, lost in meditation, fails to come at the auspicious hour of marriage. The pertinent question here is, who is Lord Shiva in terms of the novel's political context of Indian nationalism? The text offers apparently no visible clue and Parvati is left forever awaiting her indifferent bridegroom. The narrative insists on the failure of the Indian communists to join the Gandhian national upsurge, and since Parvati is "India," to fulfil, the expectation of a formal coherence the forgetful consort should point towards the recalcitrant Indian Marxist. But the Communist, the Marxist in Rao is "above all a realist" for whom "metaphysical enquiry" is due to a physiological disorder and "God is lie." On the other hand it is the orthodox brahman bent on salvation alone, who "asks for more inquiry into your biological, psychological, and psychic self delimiting you bit by bit into acute dissolution. . . ."

"A symbol," says Camus, "indeed assumes two planes, two worlds of ideas and sensations, and a dictionary of correspondences between them" and further it "transcends the one who makes use of it and makes him say in reality more than he is aware of expressing."[39] So in the inference of the reader, Rao's Shiva may represent what the author is not perhaps prepared to admit, namely, the failure of orthodox brahmanism which disdained the young Indian nation at a crucial point of history. So, for the orthodox brahman intellectual, India, like Parvati, deified in the temple as Kanyakumari, remains an abstraction, a metaphysic, cold and formal like the stone idol even as remote. The quest for an "Indian" identity of an orthodox brahman ends in an obsession with form, the abstract *image* since the Indian reality of sight and sound, touch and taste lies for ever beyond the grasp of transcendence.

This interpretation of the legend may of course appear perverse to Rao's admirers, to whom Rao may represent the soul of India, but it is the only meaning that emerges from the structure of the novel as an artistic venture. *Comrade Kirillov,* as we have seen, is not a traditional fiction involved in the contemporary political context as Koestler's *Darkness at Noon* so obviously is. For Koestler, the realistic form could be easily grounded in his personal sympathy with the victims of the Moscow trial, crystallized in his central character Rubashov. The Western critique of the "purges" derives from liberal humanism which however is not at all valid in Rao's stand on orthodoxy. Besides written so long after the actual incidents and with the background of Rao's own transformation from an ardent socialist to an uncompromising orthodox, the novel is a symbolic presentation of selfcriticism which can be apprehended only in terms of its language. The stylistic caricatures of *Kanthapura* and *The Serpent and the Rope* are manipulated to arrive at a new signification which upgrades the legend of Kanyakumari from a mere finishing touch into a determinant factor controlling the whole structure. The satiric devaluation which occupies the greater length of the novel leads to romantic idealization in the legend at the end. This mixture however is in consonance with the Western tradition because the form of allegory offers ways of combining satire and romance.[40]

If we apply Rao's own theory of *Sphota*—the Indian philosophy of grammar—to the organization of the text, the last section immediately becomes the most revealing. The novel may be taken as a linguistic whole, like a *word*; each of the four sections is an individual letter arranged in temporal succession. So the satiric portrayal of the communist self of Padmanabha, the sentimental identification with the brahman, scholarly, and Gandhian Padmanabha, cannot indicate either separately or conjointly, the real meaning of the whole. It is the "structural nothingness," the void generated by the impasse of the author in relation to reality, by the very ambiguity of the concept of India, that functions as *sphota* and has made the different permutations of form in those sections possible, and ultimately manifests itself as meaning, fixed by the last unit even as the last sound, according to the *Sphota* theory and upheld by Rao here, determines the sense of a word—composite of letters pronounced in succession.[41] It is the stone form that lends permanence to the rejection of Parvati's womanhood and embodies the final dehumanization of art as the desperate refuge of a brahmanic self, bent on transcendence.

NOTES

1. Roland Barthes, "Style and Its Image," *Literary Style: A Symposium,* p. 10 and the discussion following his paper, p. 11.
2. Roman Jakobson, "The Dominant,"*Readings in Russian Poetics*, p. 83.
3. Jean-Paul Sartre, *What is Literature?* , trans. Bernard Frechtman, p. 171.
4. This kind of attention to excremental activities which occur quite often in *The Cat and Shakespeare* (pp. 62, 64, 97, 116) connects Rao with Dadaism, the precursor to Surrealism. See for example Alfred Jarry's *Gestes et opinions due docteur Faustroll,* 1971, 1972, Livre II, pp. 672, 674, 700-2.
5. Claude Levi-Strauss, *Tristes Tropiques,* 1956, trans. 1961, 1966, p. 71.
6. "Wherever a sign is present, ideology is present, too" and "Any ideological product is not only itself a part of a reality (natural or social), just as any physical body, any instrument of production, reflects and refracts another reality outside itself. Everything ideological possesses meaning." V.N. Volosinov, *Marxism and the Philosophy of Language,* trans. L. Matejka and D.R. Titunik, 1973, p. 9.
7. C.D. Narasimhaiah, *Raja Rao*, p. 168.
8. An Interview with Raja Rao by R. Parthasarathy, *Span*, Sept. 1977.
9. Ihab Hassan, *The Dismemberment of Orpheus: Toward a Post-Modern Literature,* p. 79.
10. See Dostoevsky, *The Devils or The Possessed,* 1871-72,

trans. David Magarshack,pp.102-16, 122-27, 238-45, 375-80, 552-58, 566-67, 577-78, 604-21. In Dostoevsky as in Albert Camus, *Kirilov* is spelled with a single *l*. Incidentally, Dostoevsky uses an earlier literary character as a prototype of a fictional person e.g. Prince Stavrogin is compared to Shakespeare's young Prince Harry, p. 53.

11. Albert Camus, "Kirilov," *The Myth of Sisyphus,* trans. Justin O'Brien, pp. 85-92. Also, A Alvarez, *The Savage God: A Study of Suicide,* 1971, pp. 238-42.
12. For the importance of the double as a central pattern in Dostoevsky's characterization and in particular the value of Kirilov-Shatov pair, see Irving Howe, "Dostoevsky: The Politics of Salvation" and Dmitri Chizehevsky, "The Theme of the Double in Dostoevsky," *Dostoevsky: Twentieth Century Views,* ed. René Wellek, 1962, pp. 62-67 and 117-99.
13. Documents maintained by the British Government during the second World War prove that the so-called "toeing the British policy" by the Indian communists was a mask for anti-British agitation. See for details *Communism in India: Unpublished Documents 1935-1945,* ed. Subodh Ray, 1976, pp. 250-82.

    Rao's stand by orthodoxy is synonymous with a blind toeing of the establishment, for his view that the Mahatma won 1942 agitation leading to the independence of India finds perhaps sole support in the official version e.g. Tara Chand, *History of Freedom Movement in India,* 1972, Vol. IV, pp. 399-400, 414-23. That the 42 agitation was particularly violent and hence marked a defeat of Gandhian non-violent ideology is elaborated in Indian fiction and scholarly research. For details see R.C. Majumdar, *History of the Freedom Movement,* 1963, Vol. II, pp. 646-73.
14. Dostoevsky, *The Notebooks for the Possessed,* trans. V. Terras, 1968. "We have Orthodoxy: our nation is great and wonderful because it believes and because it has orthodoxy," pp. 236, 250, 225. Also *The Possessed* or *The Devils,* p. 255. "A man who does not belong to the Greek Orthodox faith cannot be a Russian."
15. Raja Rao, "I believe India is the direction of sensibilities and refinements the world never surpassed. In many ways, one can say, India is culture." Interview by Elizabeth Wohl, "Raja Rao on America," p. 35. Cf. Stavrogin: "The earth has never

seen such a gigantic idea as the one which is now taking shape here." Dostoevsky, *The Notebooks for the Possessed*, p. 144.

16. Raja Rao, "Meaning of India," *The Illustrated Weekly of India*, Aug. 12, 1962, p. 19. Cf. V.V. Zenkovsky's view: "Dostoevsky . . . emphasizes with great acuteness that to bring harmony into the historical process one must inevitably suppress human freedom." "Dostoevsky's Religious and Philosophical Views," *Dostoevsky; Twentieth Century Views*, 1962, p. 144.
17. Dante, *Divine Comedy*, trans. J.D. Sinclair, Canto XII, II, 97-105.
18. As W.J. Harvey points out: "However invisible he may make himself, whatever narrative technique he may use to conceal his exit from his fiction, the novelist must be both omnipotent and omniscient." *Character and the Novel*, p. 32. Hence "abdication of his god-like prerogative" and "refusal to allow intrinsic knowledge of other characters" form the core of the new fiction.
19. According to David Lodge, "It is in fact the transference of the writer's own sense of the problematic nature of his undertaking—making the reader participate in the aesthetic and philosophical problems the writing of fiction presents, by embodying them directly in the narrative—that characterizes the problematic novel." *The Novelist at the Crossroads and Other Essays on Fiction and Criticism*, p. 24.
20. Discussing the point of view of the novelist towards his character, Roger Fowler considers speculative verbs, interpretative adverbs and conjunctions, expressions of tentativeness as "words of estrangement" and classic linguistic signs of a narrator's isolation from his characters. *Linguistics and the Novel*, p. 92
21. Cf. Also *Comrade Kirillov*, pp. 30-31, 49, 73, 90, 91
22. Rao maintains this stand in the interview by Annie Brierre, *Paris Letter, The Illustrated Weekly of India*, March 10, 1963, p. 26.
23. For details see J. Bandopadhyay, *Indian Nationalism vs. International Communism*, 1966. Bandopadhyay clearly declares his "Indian" stand to be based on the "Hindu-Buddhist-Jain tradition of non-violence and universal peace which found culmination in the policy of Ashoka" and does not hesitate to

reject "the Brahminic tradition of unscrupulous diplomacy as embodied in Kautilya's Arthasastra, the Manusmriti and the Kuru of Thiruvuluvara," none of which being acceptable "as a guide to future," p. 93. Also pp. 45-56.

24. Romain Rolland's record of meetings with Raja Rao (July 8, 1930, August 1930, April 1932). *INDE Journal* (1915-1943), 1960, p. 472. In his letter to Maxim Gorky also, Rao declared his affiliation with the extremist socialist group of the Indian National Congress and hopes for closer ties between India and the Soviet Union. (Quoted in detail by Pyotr Baranniknov, "Maxim Gorky O Bharat," *Antarjatik*, April 1968, Calcutta: 12th year, issue 11, p. 1068). Also his admission to M.K. Naik of his socialist communist past, *Raja Rao*, pp. 18-20.
25. H. Mukherjee, *Gandhiji—A Study*, 1958, pp. 183-209.
26. Mikhail Bakhtin, "Discourse Typology in Prose," *Readings in Russian Poetics,* eds. L. Matejka and K. Pomoroska, p. 185.
27. Rao's hero actually represents the author who states: "I admire the Albigenes for their courage, their disinterestedness. But I am always for the Church and the orthodx faith. The Church is always right, always superior to any revolt." "An Interview with Raja Rao: Paris Letters," p. 26.
28. E.g. "I wanted to show Kamal my India. I at least owed this to Irene." (p. 122) We are informed that "Rama once told" P. of a 13th century peasant mystic (p. 40), advised him to visit *ashrama* (p. 73), used to mock at him (p. 72), but we are not shown when and how. The same mystery hangs over Irene's journal being left to Rama's custody.
29. So Padmanabha Kirillov repeats Ramaswamy-Rao's views on Albigenes—its relation with Buddhism and romantic love which is the thesis of *The Serpent and the Rope* as borrowed from Rougemont's *Love in the Western World.* So narrator Rama's "true home" is Trivandrum (p. 80) where Ramaswamy ends his journey for here Raja Rao met his Guru—the same Trivandrum is the place of happenings in *The Cat and Shakespeare.*
30. Roland Barthes, "To write, an intransitive verb," *The Structuralist Controversy*, pp. 139-40.
31. Rao's interview with Annie Brierrie, "*Le Serpent et la Metaphysique,*" Nouvelles Litteraires, 28 fevrier, 1963. Also "He

who possesses Sanscrit, can possess himself," p. 35. Hence Rao's insistence on his medium being "Sanscritic English," Preface to *The Policeman and the Rose*, p. xv.

32. Take for example the following opinion: "There is a great difference between the metaphysical conception of *sabda* (sound) and the scientific concept of sound. Sound of physics is really the shadow of real sound." Lalan Prasad Singh, *Tantra, its mystic and scientific basis*, 1976, p. 85.
33. Contrast for example the Marxist viewpoint of V.N. Volosinov's *Russian Marxism and Philosophy of Language.* 1930, trans. L.Matejka and I.R. Titunik, 1973. Presenting a semiotic view of language, Volosinov holds: "The structure of the utterance is a purely sociological structure" and regards it as the basis of Marxist theory of ideologies, p. 98.
34. Roger Fowler, *Linguistics and the Novel*, p. 104
35. Ajit Mukherjee and Madhu Khanna; *The Tantric way: Art, Science: Ritual*, p. 105
36. Volosinov, *Marxism and the Philosophy of Language*, p. 12. Also Fowler, *Linguistics and the Novel*, p. 77
37. Cf. Roger-Fowler's view: "Language is a powerfully committing medium to work in. It does not allow us to say something without conveying an attitude to something." *Ibid.*, p. 76.
38. This obsession with a few objects is a marked character of the anti-novel e.g. Sturrock, *The French New Novel*, p. 20.
39. Albert Camus, *The Myth of Sisyphus*, p. 102
40. Robert Scholes, *Structuralism in Literature: Toward a Structuralist Poetics of Fiction*, p. 138.
41. "The *sphota*, which has been linked to the neo-platonic logos, is often translated by the terms "expression," "concept" or "idea," but none of these terms brings out its essential nature. Some philosophers propounded and the grammarians took it for granted that a word has intrinsically a word-prototype, but it may be explained as the sound of a word as a whole, and as conveying apart from its component letters (*varnas*) . . . when a word is pronounced, its individual sounds become reflected in some degree in the order of the *sphota* in which the particular sounds are comprised; and as soon as the last sound dies away, the *sphota*, in which the idea corresponding to all these sounds is comprised, becomes manifest and raises to our consciousness the idea thus associated. The sounds of a word as a

whole, therefore, and apart from those of the constituent letters, reveal the *sphota*." Sushil Kumar De, *History of Sanskrit Poetics*, Vol. II, p. 13. It is however to be noted that the philosophy of *sphota* known as Verbal Monism (*Sabdadvaita* or *Sabdabrahmavada*) is confined almost to its founder Bhartrihari. See for details Gaurinath Sastri, *The Philosophy of Word and Meaning: Some Indian Approaches with Special Reference to the Philosophy of Bhartrihari*, 1959.

Conclusion

In the analysis of the novels of Raja Rao we have considered the structure of each work, the hierarchical arrangement of the different components of plot, narrative technique and language which constitute the total form. It is now apparent that in the quest for an Indian identity, the novelist has tried to develop an individual form, groping for a proper dominant which should satisfy the inherent logic of each structure. In the beginning the theme of Time dominates in the pattern of novel. In the juxtaposition of the mythical potential of Mahatma as an incarnation and the actual political and social reality of the time controlled by forces emanating from elsewhere, it is the principle of conflict that operates. The representational form is quite effective in the delineation of the traditional activities of a Hindu village, but fails to integrate the historical reality into the pattern of myth for the complexities of the present life prove to lie beyond the control of artistic form. The realistic aspect is further emphasized by the technique of *Skaz*, the orientation to the common man's speech habits, realized in the peasant grandmother-narrator with plenty of local colour and colloquialism. At the same time there is stylization clearly originating from the author's poetic sensibility, and the reality is sought to be distanced through a handful of rhetorical devices. The whole experiment is severely limited to a few constructs, a few figures of speech which are repeated ad infinitum. So the climax registers a failure of technique and style since the intention to present reality in dramatic immediacy confuses the hierarchical relationship among different components and reveals an undue emphasis on the foregrounded elements of style without the relief that a background of normalcy alone provides. A long unfocused flow of narrative, from which the main characters have disappeared, imitates speech, and at the same time punctures it ineffectively with literary rhetoric.

Here is a total surrender to actuality although traditional realism depends for its aesthetic tactics on a balance between mind and world at a specific point of time. But in *Kanthapura* this balance is upset with the reality of time posing a fundamental problem for the authorial personality self-divided between the Gandhian ideology of Indian nationalism and his strong, latent brahmanic orthodoxy. His concern with the contemporary reality of India, fraught with the urgent problem of ousting a foreign rule, adopts a traditional form, imitative of reality. But his personal situation, the conflict between orthodoxy and nationalism, impedes the development of characters and their role in the destruction of *Kanthapura*'s archaic existence. He is unable to indicate the contribution of the orthodox brahmans to the tragedy of annihilation nor is he prepared to assert his identification in unequivocal terms with his hero Moorthy, who finally leans towards the even more radical politics of socialism and plunges into the reality of time with despair, whereas the grandmother-narrator, the archaic soul of *Kanthapura*, takes refuge in fantasy with hope. *Kanthapura* may not be perfect, but it is undoubtedly a remarkable achievement in the close approximation of thought and technique, in the attempt, however flawed, to build a structure.

In *The Serpent and the Rope*, there is a determined endeavour to restore the balance which was snapped in *Kanthapura*, to rearrange different elements in a more orderly structure which is conceived as a far more ambitious plan. The concern with Time which as social and political content dominated *Kanthapura*'s fictional world and disrupted the orthodox Hindu life is now presented at two levels, in the psychological entanglement of a triangular man-woman relationship as well as in the historical thesis the hero is engaged in. The brahmanic orthodoxy, deeply rooted in the author and not assimilated in the contemporary context, changes into an idea, a grand metaphysic of identity, equating Truth with Orthodoxy which is stripped of its socio-economic implication and presented as a basic attitude to life in conceptual terms. Gandhian humanism, one of the mainsprings of Indian nationalism, is diffused into a generalization—an approach to life which is humanistic in quintessence. In the rejection of the Christian-Buddhist French wife of the brahman Ramaswamy, the pendulum that earlier tilted towards humanism in *Kanthapura* swings to the other extreme of rigid and uncompromising orthodoxy. In consonance with this gradual transformation of content into abstraction, the mode of *The Serpent and the Rope* develops from *Kanthapura*'s socio-political realism into a psychological variant of the distinctly romantic type because it utilizes abstract thought in the methodology of the novel to distance and defamiliarize the mundane and hackneyed reality of an extramarital set-up. The mingling of love and quest in the plot functions as the ground for the display of intellectual acrobatics playing with parallels and analogies from an intensely subjective interpretation of history with a fixed goal of Transcendental Reality as Truth. But the journey to this destination is through a pattern of human relationship which is distinctly existential in its dependence on interaction with the Other. The whole narrative structure is phenomenal whereas the ideal of the Indian identity lies in the Truth beyond the phenomenon of appearance. Here is the fullest expression of the original disjunction in the self, now developed into an acute crisis which divides the philosopher painfully from the artist. Although the thesis proclaims the triumph of the transcendent ideal, the narrative technique follows all the rules of the phenomenal game of the Western tradition in fiction. At this stage one is convinced that what Rao poses to reject as "Western" (historical, romantic, personal, poetic) is actually as much a part of his own self as the ostensibly applauded "Indian" (traditional, classical, impersonal, antipoetic). The ambiguity inherent in the very notion and experience of self is revealed in the elaborate linguistic structure which is traditional in the conventional manipulation of local colour and modernist in the bold use of deviances. By a careful collocation of a particular class of words, Rao tries to extend the experimental at the semantic level. On the other hand there is a distinct exploitation of the poetic mode in the utilization of rhetoric, linguistic recurrences with a strong symbolic overtone in the form of distinct motifs emerging from the context. The unifying principle which coheres such diverse aspects lies in the metonymic association which progresses syntagmatically and, according to the structuralist poetics, constitutes the basis of the realistic mode. Since the avowed object of the Indian novelist is to reject Time and the West, this dependence on the realistic mode is by itself a piece of irony which is further strengthened by the almost incessant eclecticism drawing heavily on the West, especially French literature—a feature which irrevocably binds the form to personal biography, consequently to history and time. From the inter-relation among the different elements therefore, no assertive meaning, either positive or negative, can emerge. This deepseated impasse is responsible for the tension inherent in the form which constantly puts the fictional reality to test. The idealization of the protagonist-narrator, who is a scarcely-veiled projection of the author, combined with a mass of generalizations, often aphoristic with strong prescriptive flavour, deals perhaps the most damaging blow to the fictional texture which, despite the wealth of symbols and images, is constantly rent with holes of authorial intrusion. The discrepancy between the thesis and the human situation highlights the unreliability of the narrator. This ambiguity in the relation between the author and the narrator culminates into straining the very boundary of fiction when the characters themselves assume independence and act out mythical roles consciously without any seeming authorial control. The interior monologue in which the whole story is presented, instead of revealing, conceals the complexities at the depth of the psyche. There is thus in this novel an acute problem of form, corresponding to the intense crisis in the pattern of thought, resulting in an uncertainty in placing the dominant—the thesis tries to distort the narrated reality; the style challenges the thesis; the narrative technique, as though in desperation, turns on itself. *The Serpent and the Rope* is a record of the deepening crisis in the artist whose problematic relation with Time now assumes a magnitude that simply clamours for an explosive expression. The language therefore constitutes finally the dominant in the total structure, because the artist cannot establish himself anywhere else, neither in the horns of the intellectual dilemma of two attitudes to life, orthodox and humanist, nor in the traditional modern poetics of fiction which cannot correlate the thesis.

It is therefore inevitable that in the next work, *The Cat and Shakespeare*, there is a desperate attempt to stabilize at an equilibrium related as well as distant from polarized opposition. In order to come to terms with Time, Rao at last turns away from the traditional-modernist form to an allegorical mode which can hold representation and intellectual preoccupation in a balance. The much sought for synthesis between orthodox values presented as Truth or Wisdom and the humanism felt to be essentially moralistic and Western, is achieved by turning both into pure conceptual patterns realized as symbols, some of which are traditional and others personal. Here we can identify a distinct, recognizable configuration in Rao's relation to reality which, since his inability to assimilate brahmanism with Indian nationalism in *Kanthapura*, tends towards a persistent equivocation. In *The Serpent and the Rope*. Buddhism serves as a scapegoat to bear the thrust directed towards Western humanism which is centred in Christianity. In *The Cat and Shakespeare* we find the same equivocation, but attuned here to acceptance, to a positive affirmation. In the symbol of kitten-and-Mother-Cat, indicative of a total surrender to faith which may fall on the undeserving, we find an acceptance of the basic humane core of Christianity. Since grace is feminine and the mother cat conveys the creative and sustaining values of life, there is an assertion of the reality of this earth. Rao's metaphysics of Truth as Transcendental Reality or Absolute Consciousness has to seek expression in a private symbol of *Shakespeare* who as an artist is a creator and in his negative capability is beyond the relative existence of the world which is like a ration-shop, ruled by scales. This cross-cultural stasis is typical of Rao in his maturity as an artist; so the ostensibly Indian symbol derived from a minor subgenre of one particular system of Vedanta serves as a means to approximate the West, whereas the obviously Western symbol, *Shakespeare*, is built into the structure as a symbol of another system of Vedanta. Both Cat and Shakespeare mean what they are apparently not, or, to put it another way, they are meant to suggest far more than the normal connotation can *logically* conceive of. The fact that the two different systems of Vedanta that are utilized here are considered to be mutually exclusive in Indian thought lends the technique in the novel the utmost importance for it has to present in a coherent whole a synthesis which is based on rejection of logic. In the process it grows into a unique technique in the manipulation of surreal poetics, mixing dream and reality. The rejection of rationality presupposes a rebellion against the traditional form of the novel controlled by causality, and *The Cat and Shakespeare* anticipates the post-modernist fiction as a consequence. There are however two important conclusions that emerge at this stage. Rao can effect a synthesis only by a radical reduction of the complex problem of contingency into a simplified abstract form of either/or—*to-be* or *not-to-be*. The content therefore tends to become more and more formalized. This leads to the second finding, the gradual diminution of the narrative as well as of characterization, the former approaching to a crystalline symbol, the latter to typification. As a consequence, form depends almost entirely on language to present a symbolic mode. But the linguistic structure does not appear to revel in that kind of baroque luxuriousness which is so much admired in the purple patches of *The Serpent and the Rope*. It is the gradual desiccation of ostensible poeticism in Rao's mature style that finally points to the truth of his situation as an exile.

From *Kanthapura* to *Comrade Kirillov*, an interesting patten of evolution is evident in Rao's handling of the English language. In the first two stages he is deeply immersed in the creative potential of the linguistic experience. His emphasis, at the early stages, falls largely on a type of innovation at the lexical level which usually offers an artist the greatest freedom and is also regarded generally attuned to the realistic convention of the traditional-modernist novel. At the same time his desire to utilize the poetic dimension of the English language is revealed in his frequent use of rhetorical devices. The vocabulary is therefore replete with both colloquialism and archaism, not to speak of his obsession with the figures of sound, notably alliteration. The interaction of two opposed tendencies produces a pattern which is characteristic of *Kanthapura*—an incessant repetition of the regular structure—subject-verb-object/complement, predominant in speech, which is frequently punctured by the essentially literary and formal device of inversion in long units of paragraphs. A simultaneous emphasis on the realistic and the poetic, the colloquial and the formal brings out the inherent opposition because these are not placed in an hierarchy of order. So the quest of the author starts with an attempt to bring together disparate elements and to utilize a definite model for his prose.

The growing maturity of Rao as an artist is instantly marked in *The Serpent and the Rope* where the opposition between elements is reduced or muted with the help of a stylistic model from a great European tradition. The linguistic realism so dominant in the portrayal of daily life in *Kanthapura* is now employed in a much larger as well as deeper connotation, for, the direct borrowings from the French, the sprinkling of Indian words and unusual frequency of certain English words related to inner life produce altogether an atmosphere, exotic and spiritual. This does not therefore ostensibly conflict with the use of literary devices at every level of the total construct—vocabulary, syntax and imagery. The poetic devices too reveal a greater mastery over the English literary tradition in the sensitive manipulation of rhythm, combined with a whole paraphernalia of rhetoric—synaesthesia, inversion, parallel construction, repetition, in syntax and vocabulary from which quite often emerge strong and definite symbolic motifs. The irony lies in this very excellence, this successful assimilation of the Western tradition by an Indian since the theme of *The Serpent and the Rope* is the eternal opposition between the "metaphysical" India of the non-dualist Raja Rao and the "poetic" West of Christ, the rock on which the brahman Ramaswamy's marriage with the Christian Madeleine flounders. So an analysis of the inter-relation between the narrative strategy and the language structure reveals an impasse without any hope of resolution leading ultimately to an ambivalence which the heavy stylization constantly tends to underline.

A break-through from this stylized convention bordering perhaps on preciosity is attempted in *The Cat and Shakespeare*. The mature Rao, who admittedly ends his quest here, emerges with a simple, amodal style, free from heavy rhetoric and the consequent bond to any specific literary tradition. It is here that we at last find a conscious operation of an order; colloquial and literary devices—residue of former experiments—are graded in a clear authorial perspective. Thus the literary device of inversion here does not conflict violently with the predominant regular pattern for the latter is not exactly colloquial, but rather devoid of any recognizable literary association in its pervasive over-simplification. Foregrounded against the predominant amodal texture, inversion therefore produces a touch of humour or gravity depending on the context. As a conscious artist, Rao here delves deeper into the language structure insofar as he gradually discards the obvious effusion of creativity found at the lexis of the preceding novels and concentrates on a sparing use of experiment and that too, in syntax. In *The Cat and Shakespeare*, there is a single deviation which is repeated—the scarcely perceptible and yet deliberate omission of the definite article to establish the unity of the particular with the universal. Yet this singular innovation occupies a central position in the total structure of the novel which reaches conclusion in the revelation of Truth in the universal as the Form. But the weight of the various symbolic connotations of ordinary English words derived from a subjective and exclusive belief—a composite of heterogeneous elements bordering on mysticism—forces the language into a hermetic system, distant from the world of human communication.

So in *Comrade Kirillov* we find the inevitable consequence, an artist devaluing his own art in a virulent parody of his own former styles. The whole attention is shifted from vocabulary to syntax, repeating a conditional pattern so that the fictionality of the fiction is exposed and the author abjures the authorial omniscience and joins the characters of his own creation. The crystalline world of *The Cat and Shakespeare* resisting communication leads to a reductive rage at meaning in *Comrade Kirillov*, when a linguistic statement uttered in a historical situation evaporates as nothing but a series of "physico-chemical vibration in ether." Language is no longer the very stuff of literary creation, but the prison shutting the Indian writer in English from the reality of human existence. It is therefore inevitable that the most vocal expounders of the "Indian" identity of Raja Rao's works cannot compare Rao with any ancient, medieval or modern writers of this subcontinent and thus seem to acknowledge, perhaps unwittingly, the truth that the very medium of English binds the artist in Rao forever to the literary tradition of the West.

In his attempt to forge a distinct "Indian" identity, equated with a metaphysical rejection of reality, Rao realizes that he is being enmeshed more and more in the West, not only in the "realistic" tradition of the novel form, but also in the poetic convention inseparable from a linguistic system. His whole endeavour is therefore to construct an enclosed self-sufficient system of his own. So, in *Kanthapura* and *The Serpent and the Rope* his form tends towards expansion, from *The Cat and Shakespeare*, it starts to contract, so that from now on the movement of his thought as well as his literary form may be placed and evaluated not against any particular *national* tradition but against the background of his own former works. It has to be borne in mind that there is no fundamental disruption which may suggest erratic performance, but a totally comprehensible development. The attempt to pass from the representational to the illustrative in Rao is marked not so much by an apprehension of greater truth or permanent values, but by a change in the compositional elements which are present in the former realistic mode at perhaps a lower level of intensity than these are in the mature form that has now evolved. In other words, there is a gradual shift of the dominant in the successive works. In *The Cat and Shakespeare* the surreal technique fuses form into style—a unique formal achievement. But surrealism which is here the technique of the allegorical mode has always been present in Rao's former works which are otherwise attuned to traditional realism. In *Kanthapura*, we have the surreal in the description of the festival of Kartika lights when gods and men mingle in the streets of the village and in the mystic experience of Moorthy when the solid reality of the external world seems to melt in his meditation. In *The Serpent and the Rope*, surrealism pervades Benares and the other world of Madeleine so strangely and so strongly evoked in sights and sounds. Finally, in *The Cat and Shakespeare*, surrealism assumes dominance in the easy exchange between the actual and the fantastic, in the macabre humour playing with thought, and turns the fictional reality into a dream-like fluidity. This gradual dominance of surrealism does not by any means completely shatter the realistic mode, although it definitely supports the symbolic. Surrealism, we must remember, is *not* a substitution of reality by transcendence, but an extension of its frontier. In the dependence on the personal and the visionary, Rao's allegorical mode with surreal poetics finally emerges as an intensification of realism. It is therefore inevitable that the synthesis achieved in *The Cat and Shakespeare* should be a surreal *point*, a delicate balance, a momentary freeze in Rao's tight rope walking along the realistic mode of the novel. The growing desperation of the artist who is unable to accept his own art in the light of his philosophy, leads him ultimately to a gesture of self-annihilation.

So in *Comrade Kirillov* we find the novelist baring himself in his task as an artist. The apparent abrogation of form Rao has so far used—the socio-political realistic mode of *Kanthapura*, the worship of orthodoxy and pragmatism in the sentimental romanticism of *The Serpent and the Rope* and finally in the allegory of Kanyakumari remains the residue of *The Cat and Shakespeare*. All the basic elements of Rao's thought are present here, Gandhian ideology, Vedanta, Buddhism, Marxism in terms of a professed polarity which is totally deceptive because the identity in focus is a perpetual enigma, participating in both sides. Yet *Comrade Kirillov* is not a mere repetition, but a stage in the developmental process. Combining intellectual content with representational mode in symbols derived from Dostoevsky's famous double, Kirillov and Shatov, it marks an evolution in the allegorical form of *The Cat and Shakespeare*. Indeed the black humour of the preceding novel becomes the dominant in a violent satire on self which is not adequately set off by the serenity of the end in the legend of India. The prevalence of heavy parody signifying complete dissociation of the author from the discourse serves as an antipode of the positive affirmation in *The Cat and Shakespeare*. The synthesis between Hindu orthodoxy and Western humanism which was so delicately held in a balance is totally shattered as "Western" Marxism is supposed to be incorrigibly alien to "Indian" spirituality. That the concept of India now seems sufficiently humanistic to include both Gandhi and Buddha rejected earlier by Rao's own rigid orthodoxy adds only to the deepest self-alienation. The spirit of negation has the most immediate effect on language which is reduced to mere husk, a *form* without content or meaning since the reality is permanently beyond comprehension. In a professed combination of the ancient Indian theory of *sphota* (the Word Principle) with the physicist view of language supposedly Marxist, the author presents an interpretation of Stalin's congratulatory telegram to Hitler as nothing but "some seventeen hundred wave-components." This violence against logic and the very basic of human communication marks the final mutation of Rao's surreal anti-rationality exhaling an almost Dadaist rage.

The very fact that *Comrade Kirillov* succeeds *The Cat and Shakespeare* proves that there cannot be a permanent resolution of the struggle that goes on in the soul of the author because he is alienated ultimately from himself. Raja Rao started his literary career as a romantic with a typical disjunction with the surrounding reality of India—the debased brahmanism as well as the new anglicized vulgarity. In his first two novels, he follows the very authentic tactics of Western realism, that of opposition between appearance and reality, ideal and achievement, great expectations and lost illusion. It is perhaps ironical that these two novels which incorporate the Western traditional poetics of fiction so plainly are dearly cherished by his admirers as profoundly "Indian." The relative lack of enthusiasm over his later works indicate how pathetic is the whole fallacy of "Indianness" in the concept of the Indian novel in English, for Rao's "Indiannness" is no less a controlling force in the later works than it is in the beginning. Besides, it is basically the same romantic aesthetic with which he starts, that leads him irrevocably to the later experiments. The sovereignty of symbols over representation or imitation is derived very much from Romanticism, in the quest for transcendence "when one is not one, but the 'I'." The modernist nature of *The Serpent and the Rope* in linguistic experiments is only a desperate mask for the pervading melancholy at the failure to attain transcendence and leads to the later postmodernist endeavours which question reality and turn the aesthetic order into provisional and relative. Just as the Byronic romantic spleen supplements the visionary ecstasy of Blake, self-contempt alternates with Narcissism in Rao's works. *Comrade Kirillov*'s violent self-abasement is therefore inevitable, the logical culmination of the self-adoration in *The Serpent and the Rope*. It is only in *The Cat and Shakespeare* that the obsession with self transmutes into the negative capability which is the primary principle of formal perfection. So the blessing of the Lord falls on Ramkrishna Pai who does not claim to be Indian or spiritual, he is "just a man."

We may find in this evolution of the form of the novel a distinct Western pattern of development—traditional, modern, postmodern, opening toward futuristic novelties. What characterizes Rao is his radical obsession with the construction of an enclosed system of his own in which his works are so intimately related with each other that his later works are actually incomprehensible without the background of his earlier novels. Thus the whole satiric form of *Comrade Kirillov* is dependent on each of his preceding creations. The pattern of this kind of development is not exactly linear progression opening out in new untrodden space along the horizontal, but tends to be circular, revolving round the same axis of the divided self of an orthodox humanist, a conservative rebel, which expressed its dichotomy in the very first novel *Kanthapura* (1938) and remains the basic core in *Comrade Kirillov* (1976). With this fixed centre, the evolution of the artist as thinker from one novel to another is marked in concentric patterns growing into successively inclusive circles, so that the predecessor is always contained in the successor, but in a new form. One may find it assimilative or accumulative in its spiral nature. On the other hand, the style develops, from *The Serpent and the Rope* onwards, in the opposite direction, that is, of gradual exclusion of the former freedom of experiments, a marked denudation of poetic exuberance in an attempt to disconnect links with an alien literary tradition irrevocably connected with a linguistic system. Its nature is to discard, to renounce. It will not perhaps be unreasonable to read in these two tendencies, the modern Indian intellectual's ambivalence towards the West, his perpetual oscillation between a natural desire to accept the inevitable and an atavistic urge to reject the alien. In the inter-relation between the development of thought and expression there is thus an acute tension which becomes permanent in the mature Rao. As a result, one finds a growing concentration on abstraction, of content transforming into form until his very theme of the "Indian" identity, the magnificent obsession, ends as the very form of a stone idol in *Comrade Kirillov* realized in a deceptively simple style charged with concentrated personal reference. Indeed in Rao's typical utterance—singular not only as a deviance but also as a recurrent pattern, "I saw my eyes see that I saw" or "eyes seeing eyes seeing" we may find his whole artistic form represented in a crystalline symbol of involution centred in self which utilizes the simplest of English words to express perhaps an intensely personal meaning. That the sentence derives its stylistic echo from Paul Valéry, as we have seen, may perhaps suggest the final judgement on an Indian novelist in English whose first and foremost concern is to establish an "Indian" identity.

If this thesis can suggest a lesson or a moral, it surely is this that the very concept of identity for an Indian writer in English is dependent on his definition of the West. Among all our writers, it is perhaps Raja Rao who places greatest emphasis on "Indianness." yet it is in his evolution as an artist that India fails to emerge as clearly outlined construct of harmony which may form the still centre of a being tossed in the perpetual flux of time. In *The Serpent and the Rope*, Rao's concept of Indian identity is impersonal, amoral and agnostic; in *Comrade Kirillov* the same Indian self is conceived as personal, moralistic and even faintly theistic with its "Godward beckonings." This mercurial shifting from one pole to another is propelled by the author's varying definition of the West which is personal, moral and Christian in the former and impersonal, amoral and Marxist in the latter, Unless the background of the West is constantly in view, the quest for an "Indian" identity seems to become meaningless. It therefore follows that such a writer faces the threat of self-annihilation if he is obsessed with an "Indian" identity based on a Hegelian dialectic of opposition between India and West. To establish oneself by proving what one is not is a blind alley for the artist in him because the attempt, however noble in nationalist fervour, rich with existential overtone, dangerously lies about the inextricable and living bond between language, literary tradition, and a whole ethos. The elasticity of English has generously accepted exiles from other languages but has never perhaps established a literary heritage opposed to the West. However singular may have been the stylistic nuances of American or Australian varieties of English, the literatures produced in the United States and Australia are more closely attuned to the literary tradition of English and to the whole Western culture than it can conceivably be to the Chinese or even Arabic, so near home.

It may not be totally irrelevant here to mention the role of religion as the stasis of a whole ethos. Whether Christianity is practised or not, it is still the foundation of the modern Western mind which facilitates cultural exchanges among members of the same ethos in fruitful possibilities without seriously undermining harmony in individual identity. Han Suyin, who writes in English to prove her Chinese identity, admits: "Asians like myself belonging to a small 'upperclass' are intellectual Eurasians. We are all brought up between two worlds." For a Christian with a Chinese father and Belgian mother, the term "Eurasian" seems acceptable (although as a writer Han Suyin prefers to use her Chinese name to the original Eurasian one), but for a proud brahman like Raja Rao with a centruries-old family tradition in brahmanic orthodoxy of exclusiveness as a holy burden, such a designation would simply be intolerable. Neither the historical context of Western colonization nor the Hindu horror of pollution favours an admission of mixture even at an intellectual level. The problem of identity for a Hindu magnifies itself for another inexplicable mystery—the intimate relation between the Indian soil and the Hindu roots which stubbornly refuse transplantation anywhere else in the world. Indeed "Hindu" tends to be a geographical concept which seeks to disregard time. So the *Mahabharata* points out that a happy Hindu is one who is never an exile. The fear of extinction strikes a modern Hindu, who has chosen the west, with an atavistic force, which seeks desperately to resist the undeniable impact of what is assumed to be an alien culture. This complex love-hate syndrome is particularly noticeable in a generation of Indians belonging to a privileged class with sophisticated Western academic background and nationalist aspiration—a class of which Raja Rao may appear as a representative. If we remember Claude Levi-Strauss's triadic concept of communication in society consisting of exchange of message, service and women, the brahman Raja Rao's whole communication with reality may be found entirely directed towards the West in his irrevocable choice of English as the medium of expression, in his half-a-century stay in the West which provides him his living as well as his three wives. In this situation, the desperate urge for a specific "Indian" identity in English fiction acquires a romantic halo of heroism which ends perhaps in martyrdom. It is because Rao equates Indian identity with uncompromising non-dualism, his rejection of reality inevitably progresses towards the annihilation of the form of the novel which centres in pluralism and acceptance of reality. His attempt at a synthesis is achieved at such a cost of human concern and rationality, it emerges so very unique and individual that the author seems gradually lost in a labyrinth of self from which there is no exit. The aggressive flaunting of Hindu spirituality, Sanskrit words (often in careless and atrocious transliteration), esoteric doctrines which lie buried in oblivion among the Hindus themselves, are all nothing but magnified reverberation of the clanking chain, the most tragic proof of self-imprisonment. For an artist who is astride two worlds, the quest for form can reach the harmony of conclusion only when the duality between India and the West is resolved. Yet the irony is, for such a writer it is precisely this duality, this tension which is the source and spring of his whole creativity. The structural pattern of this creativity is basically non-Indian for, it rests on the principle of opposition which has dominated the Western mind producing heresies, Inquisitions, Pogroms, Moscow Trials and Concentration Camps. This attitude leads to an emphasis on the difference between India and the West. Although Advaita is one among many schools of Vedanta, and Vedanta is only one of the six major systems that comprise the orthodox branch of Hindu thought, yet it has received an overblown importance in the Western intellectual preoccupation with India because the concept of the non-duality between the attributeless Absolute Consciousness and the individual offers the greatest possible contrast to the Christian West which believes in a personal God and in the existence of the individual in his own right at a level qualitatively different from the Divine. It is because Rao seeks an "Indian" identity in English and his works are addressed to the West that the socio-linguistic dimension of the novel-form defines the very pattern of his creativity and ultimately imprisons the artist in a simplistic "Indian" image which is to a large extent superimposed by the West on our complex reality. The desperate attempt at a break-through, for a true synthesis, hardly succeeds in modifying the original theoretical stand: "Duality is anti-Indian, the non-dual affirms the truth." The basic *either-or* principle establishes Rao's "Indian" identity once for all to his Western readers for whom he writes, obliterating the Indian truth that this is a stand no Indian thinker or artist has ever struck in the whole course of the history of this sub-continent; because it reduces spirituality to the level of a mere attribute of nationalism, and above all its rigidity denies that core of heterogeneity which is the dominant motif in the vast and variegated Indian culture. If there is any spiritual essence in the whole corpus of Rabindranath Tagore's writing, it lies—according to Tagore himself—in the life-long endeavour to realize through his total experience "that complete and fulfilled love between the Divine and the human of which duality and non-duality are the two aspects, one complementing the other." When Raja Rao declares, "I don't want to compare myself with Kalidasa" or describes himself as "an Indian who wanted to forget Tagore," he is bound to "continue the adventure in lone desperation" as he confesses in the Preface to the *The Policeman and the Rose*. Exile therefore is predestined for Raja Rao, his *karma*. The beautiful rhetoric of his celebrated metaphysic of Indian identity— "India is anywhere and anywhen"—will perhaps remain a piece of profound tragic irony. The ideal of transcendence annihilating time and space seeks roots in the temporal and spatial reality and in the intricate pattern of relationship binding language, literature and thought; this reality is not so much Indian as Western confessing the victory of Plato enshrined in an alien linguistic structure, complete with the finishing touch of a modernist poetics. The quest for form therefore goes on because in the very self of the brahman novelist in English, the crisis is perpetual.

Postscript I

The Chessmaster and His Moves

Raja Rao's magnum opus *The Chessmaster and His Moves* (1988) which has been awarded the prestigious Neustadt International Prize of the Okalahoma University presents yet another challenge to the traditional aesthetics of the novel. Granted that the novel as an essentially open form is not bound to any distinct typology or even convention, it does work out some sort of relationship between an idea of reality and a particular fictional form. In Rao's own evolution as novelist, from *Kanthapura* to *Comrade Kirillov*, we find a close approximation to this century's rebellion against the overbulk of reality in the traditional fiction. Like all major novelists, Rao too has tried to redeem the "story," "character" and "realism" by an alternative base for order through speculation, leitmotifs, linguistic recurrences; in short, the dramatic immediacy of the traditional narrative is replaced by elaborate tactics of poeticization, which now at the post-modern stage rests solely on authorial consciousness.

The Chessmaster and His Moves which is a formidable assemblage of written matter with 708 pages of close print followed by 25 pages of Translations and Glossary, presents a vast mosaic of narration, reminiscences, confession, allusions and above all, what he terms "cogitation" generated by loosely associative principles revolving round a thematic centre that is, the protagonist's quest for a lost age through encounters with men, women and himself.

This centre is held firm by not allowing the fragile framework of imitation, that is of "realism," to lapse completely. The human situation involves Sivarama Sastri, a Tamil brahman engaged in combining metaphysics with mathematics (supposed to follow the famous Indian mathematician S. Ramanujan), Suzanne (S.) a spiritually-inclined French actress of classical comedies; Jayalakshmi (J.) a sick North Indian orthodox woman born in a princely state and married in another, surrounded by minor characters like Siva's friends, sensual Jean-Pierre, his libertarian wife Mireille, Jew linguist Michel, a survivor of the Nazi Concentration Camp, and the last but not the least, Siva's sister Uma, an unhappily married, average, Hindu middleclass woman. This framework is an obvious repetition of the narrative presented in *The Serpent and the Rope* with the triangular relationship of Ramaswamy-Madeleine-Savithri, interspersed by Lezo, Catherine, Georges and sister Saroja. The outcome of the human interaction is also similar—the disintegration of the intercultural human bond accompanied by an arrogant declaration of the superiority of the so-called Indian, eternal, asexual love transcending marriage, and the ultimate loneliness of the hero, left in the West. The scene, too is Paris; "the home of all refugees," the "Brahmapuri" which is admittedly the only "sanctuary." Events are also repetitions, for example, a short-lived adultery—this time with Mireille in place of Laxmi; a major surgery performed in London—a cyst is removed from J.'s brain in place of the hero's lung operation. Once again an elaborate rite is performed to symbolize the ideal union of the two Hindus and a gift is exchanged as the only possible concretization of their abstract love—a drawing of elephant which forms part of the marriage ceremony in Siva's community, a substitute for Rama's toe-rings. Above all, the same speculative teacher-pupil sort of dialogues between the protagonist and all other characters with the foregone conclusion of upholding his point of view alone. Again, ironically, despite the much-vaunted intellectual superiority which produces an obsessive notion of self-idealization—a constant irritant to the readers—the hero's research work arrives at a dead end. The reason is, we are told, "I was not interested in going out to prove anything to any one. I wanted to prove everything to myself."

This concentration on the ego offers a clue to the unabashed repetition of the earlier creation. The etymology of the word "novel" indicates something "new." So a novel, remarks John Fowles, "must have relevance to the writer's now." The "now" of Raja Rao seems to be a re-play of his "then," since any interaction with the present is no longer even fictionally possible. Perhaps the separation from his second wife, the American stage actress Katherine Jones re-creates the trauma of the breakdown of his first marriage with the French intellectual Camille Mouly and shifts his creative focus back to Paris with the post-war ambience filled with the memories of the Resistance, Maquis, Concentration Camps, ("when death lurks at every nook and corner") even though it is emphasized that the action (in so far there is any) takes place in 1963. Time, therefore, is the first casualty in Rao's warfare against "realism," fusing constantly past and present, incessantly going backward and forward recounting a character or an incident sometimes in such a way as to defy logic. So Suzanne, who is introduced as a grownup woman working at the *Comedie Francaise* during the War, mother of a child by a fellow actor who disappeared later in Vietnam still under the French, develops as a girl of only 23 or 24 in the early sixties and, miraculously still a virgin. It is even specifically mentioned that the new sexual revolution of sixties has not touched her nun-like chastity. All characters participated in the Resistance and yet appear quite young now in 1963 in their acts and manner, matching of course Sivarama who at 31 is already an internationally acclaimed scholar worthy to be considered for the Nobel Prize. His "India" of 1963 seems no less mercurial with both Patel and Nehru dominating the political scene with the Maoist, Naxal extremists of Bengal and Jayaprakash Narayan's leadership around. The life styles of the Indians belong to the past when even middle classes could afford foreign cars, Hindu-Muslim domestics, treatment of common maladies abroad and "dancing girls," not to speak of the aristocracy's constant extravaganza of silk and jewellery (at Calcutta-Ghazipur-Vilaspur) foreign trips, Swiss finishing schools for princesses and English public schools for princes—all of which recall a milieu long vanished. Hence his Calcutta is a city "of Scotsmen, marwaris and Jews." One effective way of undermining time is to insist on agelessness. So Jaya, "the only woman who is the complete woman" for "she makes you man" seems almost a mythical Hindu wife whose calm and contented acceptance of her husband's liaison with a maidservant is matched only by her equally phlegmatic acceptance of her father's ward Raja Ashok who happens to be her constant admirer. This Indianization of the French high life of the eighteenth century is rendered distant from time with the contextualized symbols of the Tiger and the Turk as well as a bit of flesh-denial— "her body seemed not to want anything very much." Almost literally "she belonged to another age." Hence her wish that in the next birth

Siva would be "King" (implying, her husband) might have been tragic for the proud brahman but natural to J. as her "sense of time was epic." it is, therefore, necessary for Siva to defeat his predecessor Ramaswamy who "belonged to the age of the *Mahabharata*" and retreat back further in the mythical no-time of "Siva and of the Kamasutra."

This aggressive atemporality attuned to the post-modern rejection of linear time extends to the internal sequence of the fiction as well. Sivarama's intimacy with Jaya starts and develops fully in India long before his arrival in France and meeting Suzanne. Yet Suzanne's supposed inadequacies are constantly blamed to defend the very existence of this love. The operation J. undergoes is reported successful with no hint of any further danger and Jaya after a few days at Paris bids Siva farewell leaving for her husband in Calcutta. The story is stated to end here. Yet a few pages earlier, Siva states almost casually that he meets J. for the last time, "one dramatic afternoon in Vilaspur, a year later" when her brain had "eaten itself" a great deal, and, "death was seated by a babul tree by her window." This "future" which does not take place in the fictional time makes one re-read the beginning of the novel. "You remember J., you said to me: tell me you need me, and I will come." This promise is never uttered by her in her whole fictional life and presumes an existence beyond the reach of her creator, the author. In fact the wish, "Would you *return* as parrot, betel vine or bodhisattva," may make one feel that she is dead. As it is never stated, the most crucial fact remains a mere supposition of the reader. In other words, here is a "historyless reality" where silence is eloquent, and pages of incessant chatter speak nothing. Similarly, Suzanne appears only in glimpses, Sivarama spends most of his time—when he is not cogitating—with others, Mireille, Jean-Pierre, J., her relations and friends, Madame La Fosse, Michel, even strangers like the Algerian leader Abd'l Karim and the Jain jeweller Ratilal Javery and his family. Yet throughout the novel, hints are scattered to indicate a degree of intimacy which assures her that she is practically his "wife and only wife and no one (can) take her place." So being actually absent, her presence is, as it were, everywhere. Indeed it is the rumour, the report of her drawing close to Michel that perhaps prompts the great intellectual duel between the brahman and the rabbi with the probable end that she may, in future, marry Michel. Siva's journey back in time based on the Proustian belief that the true paradise is the paradise one has lost, comes to an end when he realizes, "just as each man has his dharma, each age also has its laws" and so confusion of epochs is the "only sin of man." He behaves like an adolescent whereas he should have been a responsible householder. This realization does not form any epiphanic climax but rests on a plateau of understanding and is stated almost casually sometime before the end of the story with Jaya and Uma. So the beginning does not begin and the end does not end the novel.

The complicated interpenetration of the past, present and future forms a vast labyrinth of vocables at the centre of which reigns silence. The writer, the creator finds his own creation assuming as though independent life beyond his traditional omnipotent control. This inabiiity or refusal to create a self-contained illusion of reality may owe its genesis in the direct intrusion of autobiography which disturbs the verisimilitude or plausibility of narration. Sivarama, a Tamil research scholar on fellowship, son of a retired provincial bureaucrat, is unaccountably so familiar with the feudal ex-rulers of North Indian princely states, that princess Jaya after her brain surgery is left in his care by her parents and husband. Famous figures of contemporary France like André Malraux are the personal friends of such a young Indian. Though ostensibly a mathematician, Siva spouts all Rao's pet notions about men and women, displays the same anti-modern medievalism in social and political ideas and upholds a distinct Advaita-Platonic metaphysics. He alludes to modern European literature, quotes the Vedas, Classical Sanskrit, Hindi Tulsidas. In other words, the hero is almost identified with the creator Raja Rao who has dropped anchor in the West, whose "Indian" roots are aesthetically stunted by selections from an archaic-classical heritage, resisting a natural growth beyond the medieval. A prolonged interregnum makes such a person's existence in modern India problematic if not impossible, since the North Indians, especially the Punjabis are so "Westernized," Bengal being no less alien in her proximity to China. He is an alien in his own country, in his own time, "a man lost in space, in the immensity of such silence, the eardrum would tear."

As the reality of time and space defies imitation, the *récit* of Siva which is the novel, can offer mimesis only as a play, a game of chess. *The Chessmaster and His Moves* is a novel-about-itself and, as such, constantly reminds the reader that every happening (if anything happens at all) is a play and even the much-idealized protagonist is only a chesspiece whose actions are nothing but movements manipulated by a mysterious omnipotent masterplayer who, sometimes clad in Kerala-type dhoti, may resemble for a moment Rao's own preceptor Shri Atmananda Guru. Since there is no opponent in this unique variety of chess, he may remind one of Herman Hesse's masterplayer in *The Glass Bead Game*. The player enjoys the game for the sake of the game alone. It is an activity complete by itself without any reference to the fury and the mire into which the miserable humanity is immersed. On Jaya's decision to return to her husband, Siva muses: "How mysterious, how congruously inconsistent our lives seemed. The stars played games with us, and behind the stars, he, the chessmaster, rubbing his head in glee, played for you, making you think he played for himself."

So confined to the alternative of Suzanne or Mireille, the concepts of freedom and choice are charged with a new existential anguish. "Had life no freedom, and was freedom always so desperately accidental, lonesome." The only way out of this "timeless grinding process" is to play the game.

Hence words, images, metaphors connected with game or play are repeated throughout the novel which emphasize the fictionality of the fiction, that the happenings narrated are not even empirically true, "Nothing ever happened." The gravity of external incidents is smudged and lines of crucial events blurred with playful "cogitation." Siva's belief in Advaita Vedanta, that is in the non-dualism of the Absolute and the Relative, renders his adultery with his friend's wife and mother of three children a "playful drama of the two becoming not-two." The question of morality is as irrelevant in such promiscuity as in the innocent kite-flying of children at Luxembourg. The love between Siva and Jaya which even in this play-novel assumes some seriousness, is realized in the one union which is compared to "the festivity at a doll's marriage," it is "the toy-wedding feast." The intellectual marathon between the brahman and the rabbi loses some of its heavy burden of fabular history when it concludes as an item of sport in a medieval tournament. Even the interminable "cogitation" is actually nothing but a play with self— "undistractedly I played with myself"; he admits all his ideas with encyclopaedic pretension, are just "mathematical equations for a lazy mind to amuse itself." Indeed the very life is nothing but "a cosmological game."

Nothing therefore happens in this make-believe world except the basic physiological functions—eating, sleeping, defecation and sex. No other kind of action seems permissible. Siva incidentally takes no initiative in any activity involving responsibility. When Uma lands in Paris for medical consultation, all arrangements for her stay and treatment are made by his friends. Each and everything he requires in his daily life is provided by others, particularly Suzanne, helped by her mother, (perhaps Rao's fictionalized mother-in-law who took care of him at Austen). It is she who comes to clean his kitchenette, cook his food, administer medicine, prepare his diet and nurse him in sickness, even take care of his mail, not to speak of her readiness to offer him her body. All Siva gives her is a nagging succession of complaints against her hankering for a child and her spiritual desperation (again a re-play of Ramaswamy-Madeleine tragedy). After enjoying all her services, he feels no compunction, declaring union with her "so dry, so melancholic" and "Jaya's simple touch of hands" possesses "more wealth than all this psychodrama." In other words, Siva is the greatest beneficiary of the system he himself despises so much—namely the modern Western democracy where liberal humanism has given women enough liberty to help aliens like Siva live a parasitical existence on the periphery of the Western society.

The absence of a meaningful participation in the life of a community perhaps lays the foundation of man-woman relationship in what is considered asocial, aberrant and incestuous, namely brother-sister attachment in terms of sex which has incidentally some post-modern parallels (for example John Irving's *Hotel New Hampshire).* Siva, however, claims that such a tie is a unique "Indian" phenomenon as he says in a deceptively casual manner, "You know, Mireille, in India the brother is even more important than the husband, the father." It is repeatedly shown and hinted that any happy or ideal union of man and woman is based on the pattern of brother and sister because it is supposed to be the only relationship in which "though there is one and the other and yet in a way of speaking, the same—the two halves of the whole." Therefore all partners in actual or potential sexual act or relation are repeatedly referred to as brother and sister—Jean-Pierre and Mireille, Raja Ashok and Jaya, Siva and each of his women.

It is significant however that this rebellion against society is at the same time sought to be legitimized by constant references to the custom of cousin-marriage in some communities in South India. This attempted defence highlights the silence of the author as to the normal and usual practice throughout the subcontinent, particularly in the valley of Ganga, he himself calls, the *aryavarta* identified with *Bharatvarsha*. The compulsion to justify what is considered abnormal is so intense that a whole set of symbols and motifs have been built up, invoking the Egyptian antiquity in the royal custom of brother-sister alliance. This supposed defence even draws upon the geological theory of the continental split which took place aeons and aeons ago when the landmass now known as the South India was to have formed part of the same continent which contained also Egypt. Hence Egyptians and Dravidians are sort of cousins— "So people say"—and hence the continuation of cousin-marriage through some pseudo-genetic anthropological mystery. However, the scientific aspect may be subsumed by the far more important psychological reality which is indicated in the reminiscence of Siva's father describing his own marriage to his cousin: "When we were married, it was not as if I had married a woman, my cousin, but I had so to say, married *some one like myself*."

The basic inability to sustain any relationship with someone who is *different* reveals the Narcissist core of all Siva's encounters with women, which may tempt one to suspect profound though incipient misogyny seeking an elaborate disguise in the whole paraphernalia of symbolist embellishment, often associated with Rao's description of the female form. If Suzanne is an apple of Normandy and Mireille with the "goblets of Shiraz"—a melon of Africa, it is evident that they are but objects of consumption. Jaya whom Siva calls "My queen, my sister," is acceptable perhaps because her birth name is Haimavati. "Haimavati and Uma being both the name of Parvati, so Uma and Jaya are some sort of equations." Siva's succession of women is actually a quest for that one Woman in a series of encounters with substitutes. Quite early in the novel Uma states categorically that Siva her brother is the only man in her life and no matter how many women he plays with "*he has only me in his heart*." She treats him as her lord and master and this pattern of hierarchy repeats itself in each of Siva's adventures with women. Suzanne, despite the blame of intellectual contrariness, declares, "you are still my master"; Mireille writes, "I am a slave"; Jaya says "mai to apki dasi hun" and is eager to mount his pyre. Each one of them, however, falls short of the original and leaves Siva. The psychology behind such affairs and terminations is deemed less important than the theme of substitution.

The theory that "everything in life seems a substitute for something else" and "similarity is identity" assumes a surreal dimension annihilating the distinct contours of individual characters and events. Michel the Jew, "the brahmin of Jerusalem" substitutes the "brahmin from Chidambaram" for he may give Suzanne the "would-have-been child" she desires from Siva, again as a substitute for her dead mongoloid son, Robert. Indeed the mystical properties of substitution may even perform a medical miracle. Siva's sexual union with Mireille is expected to cure Uma's infertility:

> Mireille knew me (in the biblical sense), thus this knowledge was somehow going to illumine Uma's procreative inside, which, if its valves were closed or lazy in functioning, could be activated by my talismanic presence through Mireille, in a way bringing freshness and wholeness to Uma's feminine organs, fulfil them by me, her brother, her guardian, her hero-companion.

This surreal expansion of the frontiers of experience terminates in a simple return to reality, lonely Siva after the departure of all his women—Suzanne, Mireille and Jaya—accompanies Uma to her bed and a series of suggestive equivocal gestures and acts follow at the end of which, she pulls his head on her bosom where he falls asleep. The ambiguity persists to the last word, "I was home, Was I?"

This doubt, this consciousness of an inner division marks the irrepressible tendency to pull out the very base of the elaborate edifice erected by the author himself and points towards a self-conflict which defines the avant-garde thought. So Siva is admittedly a "half-Westernized brahmin," "a royalist communist," a scientist trying to link the Upanishads with existentialism. The constant struggle within finds a pathological manifestation in the mysterious trancelike brain disorder of Siva in Paris which is supposed to be related to Jaya's brain surgery taking place in London, as "the same phenomenon, seen from two different points." Suzanne's Yoga-trained "inner voice" and special power to see colours and shapes is on the other hand "mere trickeries of spirit."

It is however in the sphere of intellection that Siva's inner conflict leads him to a point of self-negation. Apparently he rejects the narrow concept of nationalism (even though "India is culture") which seems to be similar to territorialism and both based on animal demands. Apparently, too, he pitches "his intent on the universal that is the transcendent" making a reference to Sankara's famous declaration: My native land is in the three worlds (*Svadeso bhubanatrayam*). The real conflict accordingly is not between the East and the West but between the two world views which determine the two races of men, "those that look the horizontal way, the way of infinity. And those that look vertically, the creatures of dissolution, the zero way." This is however a formalized repetition of the basic stand in *The Serpent and the Rope*, which claimed: "There can be only two attitudes to life. Either you believe the world exists and so—you, or you believe that you exist—and so the world. There is no compromise possible." The Hindu is identified with the vertical and the Hebraic with the horizontal, "historylessness or chronicling: Krishna or Moses." Gradually the "horizontal" group expands considerably to include the whole gamut of the Judaeo-Christian-Islamic thought and Marxism, as well as Jainism, Buddhism (even though "zero is after all Buddhist," "The Buddha and the Jew meet" and "Jainism has failed us like Buddhism has"), Confucianism ("Judaic justice and Confucian Li are cousins of sorts") and other branches of Indian philosophy even modified non-dualism of Ramanuja. The vertical becomes Raja Rao's exclusive Platonic-Advaitic-Indian belief. ("India is a metaphysic, it is like zero.") Siva's encounters with men, Abd'l Karim, Ratilal or Michel point toward the impossibility of any relationship. Each attempt reinforces a permanent divide, "the zero and the infinity could not be true at the same time." He finds that being "free," he has nowhere to go, no one to do anything. Any relationship with another presupposes the existence of the other which his *Advaita* denies in its insistence on the transcendence of time, space and causality. He cannot marry S. because S. remains a distinct individual ("S. was S.") who is not totally assimilated in him. Love is "being—where there is no otherness—not merger, but transcendence." So the ideal couple Siva and Jaya cook the typical dishes of their individual community, take the meal with all formal trivia, talk about the possibility of any meaning of life and lie on bed side by side with "a clear distance between them," like in "an egyptian pyramid." They are supposed to be free, "the line could be crossed" but this deemed "not congruous" "because you could win nothing, gain nothing, by the concrete." The detailing so far of all sexual acts in literary and esoteric extravaganza is thus rendered meaningless.

Since this atrophy of the body is true marriage, "Marriage is marriage that never takes place," the realization of the Absolute as the self turns happiness into "pure nothingness." There is but the terrible doubt: "Jayalakshimi, do you hear all this that I mumble: And are you there?" Siva's solipsistic universe necessarily excludes everyone else and life remains "Just one exhausted emptiness." The absurdity of life acquires a monstrous dimension as Siva regards human relationship with Suzanne or Jaya "metaphysical interlocking—with each other's postures only," to be compared to the streetcurs joined in the act of copulation, unable to get themselves free from each other till forcibly separated by some passer-by. The sublime, the erotic and the vulgar converge in a soul bent on self-destruction.

It is the use of language which finally enables the writer to express such a core of agonism in constant equivocation. An obvious element of linguistic realism assimilates mainly items of spoken French as well as some Sanskrit-based words, on the other hand the literary fabrication in careful rhetoric, luxuriant imagery and allusiveness poeticizes the medium, yet the whole emphasis of style is subordinate to the length of the sentences and paragraphs. A sentence may run to 30 lines and a paragraph to pages. The sheer volume of written matter, spinning words as though Siva's asthma is physically rendered into his style. However irritating and confusing are his loose constructions, his imperceptible changes of tone from the sublime to the ridiculous, Rao's style alone holds together the disjointed patterns of narration and meditation by infusing opacity, that peculiar dense quality which demands the participation of the reader and at the same time resists communication. The whole design resembles modern art in which men and events are treated like abstractions of shapes and colours, cut and repeated with a central music somehow connecting vaguely the dissimilarities. Language alone in its temporal dimension can provide that "music." However, the narrator has declared: "I am my music and player as well." So both the chessmaster and his game are created by the writer who is unable to believe in the objective validity of meaning and yet cannot do without meaning. Hence the importance of silence. The seeming disjunction between the "horizontal" world-view of the Polish Jew and the "vertical" transcendence of the Tamil brahman, despite one's history of persecution and the other's glory of domination has one unstated unity: each prays to his Supreme in his specific language of the gods watched by amused French children in the terrace of Trocadero in Paris. Both are residues of archaic modes which ignored the living communication of human existence, the medium of exchange between the child and the mother. Both stand as outsiders in the soil of a modern country which has taken that very living speech of all her inhabitants, regardless of class or gender, to a height of the greatest achievement. The conflict is really no longer between the East and the West but between the modern and the archaic. The brahman and the Jew are companions in the same adventure of exile.

Postscript II

On the Ganga Ghat and Other Stories

Although Raja Rao's early short stories often find place in different anthologies, his fame so far rests on his novels. Till the publication of *On the Ganga Ghat* (1987), his stories were regarded largely as by-products of the novels. Indeed his concern for humanity in *Kanthapura* finds added reflection in *The Cow of the Barricades and Other Stories* (1947). When he portrays the low caste, faithful maidservant Javni's acceptance of fate, childwidow Akkayya's pathetic clinging to other women's children, sick and oppressed Dattopant's death leap before the train supposed to be carrying the Viceroy and the Maharaja, the tortuous lives of the crazy miser Motilal and his wayward son Chhota's desperate wife revolving round the little Gram Shop, his preöccupation with the actual human experience establishes itself with a wealth of concrete details and acquires life-likeness with the help of realistic linguistic devices. This realism sometimes stark and powerful in the delineation of the negative is tempered by poeticization which marks the style as well as the imagery: women are beautiful as "new-opened guava" or "tender as April mangoes"; the barren Maratha land, fissured in ravines like "loamy python" produces "thin, unmoving bonelike plants with little skulls" of cotton. The writer who is here essentially a sensitive observer of the reality around offers glimpses of a dying world—sometimes even deprived of nature's vital bounty—ruthlessly exploited by a rapacious foreign rule as much as by its own proto-feudal socio-economic system.

This serious concern with the contemporary existence expressed in a form which drew heavily on the Western realistic mode is complemented by a complete distancing of reality in pieces like *The True Story of Kanakapala, Protector of Gold* and *Companions* which utilize the indigenous oral technique of narration.

In this "other" world of Rao, animals play no less an important role than human characters, one serpent fights the vices of greed and crime, another forces ordinary mortals entwined in the coils of flesh to look for God. The situations are non-specific in time and the "moral" potential in each fable approximates to a kind of pre-fictional mode. *The Cow of the Barricades* attempts to strike a balance between myth and realism (as also *Narsiga* an orphan pariah boy's nationalist fantasy). The mysterious cow Gauri, who comes to visit the Mahatma's disciple the Master and brings in a note of harmony among men and animals in the household, gets killed by a British bullet on the barricade put up by the agitating nationalists. Her martyrdom is duly commemorated in a huge statue larger and sterner than her original self and becomes a legend as well as a perennial source of commerce for toy-Gauris are sold in plenty. This delicate and perfect balance proves to be precarious in the later Gandhi stories like the *Fables for the Feeble*. Obviously. Rao's Gandhian belief, no matter how fervent in real life, ceases to supply an adequate artistic form as is also seen in the later novel *Comrade Kirillov*.

The broad humanist concern about others, typical of romantic liberalism, is replaced by an insistent quest for self as the author's attention turns inward during *The Serpent and the Rope* period. Based on the same French locale, *Nimka* and *India—A Fable* in *The Policeman and the Rose* (1978) explore the human condition in multicultural encounters where the state of exile provides a constant framework of reference and grounds the presentation to a semblance of actuality. The same "India" whose absence in life turns the experience as distant as a fabular world of prince and princesses, resides ironically at the core of the self as a source of atrophy to resist any "alien" touch and impedes the growth of a lasting relationship with a foreigner. Hence the white Russian Nimka is left alone with her identification of Gandhi, India and the Indian hero.

These stories create a world that is dense, multi-layered with all the rich manipulation of symbols, linguistic recurrences, allusions and stylistic innovations that we associate with this period. *The Policeman and the Rose* utilizes the theme of human bondage, quest and liberation in an extravagant surreal-symbolic narration where the metaphysical abstraction so heavily informs the details of concrete imagery that the narration of felt experience is drastically foreshortened. If the Policeman, a Kafkaesque symbol of the ego, represents the bondage of the self, the journey of the Christian red rose extends through ages and lands till it becomes the white rose of Travancore, where Rao met his guru. Rose symbolizes the pilgrimage and liberation as it acquires the fragrance of lotus, the apocalyptic flower of the Hindus. The base of abstraction perhaps lies in the Vedantic notion that once *avidya* or ignorance which resides in the consciousness of the ego is removed, the Truth is revealed and one becomes a liberated soul, free from the recurring cycle of time. In the narration however the distinction between the ego and the self opens up a deep chasm ("the enmity between him and me") as the Policeman is both "he" and "I" and the constantly changing perspective surrenders to a surreal fluidity which is mercurial. The Policeman going through innumerable incarnations—vegetable, animal and human—at last born a South Indian brahman leads a sad existence in France with a dead child and (possibly) a foreigner, selling spiritual junks which earns him lot of honour and fame. Despite the constant police watch, the hero has a moment of illumination which demotes the Policeman. A visit to India restores the shrunken ego, but makes it impossible to return to the old life, so he travels till he finds Truth in Tranvancore where the Policeman vanishes, and the "I" is freed from prison. Thus the well-known western quest theme becomes an intricate web of symbols and leitmotifs based on metaphysics and personal experience that completely replaces narration and not surprisingly has generated a feeling of confusion even among appreciative readers.

During the same period, however, Rao wrote pieces like *The Moon over Lucknow* (1961) and *Divali comes to Ramu* (1963) which offer little sketches of the daily lives of ordinary men and women in North India—Rao's *Aryavarta* or the heartland of *Bharatvarsha.* Without any aggressive metaphysical pretension, the stories are narrated with a cultivated simplicity in style and above all in a new narrative technique which eschews the "story" that is the sharp rise-and-fall plotting and presents reality in its true form of contingency as a uniform flow in a plateau.

Collecting threads from all these stories, particularly the new narratology of non-happenings, Rao's latest work *On the Ganga Ghat* (1989) marks a brilliant achievement as a classic of fabulation. In this final stage of evolution, the new form emerges as a fusion of the short story and the novel as he himself tells the readers. The post-modern reduction of the realistic form acquires a fabular transparency with a neat circular arrangement of imaginary characters round a central theme which is the dominant mood of the author. A meeting of the artist and the pilgrim brings to life India as a timeless existence ruled by orthodoxy, peopled by men and women content to live in an age-old hierarchy of structure. For the lifelong exile in the modern West, India is all that the contemporary age is not—a mythical entity in wish-space and wish-time built with deliberate simplicity and apparent innocence that mark the height of Rao's success as India's greatest anti-modern modern writer in English.

The title sets the tone of traditionality—the stone steps of the Ganga, the river of redemption at Varanasi, proverbially the last stop in the Hindu's journey of life. "Home is Ganga Ghat." Hindus from all corners arrive here for absolution. Retired from action, householders come here to spend the rest of their lives in contemplation and prayer like Muthradas from Vrindaban, Rani Rashomani from Bengal, Ranchhoddoss Sunderdas from Bombay. They join a variegated procession of life with others, who live around the ghat—Chhota Munnalal or Madhoba carts logs for burning the dead bodies and is in love with a spirit who sings a wordless song, his friend is Shankar of the 3 B's ("Barbarian, Benaras, Brahmin") the only character who is allowed modern education; Bhedia the idiot tramps, Putli and his father a snake-charmer and street-juggler, confound the reality; Mohendra and the gang of delinquents tease Sadhus on Dashashwamedha Ghat and live on petty thieving; Bhola the motor-mechanic doodles tantric triangles and circles on the ghat, keeps himself and his preceptor; Shivlal the pimp serves a "fat Punjabi bitch" as faithfully as his bad-tempered, foul-mouthed, bhang-addict guru; daughter of Ranchoddoss, Sudha, the female ascetic reads the Vashishtha Ramayana off the Hanuman Ghat.

Each thumbnail portrait, replete with telling concrete details yet stylized like a Rajput miniature, is complete by itself and at the same time relates to the centre of a total design as segments of a circle. The message of the Ganga Ghat, a platform to start the last journey, lies in the place itself—a place of redemption. Therefore, renunciation and abstinence form the core of most of the lives described. Yet this search for deliverance *(moksha)*, the last of the four-fold objectives of life enjoined by the Hindu orthodoxy, does not totally ignore the other three, namely performance of duties *(dharma),* earning livelihood *(artha)* and sexual satisfaction *(kama).* As befits the archaic existence, the pattern of human happiness and woe, failure and success are moulded by the family and the gods, no other concern—political, ideological or social—ever intrudes the closed existence, nor is there any attempt to better any one's lot, no protest either. For "Life is so simple. God gives when He gives. For the rest, man has to say his mantras assiduously, eat good food, sleep, wake and work."

This "simple" life revolves round preassigned rituals and conventions. So the story of Ranchhoddoss Sundardas begins with a detailed description of how his family built a temple and organized regular *Kirtanas* to commemorate a vision of Lord Pandurang. Madhoba, the strong man who wins wrestling matches, goes to the Hanuman Temple regularly to worship the monkey god, the bestower of strength. As soon as Shankar, a student of science, learns of his wife's pregnancy he offers a "thousand-and-eight-name-of-the-name" to Devi Annapurna in the temple and buys for his wife a ruby nose ring though he may dream of a modern future. For more than half-a-century Rani Rashomani's life has moved around bath, worship and listening to the recital of the *Mahabharata.* Life indeed is "simple."

Simplicity however costs money. The inhabitants of Rao's world are carefully selected from a class which derive their livelihood either from ancestry or tradition. Muthradas belongs to a hereditary trading family, Ranchhoddos heads a very old jewellery business, Rani Rashomani, the princess of Darbhanga, widow of the Raja of Bankipur naturally has no concern with money. Earning money incidentally is as normal as the practice of religion. The sons of Ranchhoddoss are "honest, devout and moneyminded." Shankar's grandfather Tyagaraja Shastri amassed fortune, reading sacred texts to Maharajas and giving astrological predictions to their concubines. His son, the astrologer, tells "lies ten annas to the rupee." Bhedia steals, Shivlal pimps. He however has stored a large amount of money as has Madhoba. Acquisition as an aim by itself forms also part of the game.

Like *dharma* and *artha, kama* or satisfaction of desire has its appointed place in the scheme of things, presumed of course to be the duty of woman and the right of man. "The power of man is to sow, the berth of woman is to reap." Husbands may be promiscuous, wives remain stereotypes of chastity. Humiliation at the husband's lechery may rarely find protest in a suicide, like that of Anasuya, a Kanakmal wife. Transgression however does not leave any stain on men. Tyagaraja Shastri, "famous for his dharma shastra learning," was no worse off for a concubine or two. His grandson Shankar even at his young life of a student has had his share of libidinous inheritance, so has Motichand, the adopted son of Muthradas. Their wives are all uncomplaining, timid and of course obedient, for marriage is their whole existentce, "a girl is meant for marriage as a wheel is destined for a cart." The only other female condition sanctioned by the Hindu orthodoxy is concubinage. Hence Benares like all holy places of the Hindus abounds in whores. "How come to Kashi Viswanath and not taste the honey of consecrated womanhood?" If an ascetic or two like Shivlal's guru does not show immediate kindness to a whore, the author obviously does not share the contempt. "She was born a concubine and she performed what she was born to, her dharma." In fact a whore who satisfies her clients earns "credits in her next life." In this microcosm of the Hindu world, the woman is a biological entity whose only purpose in life is to satisfy either one male as a wife or many males as a whore. No other fulfilment is recognized." And all that European talk of women going to become politicians or professors is so much like making the river run backwards back." Sudha, who is neither a wife nor a whore, but a respected ascetic, is therefore explained away by her few years of convent education and exposure to European films.

At the same time there is a tacit assumption that the wife is the pivot of the Hindu male existence on the earth. Both Muthradas and Ranchoddoss retire from active life after the death of their wives, as does young Bhola, who loses his family in an epidemic in Benares. A man's activity is expected to lead to marriage as Madhoba's saving money gives rise to speculations. Indeed the bachelor and the abstemious are all slightly abnormal. Madhoba captivated by a spirit gets into insane fits of rage. Shivlal tears off the money he has stored to celebrate a Divali, an action which renders all his efforts meaningless. The only man who leads a normal life in and around the ghat is the married Shankar who is now redeemed by the imminent birth of a child, assumed to be a son. Hence the news of his wife's pregnancy receives a detailed ritualistic emphasis ("Beat the drum and proclaim"), and an exaggerated attention. This rapture for new life—the only one in the book—sets off the recurrence of death which pervades the lives of all the other characters. From the very first story where the taxi driver Motilal takes Raja Rao and his friend's son, Paul, to the Guest-House and talks of his son "who died of death," mortality haunts each person and in fact not only brings all of them here, but prepares them for the inevitable end. Rani Rashomani "waited for death as a baby-bird awaits its mother's beak" storing piles of sandalwood. The action itself, even as the importance granted to death, belies all attempts to transcend time as the goal of deliverance.

Hence the concluding contemplation which rounds off the concrete, detailed portrayals of men, women and animals explores the paradox of existence. On the one hand it is claimed, "Man is mortal is the grandest fib man ever invented." At the same time it is evident "all of structure's destiny is decay and disappearance." What is then the reality of being, of self? As the knowledge of self has no existence before birth or after death, therefore, the passage in-between does not exist either. Without a beginning or an end, the middle cannot exist. After demolishing logic and rationality all through the stories, life is *argued* to nothingness. The self remains an inscrutable enigma, life a miracle. At one level, "Ganga never flows," at another rises the prayer, "O, Mother Ganga, please be gracious and—flow."

This dual vision justifies the choice of Benares as the microcosm of the author's universe for here "the unreal and the real are so co-adjuscent." The animate and the inanimate, human and animal share the same chain of action and reaction passing through ages. Prabhavathi an unhappy queen drowned herself under the neem tree followed by her faithful maid. A rock appeared mysteriously under the tree and was duly consecrated by the royal family along with the tree. They are reborn as the extraordinary Bhim parrot and his mate Rupvathi and live in the same neem tree protected and fed by a Siddha who lives under it. With the death of the holy man, Bhim either falls into his pyre and dies, or fasts for days and disappears. Thus myth continues in actuality which in turn becomes a legend denying significant external reality. Rupvathi incidentally "sits in her austerities biding her time," like an orthodox Hindu widow. Indeed a rhetoric of personification endows the birds and beasts with pervasive "Hindutva"—a strong

Hindu identity with appropriate name, honorific, caste and prehistoric past. Here sparrows, blessed by Rama, along with Krodha the vulture belong to the "right" or "inner circuit" of Benares with "the Rajas, the concubines, the pilgrims and the temples." The microcosm excludes the "left" or "outer circuit" which belongs to "the weavers, the untouchables, the hide-sellers, the prostitute houses (of the poor and the accidental)," with whom the writer has nothing to do. Indeed the Dalhousi bridge gets more attention than these "poor and the accidental" for the bridge links the pilgrims. Deliverance being the objective on the Ganga Ghat, it falls upon Jhaveri Bai, a cow, the holy animal of the Hindus to formulate the suitable prayer, "Mother, give us no birth or death," for "birth is so mean, death is so low."

The quintessence of Hindu orthodoxy, indeed of any orthodoxy, lies in the refusal to admit change, the reality of time. Rao himself tells the readers: "All persons and places are not true—but real." This "reality" for him cannot be therefore the experience in temporality, but a perception of the mind carefully cultivated by tradition and myth. Benares is holy, because as a symbol it defies the contemporary, it is the Eternal City. Rani Rashomani believes, "Nothing in Benares has ever changed since Shiva decided to come down and emerge here for the benefit of mankind on this crescent curve where the two streams Varuna and Asi meet." Pre-history overwhelms the contingency which is either ignored or deprecated. Hence the bourgeoisie of the new professionals and administrators—a class Rao himself belongs to—is significant in its total absence. The present constantly harps on the past, the taxi is called a "palanquin" and the driver Motiram provides the "pilgrim link" through hereditary profession. Bhola, a wheel-right by birth, is changed into a motor mechanic grudgingly, forced by the British who are completely unacceptable. Even a casual contact with the alien or modern evokes all the destructive Hindu rage of pollution. The little chick of Bhim and Rupvathi is unhappy with the good English lady who has taken it and comes back home, but being "London-returned," it atones for the alien touch and dies at once. The author adds, "this makes it better for rebirth." The rejection of the modern or the alien is here an inexorable law of nature.

The only villain in this world, Shivlal's uncle Maganlal the Gunman, who usurps the property of his dead brother's wife and sons, has therefore "modern" ideas. From a hereditary landowner he becomes an industrialist, opts for a modern lifestyle with facilities of technology and new education, takes his wife out of the sanctified four walls. The author's contempt for the new "civilization" finds concrete expression in the "Western jacket" for Maganlal and his wife's "Bata slippers." The British rule is resented not because it is colonial, but because it ushers in the new age—the inevitable transition from the archaic—feudal mode to the modern existence. Rao's satire of the new rich vulgarity personified in the wife in "high-heeled shoes" with "titter mitter English" and children in the Convent decrees that if the change cannot be resisted it is to be stamped as evil.

This static view of India has to reject, therefore, all attempts of the contemporary towards social justice and better life through various reforms. Sudha's renunciation, so uncommon for a Hindu woman destined to serve men, is expiated with a lively reference to her unfulfilled desire in former life to burn herself with her dead husband in the legendary glory of Hindu wives: "How noble it was in old virtuous days. You could be burnt with your spouse, your Lord. It is a pity the British came and stopped it all." The naive lament very cleverly bypasses the historical truth that unwilling widows were burnt for commercial gain and massive agitation was launched by Hindu scholars who found widow-burning contrary to the holy texts. With the metaphysic of traditionalism, Rao not only idealizes the Hindu archaic mode, but tries to sanctify corruption simply because it was in practice. So the actual attempts to rebel against the feudal decadence and degeneration are subverted ruthlessly. The Brahmo enlightenment is parodied in the presentation of Rani Rashomani's husband as a British sycophant, drunkard and a dandy. In Rani's memory he remains as the cufflinks engraved with the picture of Edward VII—a telling symbol of insignificance. Indeed the depiction of Rani's adherence to ritualistic and traditional Hinduism serves as a living refutation of all that the Brahmo movement stood for.

However, Rao has never been an objective or impartial analyst of the social dynamics, his genius lies in the art of subversion which presents a crystalline and transparent narrative series in which myth replaces reality. So, for Rani Rashomani, Shiva is more real than her own exquisite hands. If the reality of time is to be deprecated, the experience of senses too is to be undermined.

"One of the great men in Benares" is Bhedia with his idiotic smile, tattered clothes, long nails, unwashed dirt and childish pranks. He is "so noble, so heart-clean, friend to all creatures and stones"; more important is his unusual power— "For him the world is imaginationings." The linguistic deviation emphasizes his uniqueness for he lives as much in the present as in the legendary, commutes freely from "here" whisking flies off a horse, to "there," taking "a trip to Indra's kingdom." This urge to deny the actual envelops others too. Bhola and his companions, forced into an alien war by the alien rulers, create a little India reading aloud *Ramacharitamanas* among themselves. The recital of the 16th century Hindi classic not only fills "the cold air of Flanders with utter sweetness," but transports the listeners beyond time and space. They return to their tents in "deep peace," even as the war goes on all around and wonder "which war was which, here and there." The strength of such transcendence depends of course on the casual assumption that all the Indian soldiers must have come from the Hindi-speaking states alone.

Such radical and simplistic reduction of the vast and intricate web of languages and cultures that constitute the Indian reality perhaps naturally leads to a virtual collapse of communication and social relationship. The characters are bound together only by the tie of deliverance as preceptor and disciple or pilgrims on the same journey towards nothingness. Fundamentally each of them is an isolate existence with no attachment, no memory, no hope. Rani Rashomani remembers none, goes to none, nobody comes to visit her either. "She is just somebody that was and is what was and so will be what is. Emphasis on language dissolves the contours of being for the meaning of life cannot get away from interactions with human being. So Raja Rao, the most subjective author of modern India concludes, "Raja is a name given to the nameless." The miracle of chance coexists with rigid predestination. If the totality of vision presents a verbal and psychological coherence as the only residue of fiction, one small doubt persists: is this wholeness true or false? One may read in this crystalline achievement the destination of a lonely soul reaching towards a sombre, asocial, apolitical literature of silence.

Bibliography

1. Primary Sources

Rao, Raja. *Kanthapura*. London: George Allen and Unwin, 1938, Ind. edn., Bombay: Oxford Univ. Press, Champak Library, 1947, American edn., New York: New Directions, 1963, Educational edn., Madras: Oxford Univ. Press, 1963, 2nd edn., 1974 (with C.D. Narasimhaiah's "*Kanthapura* : An Analysis" as Introduction rpt. from *The Literary Criterion*, Mysore, Univ. of Mysore, 1966).

------. *The Cow of the Barricades and Other Stories*. Bombay: Oxford Univ. Press, Champak Library, 1947.

------. *The Serpent and the Rope*. London: John Murray, 1960, Ind. edn., New Delhi. Hind Pocket Books, 1968. (French translation by Georges Fradier of the English typescript published in Paris, Calman-Levy, 1959).

------. *The Cat and Shakespeare: A Tale of Modern India*. New York: Macmillan, 1965, Ind. edn., New Delhi, Hind Pocket Books, 1971. (First published as "The Cat," New York: Chelsea Review, No. 5, Summer 1959).

------. *Comrade Kirillov*. New Delhi: Orient Paperback, 1976. (First published in French as La *Comrade Kirillov* with La Chatte et Shakespeare, trans. Georges Fradier. Paris: Calman-Levy, 1966.)

------. *The Policeman and the Rose*. New Delhi: Oxford Univ. Press, 1978.

------. *The Chessmaster and His Moves*. New Delhi: Vision Books, 1988.

------. *On the Ganga Ghat*. New Delhi: Vision Books, 1989.

------. "Pandit Taranth," *Asia*, Jan. 1935, pp. 10-15.

------. "The Premiere of Sakuntala," *Asia*, June 1943, pp. 365-68.

------. "Varanasi," *The Illustrated Weekly of India*, September 3, 1967, pp. 12-15.

------. "The Moon Light in Lucknow," *The Illustrated Weekly of India*, November 5, 1966, pp. 15-19, November 12, pp. 20-23.

------. "Trivandrum," *The Illustrated Weekly of India*, Dec. 9, 1962, pp. 46-47.

------. "Meaning of India," *The Illustrated Weekly of India*, Feb. 25, 1962.

------. "Fables for the Feeble", *The Illustrated Weekly of India*, Dec. 1962, pp 46-47.

------. "Books which have influenced me," *The Illustrated Weekly of India*, February 10, 1963.

------. "Divali Comes to Ramu," *The Illustrated Weekly of India*, Nov. 17, 1963, pp. 15-19.

------. "The Writer and the Word," *The Literary Criterion*, Mysore, VII, 1, Winter 1965, rpt. *Critical Essays on Indian Writing in English*. Eds. M.K. Naik, S.K. Desai and G.S. Amur. Dharwar: Karnataka Univ., 1968.

------. "Irish Interlude," *The Saturday Review* , XLIX, No. 26, June 25, p. 32.

------. "A Nest of Singing Birds," Preface to Toru Dutt's *Ancient Ballads and Legends of Hindustan*, Calcutta: Writers Workshop, 1972.

------. "Devant les dieux de l'Inde . . . avec André Malraux" Le Figaro littéraire-Samedi, 9 Avril 1960.

2. Secondary Sources

(a) Works exclusively on Raja Rao

Naik, M.K. *Raja Rao.* New York, Twayne, 1972.

Narasimhaiah, C.D. *Raja Rao.* New Delhi, Arnold-Heinemann, 1973.

Niven, Alastair. *Truth Within Fiction: A Study of Raja Rao's Serpent and the Rope*. Calcutta: Writers Workshop, 1978 (I thank Prof. P. Lal of Writers Workshop for permission to consult this typescript).

Rao, K.R. *The Fiction of Raja Rao.* Aurangabad: Parimal Prakashan, 1980.

Sharma, J.P. *Raja Rao: A Visionary in Indo-Anglian Fiction.* Meerut: Shalabh, 1980.

Sharma, K.K. ed. *Perspectives on Raja Rao.* Ghaziabad: Vimal Prakashan, 1980.

(a) *Articles/Reviews on Raja Rao's novels published in dailies, periodicals, collections (in English)*

Alam, Qaiser Zoha. "*Kanthapura*'s Style: A Point of View," *Language Forum*, Vol. V, No. 2, July-Sept. 1979.

Ali, Ahmed. "Illusion and Reality: The Art and Philosophy of Raja Rao," *The Journal of Commonwealth Literature,* No. 5, July 1968.

Amur, G.S. "Raja Rao: The Kannada Phase," *The Journal of Karnatak University*, Vol. X, Humanities 1966.

Anjaneyulu, D. "*The Cat and Shakespeare: A Tale of Modern India*," *Thought,* New Delhi, Feb. 5, 1966.

Dey, Esha. "A Baroque Stylization: A Note on Raja Rao's *The Serpent and the Rope*," *Language Forum*, New Delhi, Vol. VI, No. 3, Oct-Dec. 1980.

------. "Fissures in being: Anguish and Alienation in *The Serpent and the Rope*," *Littcrit*, University of Kerala, Trivandrum, June, 1981.

------. "India: the Thematic Axis of Raja Rao's *Comrade Kirillov*, An Antinovel, "*Commonwealth Quarterly*, The Centre for Commonwealth Literature and Research, University of Mysore, September 1981.

Eng, Ooi Boo. "Making Initial Innocent Sense of *The Serpent and the Rope*," *The Journal of Indian Writing in English*, Department of English, Annamalai University, Annamalainagar, Vol. 8, January-July 1980.

Fremont-Smith, Eliot. "Proverb hunting in Paradox Land," *The New York Times*, January 20, 1965.

Gemill, Janet Powers. "Rhythm in *The Cat and Shakespeare*," *Literature East and West,* Vol. XIII, I & II, 1969.

Harrex, S.C. "The Fascination of What is Difficult: Some Student Responses to Raja Rao," K.K. Sharma, ed., *Indo-English*

Lit, Ghaziabad: Vimal Prakashan, 1977.

Hartley, Lois. "*The Serpent and the Rope*," *America CVIA*, May 4, 1963.

Iyengar, K.R.S. "Literature as Sadhana,"*Aryan Path*, Vol. 40, Nos. 6-7, June-July 1969.

Mukherjee, Meenakshi. "Raja Rao's Shorter Fiction," *Indian Literature*, Vol. X, No. 3, 1967.

Nagarajan, S. "An Indian Novel: A Review of *The Serpent and the Rope*," *The Sewanee Review*, Summer 1964.

Naik, M.K. "*Kanthapura*: The Anglo-Indian Novel as Legendary History," *The Journal of the Karnatak University*, vol. X, Humanities, 1966.

------. "*The Serpent and the Rope*: The Indo-Anglian Novel as Epic Legend," *Critical Essays on Indian Writing in English*, eds. M.K. Naik, G.S. Amur, S.K. Desai, Dharwar: Karnatak University, 1968.

------. "The Achievement of Raja Rao," *The Banasthali Patrika*, Rajasthan, No. 12, January 1969.

------. "The Kingdom of God is within a Mew: A Study of *The Cat and Shakespeare*," *The Journal of the Karnatak University*, Vol. XIII, Humanities, 1968.

Narasimhaiah, C.D. "Raja Rao: *The Serpent and the Rope*," *The Illustrated Weekly of India*, September 1, 1963.

------. "National Identity in Literature and Language: Its Range and Depth in the Novels of Raja Rao," *National Identity*, ed. K.L. Goodwin, London: Heinemann, 1970.

------. "Raja Rao: The Metaphysical Novel *(The Serpent and the Rope)* and Its Significance for Our Age," *Readings in Commonwealth Literature*, ed. William Walsh, Oxford: Clarendon Press, 1973.

Natwar-Singh, K. "Return Passage to India," *Saturday Review*, March 16, 1963.

Patil, B. Chandrasekhar. "The Kannada Element in Raja Rao's Prose: A Linguistic Study of *Kanthapura*," *The Journal of the Karnatak University*, Vol. XIII, 1969.

Prabhakar, M.S. "India in dispute," Letter to the Editor, *Encounter*, January 1965.

Prescott, Orville. "*The Serpent and the Rope*," *New York Times*, Feb. 22, 1963.

Raizada, Harish. "Literature as Sadhana: The Progress of Raja

Rao from *Kanthapura* to *The Serpent and the Rope*," K.K. Sharma, ed., *Indo-English Literature.*

Rao, J.S. "Concepts of Time and Death in Raja Rao's *The Cat* and *Shakespeare*," *Littcrit*, University of Kerala, Vol. 2, No.2, Dec. 1976.

Ray, Robert J. "The Novels of Raja Rao," *Books Abroad*, Oklahama Univ., Autumn 1966.

Rajdan, B.M and S.P. Ranchan "*The Serpent and the Rope*: India Made Real," 1,2,3. *The Illustrated Weekly of India*, March 13, April 3, April 10, 1966.

Sastry, L.S.R. Krishna. "Raja Rao," *Triveni*, Madras, January 1968.

Shahane, V.A. "Raja Rao's *The Cat and Shakespeare*: A Study in the Form of Fiction," *The Journal of Indian Writing in Eng*, Vol. 3, No. 1, Jan. 1975.

Sharma, Atma Ram. "Peasant Sensibility in *Kanthapura*," K. K. Sharma, ed., *Indo-English Literature.*

------. "Raja Rao: Cats, Serpents, Comrades and of Human Condition," *Perspective*, Calcutta, May 1978.

Shepherd, R. "Symbolism in *The Cat and Shakespeare*," *World Literature Written in English*, Commonwealth General Journal, xiv, 1975.

Taranath, Rajeev. "A Note on the Problem of Simplification in Raja Rao's *The Serpent and the Rope*," *Fiction and the Reading Public*, ed. C.D. Narasimhaiah, Mysore: The Univ. of Mysore, 1967.

Thakur, Guruprasad. "Reflections on Rama. India as depicted in *The Serpent and the Rope*," *The Journal of Indian Writing in English*, Vol. 2, No. 2, July 1974.

Tucker, Martin. "Cultures in Conflict," *The Commonwealth*, Jan. 25, 1965.

Zuckerman, Ruth Van Hart. "*The Cat and Shakespeare*," *Books Abroad*, Summer 1965.

(b) *Reviews/articles on Raja Rao's Works in French*

Anon. "Le Serpent et la corde," *Lumière*, Paris, 22 juin 1959.

------. "Littérature Indienne de Langue Anglaise," *Le Livre Francais*, Paris, Sept. 1959.

------. "Vient. . . ." *Le Droit*, Ottawa, Mai 1964.

------. "Un Indien découvre l'Europe," *Figaro Littéraire*, Paris, 9 Mai 1959.

------. "Les Livres: le Serpent et la Corde par Raja Rao," *L'Echo de Tourraine*, Tours, Mars 1960.

------. "Le Serpent et la Corde, par Raja Rao," *Connaissance du Monde*, Gaeton Rouguet, Paris.

------. "De quelques aventures spirituelles," *L'Echo d'Oran*, Algeria, 7 Aout 1959.

------. "Le Serpent et la Corde par Raja Rao," *Le Courrier d'Extreme Orient*, Paris, 15 Feb. 1960.

------. --Le Peuple, 29-9-59.

------. Raja Rao, *La Gazette de hausanne* , 11/12 Juillet 1954.

------. "Raja Rao, La Chatte et Shakespeare," *Le Jour*, Beyrouth, 7 Juin 1966.

------. "Si vous mettez chaque semaine un livre dans votre bibliothèque: nous vous conseillion celui-ci," *Tribune de Lausaune*, Dimanche, 18 Sept. 1966.

------. "Le Serpent et la Corde, par Raja Rao," *Tribune De Geneve*, 24 Juin 59.

------. "Vient de Paraitre," *Le Monde*, Paris, 16 April 1966.

Block-Michel, Jean "Moments Littéraire: Le Serpent de la Corde de Raja Rao."

Brierre, Annie, "Raja Rao, la Chatte et Shakespeare," *La Table Ronde*, Nov. 1966.

Brion, Marcel. "Lectures Etrangeres: Le Serpent et la Corde par Raja Rao," *Le Monde*, Paris, 29 December 1959.

Depoisier, Claude. "Un brahmane retour de France: Raja Rao, La Chatte et Shakespeare," *Journal de Geneve*, 22-8-1966.

Do-Dinh, Pierre. "Lectures Asiatiques: Romanciers Indiens," *Le Monde*, Paris, 22-25 fevrier 1959.

Frameries, Georges. "Un manuel, un recit, un experience," *le Populaire de Bois*, Paris, 7.6.66.

L.E. "Le Serpent et la Corde, par Raja Rao" *Figar Littraire*, Paris, Juine 1959.

Mignon, Jean-Charles. "De l'Inde au Mexique: De Livres de sourire, de scrupules et de violence," *Le Soir Bruxelles*, Septembre 1, 1966.

Miguel, André. "Les Livres: André Miguel a lu cette semaine," *Berux Acts*, 26.5.1966.

Tavernier, Rene. "Aventuries du coeur et de 1 'esprit: vus de France et de l'Inde," *Le Progress,* Lyon, 7 Juin 1959.

(c) *Articles/Works on Indian Writing in English in which Raja Rao/ his writing is discussed*

Anon. "India's Search for Self-Expression," *Times Literary Supplement,* Aug. 10, 1962.

Chaddah, R. P. "The Mahatma in Modern Indo-English Fiction," *The Indian P.E.N,* XLII, Vols. 11-12.

Harrex, S.C. *The Fire and the Offering: The English Language Novel of India 1935-1970*, Vol. 2, Calcutta: Writers Workshop, 1978.

Hemenway, Stephen. *The Novel of India,* Vol. 2, Calcutta: Writers Workshop, 1975.

Iyengar, K.R. Srinivasa. *Indian Writing in English,* 2nd rev. edn., Bombay: Asia Publishing House, 1973.

Joshi, K. N. and Shyamala Rao. *Studies in Indo-Anglian Literature,* X, 3, 1967.

McCutchion, David. *Indian Writing in English,* Calcutta: Writers Workshop, 1969.

------. *The Indian Novel in English, Jadavpur Journal of Comparative Literature*, Calcutta: Jadavpur University, Vol. II, 1973.

Mehta, P.P. *Indo-Anglian Fiction: An Assessment,* Bareilly: Prakash, 1968.

Melwani, M. *Critical Essays on Indo-Anglian Themes,* Calcutta: Writers Workshop, 1972.

Mukherjee, Meenakshi. *The Twice-Born Fiction: Themes and Techniques of the Indian Novel in English,* New Delhi: Arnold Heinemann, 1971.

Narasimha, Raji. *Sensibility Under Stress: Aspects of Indian-Anglian Fiction,* New Delhi: Ashajanak, 1976.

Narayan, Shyamala. "India," *The Journal of Commonwealth Literature,* Vol. XII, No. 2, Dec. 1977.

Parameswaran, Uma. *A Study of Representative Indo-English Novelists,* New Delhi.

Reddy, G.A. *Indian Writing in English and Its Audience,* Bareilly: Prakash 1979.

Shahane, Vasant A. "Indo-Anglian Fiction and the Question of

Form," *The Journal of Indian Writing in English*, Vol. 2, No. 2, July 1974.

Sharma, G.P. *Nationalism in Indo-Anglian Fiction*, New Delhi: Sterling, 1978.

Singh, R.S. *Indian Novel in English: A Critical Study*, New Delhi: Arnold Heinemann, 1977.

Varghese, C. Paul. *Essays on Indian Writing in English*, New Delhi: N.V., 1975.

Venugopal, C.N. *The Indian Short Story in English*, Bareilly: Prakash.

Walsh, William. "Nataraja and the Packet of Saffron: The Indian Novel in English," *Encounter*, October 1964. Rpt. *Readings in Commonwealth Literature*, ed. William Walsh, London: Oxford University Press.

Williams, Haydn M. *Studies in Modern Indian Fiction in English*, Vol. 2. Calcutta: Writers Workshop, 1973.

------. *Indo-English Literature 1800-1970, A Survey*, Madras: Orient Longman, 1976.

3. Interviews

Brierre, Annie. "An Interview with Raja Rao," *The Illustrated Weekly of India*, March 10, 1963. Adapted from the French "le Serpent et la métaphysique," *Nouvelles Littéraires*, 28 fevrier, 1963.

Gokhale, Ashok. "Indians who made it," cover story in the special issue on "Indians in America: Crisis of Identity," *India Today*, New Delhi, July 16-31, 1980, p. 42.

Gondal, Yogesh. "Raja Rao: Obscure but Rhythmic Writer," *New Delhi*, New Delhi and Calcutta, Vol. 3, Issue 7, Aug. 18-31, 1980, pp. 60-64.

Kamath, M.V. "The Brahmin and the Rabbi," *The Illustrated Weekly of India*, Aug. 24, 1980, p. 47.

Narayan, Shiva, "An Interview with Raja Rao," *Indian Writing in English*, ed. K.N. Sinha, New Delhi: Heritage, 1979.

O'Brien, A.P. "Meeting Raja Rao," *Prajna*, Golden Jubilee Number II (2), Benares Hindu Univ., 1966, pp. cliii-clxxxiv.

Parthasarathy, R. "The Future World is being made in America," An Interview with Raja Rao, *Span*, Sept. 1977.

Raman, A.S. "Chiarascuro," *The Illustrated Weekly of India*, Sep. 29, 1963, p. 11.

------. "A Meeting with Raja Rao Recalled," *The Illustrated Weekly of India.*, Sep. 25, 1966, pp. 15-16.

Ranchan, Som P. "A Meeting with Raja Rao"--I, II, III, IV, *Thought*, Delhi, July 13, 20, 27, Aug. 3, 1968.

S.V.V. "Raja Rao: Face to Face," *The Illustrated Weekly of India*, Jan. 5, 1964, pp. 44-45.

Wohl, Elizabeth. "Raja Rao on America," *Span*, 1973.

Index